PAUL GARRISON

EXPONENTIAL
MARKETING

CAPTURING SUSTAINABLE GROWTH IN
AN ENVIRONMENT OF CONSTANT CHANGE

Paul Garrison
Exponential Marketing. Second edition, revised and updated.
© The Garrison Group, 2006 and 2009

Written by Paul Garrison

Comments and feedback are always welcomed
paul@garrisongroup.eu

Case studies, in chapter order, written by
Gábor Bródi, Roberto Garcia, Milena Dyankova, Milán Herczku,
Ildikó Kókai, Daniel Arnold, Dénes Tóth, Ana Matos, Julia Vahidova,
Katalin Halász, Mátyás Szalai and Sam Moorthy

www.garrisongroup.eu

PAUL GARRISON

EXPONENTIAL MARKETING

CAPTURING SUSTAINABLE GROWTH IN AN ENVIRONMENT OF CONSTANT CHANGE

MANAGER PUBLISHING

To the clients and staff of the Garrison Group who share equal credit
in creating, refining, and implementing new marketing ideas and concepts
– many of whom wrote case studies included in this edition.

A special thanks to my students at the CEU Business School
and other universities over the years who have enthusiastically
allowed us the opportunity to test some of our latest thinking
on their bright young minds.

Contents

Welcome to my Marketing Religion

People I have worked with over the years usually come away from the experience thinking I am a bit of a fanatic. They would say: 'That Paul has some good ideas and some new ways of doing things, but he is absolutely relentless about this whole customer thing.' 'Like a dog with a bone', others would add. I can only plead guilty as charged. I am a fanatic about customer focus; I have been for a long time. I didn't invent this *marketing religion*; I learned a lot of it from another fanatic named Sergio Zyman, the former chief marketing officer at Coca-Cola who became my mentor twenty years ago, and I assume he learned it from someone else. I have continued to learn the intricacies and nuances of this customer-focused religion from many other practitioners along the way, just as I suppose they have learned a thing or two from me. We talk in terms of who 'gets it' and who doesn't, as we set off to convert those who don't.

If you were to ask most marketers if they were customer-focused, they would simply answer 'of course', with a hint of incredulity in their voices – as though it went without saying. Then they'd go back to *managing their brand* by doing *marketing stuff* like hiring agencies, producing advertising, conducting focus groups and looking at sheets of brand indicators. But that isn't really marketing anymore than presuming that doing the books every day at the close of business is financial planning. It just some of the things you should do along the way. Marketing literally means 'going to market'. Doing all that other stuff well may be important, but it isn't crucial. Customer value is crucial because how successful you are when you get to the market is all about the perceived value customers place on your product relative to its price. Higher value equals a higher price, and a higher price usually translates to a higher profit. Sounds like good business to me.

Brand managers usually scare me when I see how busy they are. They are always busy doing stuff, but are they doing the right stuff? Are they developing and growing customer value? Whether they realize it or not, brand managers, like many marketers, tend to be process-oriented rather than customer-oriented. The comfort and safety they find within the 'tried and true' processes becomes an emotional safety net for them. The truth is, however, that an unyielding faith in focusing everything you do on providing greater customer value is the only compass that will keep your course on track through your busy days.

Unfortunately, unlike true north on the compass, customers don't stay in one place – they continuously move, adapt and change. Consequently, any marketing process that is driven by what has happened with the customer in the past may not be applicable in the current environment. More importantly, it may not relate to what will happen in the future. Your marketing, and the customer value focus that drives it, has an expiration date on it – it's perishable. The faithful in my marketing religion are constantly in need of new insights to bring them closer to their customers and their customers' ever-changing perception of value. To be both timely and effective, marketing requires an insatiable curiosity about what shapes and drives human behavior.

Imagine for a moment what could happen if we all stopped using the familiar marketing job title of *brand manager* and started using *customer development manager* instead. Merely semantics, you might say. But is it? The brand is only relevant to what the customer wants and needs. For a manager to focus on the brand is like putting the cart before the horse. I recently heard a young brand manager stating how much she enjoys nurturing and developing her brand. She is passionate about it. Good for her, but her passion is misdirected. It is her customers that she should be nurturing and developing, not her brand.

Focus on the customer – that's where the money is. The brand is only the tool; what counts is the customer value that the brand represents and identifies, and that is a constantly changing dynamic. Imagine that this newly named customer development manager goes through her day – each and every day – with a relentless focus on understanding customer value and how her brand can better communicate and deliver on that value in a changing world. Imagine the business impact of that!

So far we are only talking about brand managers. What about the engineers responsible for product development? How many times have you sat in front of your new TV, DVD player, computer, or mobile phone and tried to figure out how it works? Steve Balmer at Microsoft said: 'Technology is only important in what it can do for people. Beyond that it is just science.' Steve

Balmer gets it. Steve Jobs has customer focus big-time. Take a look at Apple – have you ever seen a brand and its products more intimately in touch with its customers?

The marketing religion I practice is relentlessly focused on the customer at the beginning, in the middle, at the end – and at every step in between. When I am working with one of my clients and a new ad (in any form) comes over from the agency, we don't sit around and discuss whether we 'like the ad'…or not. That's irrelevant. Instead, we do a quick review of who the core customers are, and then we discuss how meaningful that particular ad execution will be to those customers – what they will value. We ask ourselves where the customers are going and what they are doing when they come in contact with the ad. We are thinking about the customers' state of mind in relation to the medium where the ad will appear. Hopefully, all those parameters were included in the creative brief at the outset, and the agency is just as focused on these customer-value deliverables as we are. That's a pretty good way to review advertising creative. It's externally focused on the customers rather than internally focused on the people who make the ad, or work for the company. And that's just one example of applying this customer-value focus when reviewing advertising creative. Think about how it can be applied to product development, customer service, store design, and so on.

When we bring in new people to work at the Garrison Group, we typically find that the more marketing experience they have, the harder it is to convert them to our religion. Most experienced marketers have been busy for years doing stuff with the growing security that they have learned to do it well – and they do. They know the process to hire an agency, write a brief, interface with the product development guys, and so on. After many years, however, they have often lost track of the real reason they are doing all this stuff in the first place. I often find that I need to deconstruct these experienced marketers to re-build a stronger, customer-oriented foundation. If I can get them to re-learn that marketing is, and always has been, about the customer, they can then re-assemble their own marketing expertise on top of a much stronger foundation, whether they are communication specialists, political marketers, or fast food experts.

Our marketing religion isn't a rigid one; in fact, it is actually quite flexible after you take on the basics – a strong foundation in customer value. It can be easily adapted for different products, as appropriate to the skills and capabilities of the marketing people that were hired to sell those products. Their capabilities, skills, passions and experiences are important, but unless their talent is grounded in a relentless devotion to understanding and delivering on customer value, it is wasted talent.

Marketing people live in a world of budgets. One of the first questions ad agencies always ask is 'what's the budget'? When we live in a world of budgets we become focused on creating activities to fill those budgets. Our focus inevitably becomes activity-driven instead results-driven. I have seldom had a problem getting funding for what I want to do to grow the business, because I never think too much about budgets; I think a lot more about results. New product launches, ad campaigns, and special events are simply the strategies and communication vehicles I utilize to achieve business results. Don't get me wrong: adhering to a budget is a necessary operating practice. But it is most definitely not the *bull's eye* at the center of your business growth target. If you want the customer to buy more of your products and services, and you want them to be willing to spend more for it than any other alternative – *more for more and worth it* – then the point you should be aiming at is to achieve better customer value.

That is just about the marketing department, who should have been getting it all along. Now imagine an organization where the sales clerks get it, the machinists, the telephone operators, the waiters, even the fork-lift drivers! They understand why customers buy the products and services their company produces and they know how they can personally increase that value. That's a company I want to be a part of!

Effective and efficient

When the changes came to Eastern Europe twenty years ago, there was a prevailing urgency for business to catch up to the West. Two decades later, a new mindset has emerged that is much more about trying to find a better way – exploiting the much higher level of flexibility now endemic to the region as a result of living in an environment of nearly constant change. Best practices from the West are still accepted as valuable, but more as a foundation upon which to build new ideas and concepts to make them even better and less expensive at the same time. Because businesses in this part of the world are often operating on much tighter budgets, managers in the East need to discover how to make these leap-ahead improvements cheaper and faster. *Exponential Marketing* introduces some new tools and processes to marketing as a process, but it is more about improving on best practices, whether from the East or the West, with much greater effectiveness and efficiency.

CHAPTER ONE

Where's the Growth?

'You need to figure out a way to fix this thing', your boss bluntly tells you as you take on the new assignment. 'I don't care how you do it, but we have to start seeing some real growth', he adds, making sure you feel the pressure.

Fair enough, you think. After all, it was your successful track record in difficult circumstances that got you this promotion in the first place. Or maybe – the thought creeps into the back of your mind – it was because their first choice wasn't available. Perhaps this is your first management position and no one knows what to expect – not even you. It doesn't really matter how or why you got into this new position of intense responsibility, the point is that you're here and you have to figure out a way to grow the business…and do it soon!

You know the economy is tough. You know the competitive situation is brutal. You also know that the guy who had the job before you either didn't get the job done (which is why they brought in someone new), or got promoted because by squeezing every possible cost saving out of the manufacturing process, and cutting manpower so lean in areas such as sales, marketing and operations, he somehow managed to make his profit number. Pick the scenario that best fits your current situation. Regardless, you certainly have your work cut out for you. The pressing reality is that you're going to need to do something much different than 'business as usual', and to do that you are going to have to start thinking differently from day one. I suggest you try thinking *exponentially*.

Exponential

Exponential Marketing is not so much about being totally new and different, but more about marketing in such a way that momentum and impact grow

5

at an ever-increasing rate (i.e., *exponentially*) rather than diminish as your business plan moves through the organization. Difference for difference's sake is a waste of time and resources – a fool's errand.

While it's great to be a change leader, it can also be a lonely job. The truth is, you can never make significant change on your own; you're going to need a lot of help and that is the real power of *Exponential Marketing* – getting everyone else involved in adding value to your business proposition. You will probably need to make some changes, maybe even some significant ones, but more importantly, you must ensure that the necessary changes are enthusiastically embraced throughout your organization, rather than what is more typical – ignored by most and opposed by a few. The first step in the *Exponential Marketing* process – *Destination Planning* – will help you line up the necessary support from the different constituencies within your organization to ensure that you're not flying solo with a lot of guns pointed up at you.

Exponential customer value

There is one fundamental growth driver that you absolutely must get everyone to act upon – understanding and delivering customer value. If you expect customers to pay for whatever it is your company wants to sell more of, you must provide customer value. Everything your organization does, or doesn't do, affects the customer's perception of your product's value. *Exponential Customer Value* is about making sure everyone in your organization is focused on providing that value – exponential because the more people get it, the more it causes everyone else to get it. Customer value is at the very heart of marketing, so it stands to reason that everyone in your organization needs to be a marketer of sorts. Each employee has to know that providing customer value not only benefits the customer and the organization, it also benefits them by making it easier to achieve their individual career and personal financial goals. Understanding what drives customer value, and, consequently, what everybody in the organization can do individually and as a team to better deliver on that value, is key to making your business grow as it has never grown before – exponentially!

One problem we face is that customer value is usually interpreted and understood as being in the domain of a distinct functional area known as the *marketing department*. For me, marketing literally means how you go to market and thus involves everything from product development, sales, and customer service to package design. Unfortunately, for a lot of people, marketing is merely about communications, and has been dialed back to focus almost exclusively on advertising and promotion.

How did something so fundamental to the success of a business, such as understanding and providing customer value, get limited in practice to a few guys in the marketing department? The regression from the roots of what marketing meant at its inception, to what it is now has been mostly self-inflicted. The cadre of men and women who inhabit the marketing department usually spend an enormous amount of money doing something no one else in the company really understands. Marketing guys tend to guard their turf with complex theories; masking their work in obscure terminology and measurement systems, such as GRPs, reach and frequency, and KBIs. What the heck are those, and why are they relevant to growing the business? Because these marketing guys tend to speak with one another in their own magical marketing language, everyone else figures 'why bother'?

But in the end, all of this marketing magic has come back to haunt the marketing department; it often finds it difficult to get the resources necessary to do that 'voodoo thing it does so well'. No one else in the organization, particularly the numbers guys on the financial and operational side of the business, can understand what it is the marketing guys are doing – or intend to do – with their communications or 'instant win sweepstakes'. The marketing guys, consequently, find it very hard to justify – in rational financial terms – the return on investment for their advertising and sponsorship budgets – typically the two biggest ticket items in their overall marketing plan. The most troubling reason for the confusion within the organization about what the marketing department is doing is that a lot of marketing guys have become so busy doing stuff like making TV ads and putting up billboards, that they have lost track of why they are actually doing it in the first place – to create and deliver better customer value.

Before you start cutting marketing budgets, firing agencies, and reducing the number of marketing guys in your organization, let's take a look at how you can create better customer value and exponentially increase the power of marketing by getting more people across the organization involved in the creation, as well as in the delivery, of this increased value. If you start thinking of marketing as a pervasive concept of focusing on customer value, rather than merely a functional area of the business, you can make the whole process exponentially more powerful. In fact, this idea of pervasive marketing across the entire organization is so fundamental to operating a successful business that it is a colossal mistake to entrust it to any single group of people – even if they have the word 'marketing' written on their degrees or diplomas.

A good business *goes to market* and wins more customers as a result of providing more customer value than any other alternative – that's marketing.

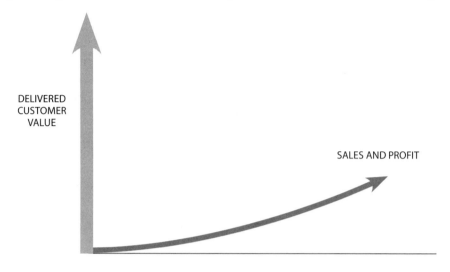

Figure 1: The power of marketing

So, how does marketing become more embedded in your business? Make marketing – i.e., providing customer value – a crucial component of every-one's job – that's *Exponential Marketing*.

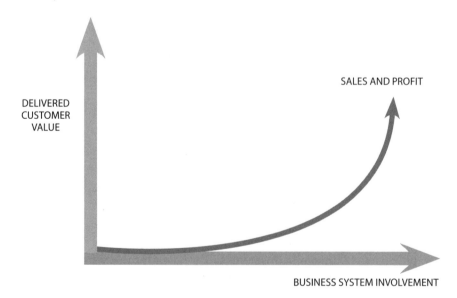

Figure 2: The power of *Exponential Marketing*

Sustainable growth in profits can only be achieved by creating sustainable growth in the business itself. You, along with everyone else in your organization, need to start thinking more about the top line as being the most important means of growing the bottom line. Driving the demand side of the equation is about increased customer value. 'Customer' and 'value' are two words that everyone recognizes, but very few seem to really understand as a linked concept. Customers will buy what you have to sell only if they believe they will receive a benefit in line with what they are willing to pay. The benefit received relative to the cost paid is customer value.

Figure 3: The value equation

The benefits of your product are often more than 'it cleans better', or that it 'connects your computer to the Internet faster', or whatever you believe the functional benefit of your particular product to be. Your product is a lot more than that. It includes emotional benefits, such as how it makes your customers feel when they use it, or how they are perceived by others when using it.

Marketers usually know, but too often overlook the fact that the capabilities and attitudes of your customer service people, the store layout, and the friendliness and effectiveness of your repair personnel greatly impact customer value. All these factors, and many others besides, can affect your customers' perception of both the functional and emotional benefits of your product. Even though you may not automatically make the value connection, your customers most certainly do. Perhaps a key benefit is something as intangible as how much more secure you can make them feel about what they just bought from your organization, particularly during the very sensitive (but mostly ignored) period which immediately follows the point where money actually changes hands.

The benefits' side of the value equation is complex and connected to more factors than you are probably focusing on; likewise the cost that the customer is willing to spend for your 'bundle of benefits' is more than simply the price in local currency. What about how much time they have to wait in line in your store, or how long they have to wait for your serviceman to pick up the phone? These are very real costs from the customer's point of view. What do you think happens to the price-value equation when you ask your customers to put up with a delivery window of between 9:00 and 12:00? Adverse factors lurking around your beautifully prepared product, with its carefully crafted advertising, will be perceived as costs, and therefore will affect the ultimate value customers place on your product.

So here is the big question: If the ultimate responsibility for delivering on all the benefits of your product extends throughout your organization, why doesn't everybody in your organization understand the concept of customer value? Why aren't the marketing guys, who are supposed to know all about customer value, talking with customer service, the shipping people, and the production department? In those organizations where the marketing guys realize that their role is a much broader one than producing TV ads, why doesn't the customer service manager, or the production supervisor, or even the receptionist at the front desk listen to them when they try to explain why it is necessary to do something this way instead of that way to benefit the customer? Why? Because senior management rarely takes the time to ensure that everyone knows and understands that what the marketing department does matters – it matters to the customer, and it affects the value customers place on the goods and services your organization provides.

In a growth-oriented company, this absolute customer orientation needs to be accepted just as pervasively as practicing sound financial policies and procedures. Strong financial controls are widely understood to be critical to the success of a business, but without customer value, you have nothing to control – you're simply not selling anything and therefore you're not making any money. The practice of limiting cost-control only to the finance department is as dangerous to the viability and health of your business as it is to assume that only the marketing department needs to understand customer value; that it alone needs to figure out how to establish, deliver, and communicate it.

Drive safely, but drive somewhere – both matter. Think of the financial controls in your business as the controls and procedures you need to safely operate your car on the road. You need to know not only how to use the accelerator, the brakes, and to understand all the gauges and lights, you also must know the rules of the road. Without an engine, however, you're not going anywhere regardless of how good the tires are, or how much you know about road signs. Customer value is the business engine that moves the machinery, spins the wheels, and gets you to where you want to go.

'Marketing is too important to leave to the marketing guys.' Sergio Zyman, the chief marketing officer at Coca-Cola used to say this over and over again, almost like a mantra. He wanted everyone in the organization to understand that each of them, individually, played an important role in how the company delivered value to the customer. Whether they drove a truck, answered the phones, or made sure the returnable bottles were spotless after leaving the washer in the manufacturing plant, everyone contributed to that value…or not. It wasn't just a 'we're all in this together' sort of thing to say; it came from the heart. It is important for everyone to understand what the business is fundamentally based on – providing customer value. It is also motivating because it tells everyone that they provide value, that what they do really does matter. It matters from the top line down to the bottom line. And, by the way, one result of this momentum approach where everyone essentially became a marketing guy was that Coca-Cola entered one of the most rapid growth periods in its history – in volume and in profits. It was also reflected in the growth of the stock price – i.e., shareholder value.

Exponential Customer Value means that everyone in the organization knows the reason why the customers buy; reasons that include a whole range of perceived costs and benefits. Customer value is no longer the sole responsibility of the marketing department; it is everyone's *raison d'être* – from the accountant to the deliveryman. Even front-desk receptionists will understand their role and consequently be accountable for adding customer value. Customer interaction will no longer be a one-way monologue of 30-second TV ads, and billboards; it will become an interactive dialogue carried out at every customer touch-point throughout the purchase decision process that will result in building stronger and more loyal connections with your best customers and prospects.

Meaningful, deliverable, and defendable

One problem we all encounter is that we don't really know for certain if we've made the right decisions about increasing customer value until the actual results come in. How do we determine if one idea to increase value is better than another? Evaluating the business impact of various plans and ideas sounds complicated – there is a whole industry comprised of expert management consultants making it so – but the plain truth is that if you want to leverage the power of a lot of people thinking about how to increase customer value in your organization, you need to make the evaluation of ideas clear enough and basic enough so that everyone gets it. I have three simple words that will help you predict success and thereby make decisions easier. Ask yourself, with as much honesty and objectivity as you can muster, if your plan is:

Meaningful?

Deliverable?

Defendable?

If you can confidently answer yes to all three, it is probably a very good idea. Try it.

Is it meaningful?

Is what you are proposing with your idea meaningful to the person, or group of people, that needs to take action (e.g., buy your product). To achieve just about anything, you need someone else to do something – whether it is for the customer to buy your product, for the retailer to display your product in store, or, if you are in the pharma business, for the doctor to specifically prescribe your brand. All of these scenarios require others to take action, and they will take action only if it is meaningful for them to do so. Your idea must also be meaningful to you, to your organization, to different departments, to employees, and to anyone else who needs to take action to fulfill your objective and execute your strategy. If it is not meaningful, start over and come up with additional strategies until you can answer this question with a resounding 'yes'.

A 'yes' answer will also help avoid considering one of the most damaging tool marketers use – deep discounts to motivate either the value chain (distributors, wholesalers, retailers, etc.) or the customer to buy now. Are deep discounts meaningful to the customer? Of course they are. A deep discount leverages increased volume via the value equation by reducing the cost denominator. But are discounts truly meaningful to the company providing them? Probably not. Discounting your product to gain short-term volume is always an option, but it is seldom a good idea because it is one-sided in providing meaningful value. A good strategy is a win for your customer and a win for your company.

Is it deliverable?

Can you do it? Don't rush out under competitive pressure to promise a meaningful benefit until you are absolutely sure you can deliver it. Customers will seldom give you a second chance.

Deliverability used to be a fairly easy question in most businesses. Unfortunately, it was sometimes never asked, or it failed to take into consideration all of the interrelated areas in your organization that actually affect customer value. There is, however, another problem that comes under the 'deliverable' heading: whether what you promise with your idea is believable. These days, with all the hype and exaggerated claims flying around in some industries (especially in telecommunications and high tech), customers have become more skeptical than ever before. The problem becomes not only whether you can actually deliver the meaningful benefit you promise, but will your customers actually believe that you can or will do it. How many people believe that the latest exercise equipment will really melt away the fat with a physical commitment of only a few minutes a day? How many really believe that the latest mobile phone will perform all of the functions promised, all of the time?

The technology boom, the dot-com boom, and whatever other boom, during the 'go-go 90s' killed the goose that laid the golden egg; incredible and far-reaching claims were made about new capabilities that seldom lived up to their hype. As a result, virtually all industries and businesses are now faced with very skeptical customers. Accept that cynical perception and figure it into your strategy – always under-promise and over-deliver.

Is it defendable?

This one is a bit tougher, but it is every bit as important to the development and identification of a good plan or idea as being meaningful and deliverable. Think at least one step ahead. If you can really deliver what you promise with your meaningful benefits, can you actually hold the ground you have taken? For example, if you are a small company, make sure you are not doing what the bigger companies consider 'missionary work'. They would prefer others do the hard conversion work of selling a new idea, and then sweep in with their higher capacity, better distribution networks, and lower prices to steal away your new customers before you – the innovator – have had a chance to get a well-deserved return on your investment. Don't fall into the trap of not being able to defend what you have worked so hard to achieve. Build defendability into your strategy from day one.

Apple is a good example of getting defendable the hard way. You know the story – two guys, Jobs and Wozniak, figured out how to build a personal computer in their garage. They envisioned a new 'personal computer' category. They had a meaningful concept of seemingly infinite computer power

13

on every desk, and in every house. They figured out a way to build this personal computer for under $2000, the maximum price they thought customers would pay for this meaningful benefit.

They didn't think hard enough about defendability. Maybe they figured that IBM was too big to get involved in little computers. After all, IBM stands for 'International Business Machines', so why would it want to mess with the small-time stuff? But of course, IBM came in and was followed by a whole bunch of 'me toos' who carved out a piece of the fast-growing personal computer pie. Desperately scrambling to find a way to defend what it had innovatively achieved, Apple opted for an exclusive computer language on its Macintosh model launched in 1984. Initially, this defendable strategy backfired and all Apple did was to give customers a good reason not to buy Apple because Apple computers could only talk to other Apple computers, something perceived by most people to be less than meaningful. Or was it? Steve Jobs was dispatched from the company he had created, but he later came back to turn around Apple's failing fortunes by using a more comprehensive strategy – one focused on the individuality and independent spirit of creative-minded users – to establish a more meaningful, deliverable, and defendable positioning. Advertising agencies and design shops have led the way, with Apple providing them with highly creative software support. Even the Apple hardware is more colorful and creative than anything else on the market. Creative individuals have jumped on board. Apple now has a customer group that it understands, and consequently can continue to offer meaningful benefits, and do so in a defendable manner. It took a long time to get there, but in the end, Apple arrived at a meaningful, deliverable and defendable strategy. Wouldn't it be nice if your idea – or strategy – was defendable from the beginning?

The *Exponential Marketing* planning process

Let's look at the basic marketing planning process (Figure 4). Depending on how you describe each step of this process from start to finish, it could include five, or even as many as seven steps followed in some shape or form by a majority of companies, whether or not they have an established marketing planning process.

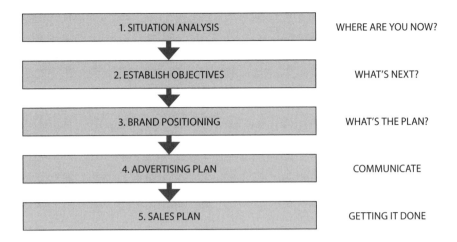

Figure 4: The 'business as usual' marketing planning process

But we're not talking about business as usual, are we? Times are tough, competition is tough and your customers have more choices and greater power than they have ever had before. You need to do things much better than 'usual'. Let's exponentially power it up by adapting the plan to an *Exponential Marketing* process (Figure 5). We still have the same five basic steps; but note, however, that every one of them, and the process itself, has been stepped up to create more impact by understanding and delivering on what matters most to potential customers, as well as getting more involvement throughout the organization by getting everyone involved in marketing – *Exponential Marketing!*

Figure 5: The *Exponential Marketing* planning process – exponentially improve the strategic planning process to create exponential growth

Step one in the *Exponential Marketing* planning process has moved. This is where the exponential thinking starts – at the beginning. Most businesses make the self-limiting mistake of focusing on *where they are* before they decide *where they want to be*. It is self-limiting because as a traditional first step it focuses the organization from the beginning on what has already been done up until now, rather than on what could be accomplished if it would only break out of its current way of thinking. By beginning the planning process with 'where we are and how we got here', managers are literally letting their past guide their future.

Exponential Marketing is more than just getting the order of steps right; it is about taking best practices in key areas and ratcheting them up a notch. Each step in the exponential planning process incorporates the best practices in that particular area with an emphasis on creating better customer value and delivering that value all the way from the factory to the sales floor.

What follows is not only a process to develop a good marketing plan; it is about creating an exponential growth plan for your business as a whole. *Exponential Marketing* will increase your bottom line by transforming the way you look at, and consequently create, top-line growth.

CHAPTER TWO

Destination Planning

Whether it is top-down, bottom-up, or someplace in between, it is typical to start the business planning process by establishing objectives based on the previous year's results. Most senior managers see these historical perform-ance numbers as a baseline to target future growth. For some businesses, the resulting incremental growth target may be +5%, or +15%, but the un-derlying fact is that most businesses are looking at the future based on what has happened in the past.

During the planning process, as line managers go through their indi-vidual operating plans, budgets, and resources to modify each of the vari-ous components that made up last year's business plans, they adjust these to the new growth number. Incremental growth objectives drive incremental planning; this in turn allows for incremental resource allocations, which in the end produce incremental growth. Sound familiar? It should because it's business as usual. And that's a problem.

The problem is that if you start with this mindset, if your vision of what can be done is based upon what has already been accomplished in the past, then this is probably as good as it is going to get. Where you go becomes self-limiting.

Incremental thinking leading to incremental results will persist in an organization until there is a down cycle that requires senior managers to ask junior managers for something extra. A new reality produces the phe-nomenon often known as the 'stretch' objective. It is a stretch because it simply adds a point or two to the current forecast, and asks line managers to do 'whatever it takes' to get the extra growth to make up for any shortfall that has occurred. What then follows is a 'stretch volume objective', and oftentimes a 'stretch profit objective'. Managers are often asked to produce extra volume without adding any additional costs. In some cases, senior managers even demand that important resources be cut (such as experienced and skilled employees) in order to get 'lean and mean'. What this really means is that you must do more with less by working harder and more efficiently.

There is a whole school of managers who actually believe that if they push down hard enough from above, their subordinates will somehow produce the required results. Because of this, there is a corresponding group of subordinate managers who have perfected the practice of 'sandbag forecasting' – they always under-promise and save something for the day when they are asked to stretch. Of course, senior managers know this because they were once junior managers, which is why they believe so fervently that they must push harder for you to come up with a bit more. And so it goes on, from one generation of managers to the next.

Most managers have already cut staff and related assets to the bone. We are at the point where every efficiency that can be achieved, and every cost that can be cut, has already been booked. So now what?

What businesses are finally waking up to is that sustainable growth in profits, and, correspondingly, in increased shareholder value, can be achieved only by creating sustainable growth in the business itself – top-line sales growth. At some point you have to actually grow the business. And if you want to grow the business in today's tighter and more competitive environment, not only do you need to transform the business itself for the future, but you also have to transform your thinking. This is where *Destination Planning* comes into play.

To significantly accelerate the rate of growth for your business, you need to start doing some things differently pretty soon, because the future starts one minute from now. The first step in the strategic planning process is your first opportunity to accelerate growth. You need to start with the end-point – the place where you ultimately want to be. Define your success.

The reason behind having *Destination Planning* as the first step in the *Exponential Marketing* process is that you need to start with where you ultimately want to be, and then look back from that end-point to establish the critical gap between that place in the future and where you currently are (Figure 6). By doing this, by planning your destination, you are likely to find yourself in a whole new game – a game with more volume growth and more profitability. I'm not talking about a destination that looks like a mission statement that you frame and hang on the wall, but rather a clear model of what real success would look like, if only you could make it happen.

By clearly identifying where you want to be at a specific point in time, you can then focus your thinking on two levels:

1. Seizing only those opportunities that truly lead you to your destination.
2. Identifying and eliminating any barriers or problems that are actually standing in your way.

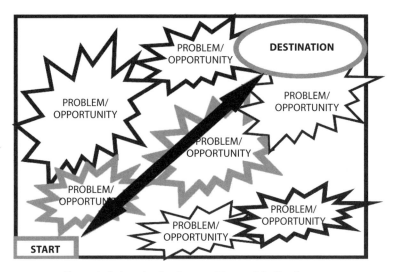

Figure 6: A clear destination provides straight-line focus

Destination Planning is a process of looking into the future and then integrating four basic forecasting elements that will provide a clear and concise model of where you want to be, and what it takes to get there – a *Success Dashboard*.

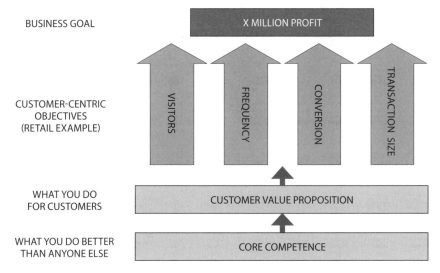

Figure 7: The *Success Dashboard* (© The Garrison Group)

With a 'one-look dashboard', you can establish the relationship between customer value and the key business objectives that will lead to your ultimate goal – all on a single page.

I doubt that any of these elements are new to you. The important thing is how effectively you can integrate all four of them to clearly define success. Each element necessarily must interrelate with the others, which gets us to the fundamental point – unless you're looking at customer value and integrating it into your key business objectives, you are going to find it much more difficult to achieve your goal.

What the CEO and the CFO will like about this *Destination Planning* model is that it gets the marketing guys to focus on measurable business objectives – something that they think the marketing guys should have been focusing on all along. And that's a good point. Coming from another perspective, the marketing guys will see this as an effective process to get the rest of the organization to focus on driving customer value – something that they think everyone should have been focusing on all along. Another good point. The reality is that both perspectives are correct and serve to emphasize why customer value (as the key driver of business growth) needs to be understood and integrated into core business objectives and goals.

Peter Brabeck, the chairman of Nestlé stated that he wanted 'marketing to be completely embedded in the business'. He then added: 'Business must be completely embedded into marketing.' He is not contradicting himself; he is simply pointing out the reality that good business and good marketing are one and the same. In a successful business you must integrate your business growth goals and objectives with the driver that makes it all possible – increased customer value.

The overall business goal

The steps in developing the destination model are important. The first thing that needs to be done is to plant the flag on the business result or goal that will best drive shareholder value. A relatively aggressive goal or description of success in this instance is critical because it will force the organization to conclude that it will never get there with 'business as usual'. The goal must illustrate the point that the organization will undeniably have to transform itself in order to achieve it. Stretch will not be enough, no matter how many sandbags have been stored away. Some may argue that to focus on just one goal is an over-simplification of a complex business; but it is through the goal's focus and clarity that it becomes effective at rallying the organization – much like a flag that must be seen by all of the troops on the battlefield. Something clear and to the point is best: *double the business by 2012*, or *put your software in 25% of small and medium-sized businesses in the market by 2015*. Obviously, the imperative is to focus on the one goal that will most positively impact shareholder value when you actually achieve it.

Transformational goals

It is very important at the start of the *Destination Planning* process not to get bogged down in all the reasons you can't do this or that. Instead, take the time at the very beginning to establish what success would look like in a best-case scenario. It isn't a perfect world, and the truth is that you may never actually arrive at the ideal situation for your organization, but how close will you get if you never think about the ideal? Start with where you really want to be without limiting yourself by predetermining what may, or may not be possible. Start with the attitude that you will have to overcome barriers, not insurmountable obstacles. Think 'what if' rather than 'why not'.

So, how far should you go? You need to stretch the rubber band without breaking it. You do that most effectively by being evolutionary rather than revolutionary. When I say transform your business, I am talking about leveraging your core competence as a business to establish an enhanced value platform that will drive renewed growth. Find a way to do what you already do better than anyone else has ever done before to create a stronger customer value platform that will achieve your goal. But stick to what it is that you fundamentally do and build on your strengths. It is about improving what you do (your core competence) for your customers (your value platform) to a level that is better than anyone else.

What business are you really in?

Understanding your core competence – and how that is perceived by customers – is often determined by how you define your business. What do you provide in exchange for customers giving you their money?

It may sound like I am talking out of both sides of my mouth when I first tell you to be transformational, and then I tell you to stick to your core competence. What I'm saying is to be aspirational about how you grow your business while keeping in mind what it is that you fundamentally do. You may need to change much about how you do your core business and how you go to market, but 'don't throw the baby out with the bath water'.

Let's take an example of how a telephone company could define its business relative to providing customer value. By taking a step back from what it does and thinking about what it does for its customer – what value it provides – the phone company may see that it has the transformational opportunity to define its business in a much more customer meaningful way (Figure 8).

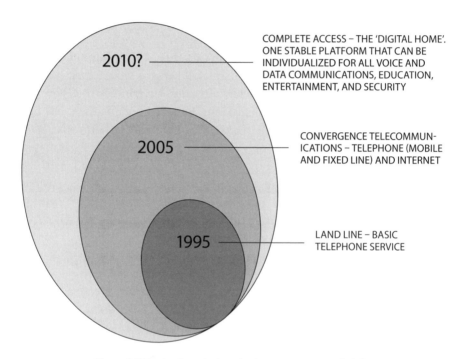

Figure 8: What business is the telephone company really in?

Imagine the effect such a business definition will have on the product development people in the newly defined, Complete Access-Digital Home business. What acquisitions should be made to strengthen the value platform to make it more meaningful, deliverable and defendable? How can support functions, such as customer service and billing, be more involved in improving value? What are the expectations of suppliers and other external constituencies? How much more effective – and efficient – can the marketing department and the agencies be in developing communication in the short term now that they know the end-game?

Catch up or leap ahead?

A reporter once asked the legendary Canadian hockey player Wayne Gretsky why he is considered the best hockey player of all time. Gretsky's answer was quite simple: 'Most players go to where the puck is. I go to where the puck is going to be.'

Nearly 20 years ago, businesses and institutions in emerging markets were faced with a significant change in the way they had operated for decades. Most adopted a 'catch up to the West' mindset, while a few others adopted a far more progressive mindset of 'leaping ahead' to enhanced competences and a better value proposition. They used an approach of learning from, and then improving upon the most up-to-date best practices from more developed markets. At the same time they avoided the past mistakes that similar businesses had made in the West…mistakes that many are still making. These more progressive businesses in Central and Eastern Europe (CEE) have developed leap-ahead business plans that take their organizations right away to where the West will probably be in delivering customer value five to ten years from now. They have set their sights on a business model and customer value platform based on where the puck will be, rather than where it currently is.

Let me use two industry examples – retailing and transportation – with two prominent regional players to demonstrate the result from playing either catch-up or leap-ahead. The Polish national airline, LOT, along with most of the other national carriers in the region, went into the early 1990s intent on catching up to what management and Polish government leaders at the time thought a *flag carrier* should be considering as fleet capability and route structure. LOT did this even though the flaws with existing Western European flag carriers were becoming increasingly exposed within the broader global airline industry. Fairly obvious, even back then, was the financial success of a new regional carrier concept that was already being executed by Southwest Airlines and others. Today, LOT, Malév (Hungary) and Tarum (Romania) all have an employee-to-plane ratios that are among the highest in the industry, costly and cumbersome fleets to maintain, and a route structure that makes very little sense in today's airline industry. Congratulations – all three have successfully caught up to the dying concept of national flag carriers in the West.

Unfortunately LOT and the others are only just now beginning to see the need to move to a regional carrier concept, but it is much more difficult to change the capabilities and structures it has today, than it would have been ten years ago. It should have known better because 'the handwriting was on the wall'.

On the other hand, the supermarket business is growing by leaps and bounds in Eastern Europe, and is currently one of the most advanced markets in the world. Even though the market leader, Tesco, is from the West (UK), it did not come into Eastern Europe with the self-limiting attitude that it would bring its new operations up to speed with its stores back home. Tesco developed an enhanced retail model that 'renovated' the best of what was working in the West, and then leaped ahead of the pre-existing barriers and limitations that the West was still struggling with – such as poorly placed small stores and limited selection.

When a business becomes focused on catching up to the West, it is not just a result of the shortsightedness of local managers in developing economies. More often than not, it is the result of veteran managers from the West coming into new markets with the lazy attitude that all that is necessary to grow the business in new markets is to dust off some old programs and strategies from their earlier experiences. Not only do they make the fundamental mistake of not recognizing that rapidly developing markets are different, but they are probably overlooking the fact that the business model they have in their minds isn't as successful as it could be back home either.

Customer value proposition

If you are really going to *double the volume by 2012*, or *put your software in 25% of small and medium-sized businesses in the market by 2015*, you must have a value-based relationship with your customers that drives that result. What do your customers need to think and feel about your products, brands and even perhaps the company itself in order for them to make the purchase and re-purchase decisions required for you to achieve your goal? It is defining how you want the customer to think, feel and act that establishes your customer value proposition. This combination of core competences and customer value proposition can be called the *value platform* because unless it is laid down as a fundamental basis for capturing growth, and acted upon by everyone in your organization, you will never reach the full potential of your business. Any significant growth in your business will necessarily have to be built on this value platform.

It is important to point out that the customer value platform is always evolving. You start with the best thinking you have today on what you think that value is relative to what you want your customers to think, feel, and act.

As you move through the *Exponential Marketing* process, however, you will be learning a lot in the *Value Diagnostics* step about your core competences and about who your customers are and what their needs are; this will serve to fine-tune and modify your customer value proposition into a more substantiated brand strategy.

Revisit your customer value proposition and core competences periodically and adjust them with input from what you are learning throughout the *Exponential Marketing* process. After all, you can't put your business on hold while you do a complete assessment and develop a new strategy; you need to be doing things tomorrow and the next day to communicate and deliver customer value in order to keep the doors open and the trucks running. Your *Destination Planning* model with your current best thinking on your value platform and the related objectives leading to your goal will help a lot in managing your way through the short term as you set your sights on the long term.

Think, feel and act

Because business growth is fundamentally linked to providing customer value, achieving your destination is totally dependant on how you can affect customers in a manner that they reward you by actually buying your product. Consequently, you need to state within your customer value proposition how you intend them to think, feel and act with regard to your product. Identifying the desired customer perceptions about your business will fine-tune the proposition and make it much clearer.

Amazon.com has transformed its business dramatically in recent years by recognizing that it is not really in the book business. It has concluded that its core competence is in the Internet retail business. This has led to an enhanced customer value proposition based on a huge base of trusting online customers. Amazon.com probably knows better than anyone else how to sell stuff online and can efficiently ship it anywhere in the world, so why should it limit itself to selling just books? It wants to compete in the much bigger and more profitable category of online retailing, and it is doing it within its core strategy of selling a wide range of 'brands' through the amazon.com site. It is also knocking down key barriers by knowing what it does… and does not do…well. It magnifies its efficiency by not warehousing all that stuff it sells in a single cumbersome site (something it could probably never do very well), but instead drop-ships from the brand manufacturer's warehouse, or from an aligned bricks and mortar retailer, through a strategic shipping alignment with UPS.

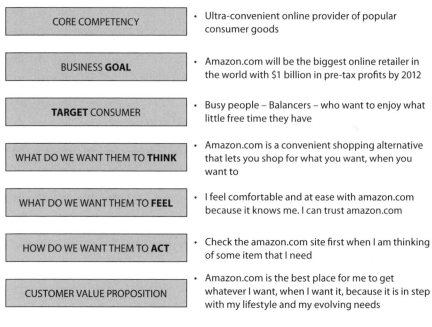

CORE COMPETENCY	• Ultra-convenient online provider of popular consumer goods
BUSINESS **GOAL**	• Amazon.com will be the biggest online retailer in the world with $1 billion in pre-tax profits by 2012
TARGET CONSUMER	• Busy people – Balancers – who want to enjoy what little free time they have
WHAT DO WE WANT THEM TO **THINK**	• Amazon.com is a convenient shopping alternative that lets you shop for what you want, when you want to
WHAT DO WE WANT THEM TO **FEEL**	• I feel comfortable and at ease with amazon.com because it knows me. I can trust amazon.com
HOW DO WE WANT THEM TO **ACT**	• Check the amazon.com site first when I am thinking of some item that I need
CUSTOMER VALUE PROPOSITION	• Amazon.com is the best place for me to get whatever I want, when I want it, because it is in step with my lifestyle and my evolving needs

Figure 9: *Destination Planning* example for amazon.com

Customer-oriented business objectives

To complete your *Success Dashboard* and thereby define your destination, your customer value proposition can be extended to customer objectives. These objectives are the four or five measurements in the *Success Dashboard* model that must be achieved to reach the goal. For a retail establishment they could be number of visitors, purchase conversion, transaction size, and repeat visits, to name just a few customer-centric objectives that would be customer-value driven. Achieving these objectives would result in reaching the overall goal. Since these objectives are a result of delivering on customer value, they are customer oriented as a matter of course. This linkage will go a long way toward getting you to where you want to be – a customer value driven business. If your destination model is based on where you want to be five or ten years from now, it is a relatively simple process to break down the yearly or quarterly objectives that must be achieved by a corresponding date to achieve the over-all business goal. You can, and should break these numbers down by business unit, brand and even location, so that everyone in the organization sees their own *Success Dashboard* and can track on a day-to-day basis how they are doing.

Can do, should do, and must do

Successful business leaders know how to focus on the two or three things they absolutely must do. They choose very carefully where they want to concentrate. Intellect is a powerful thing, but brain power can also create a situation in which you enjoy solving problems so much that you spend all your time looking for new ones to solve. Sounds strange – but it happens, whether the great problem solver consciously realizes it or not. Although this approach may keep some businesses out of the ditch, they probably aren't going anywhere very fast either.

Destination Planning is a mechanism that enables you prioritize your time as well as your resources. In your position there are probably one hundred things you and your business 'can do'. As a matter of fact, you can stay incredibly busy in the attempt. Then, there are significantly fewer things that you 'should do' – maybe 20–30. It is these 'should dos' that tend to eat up all of your time. However, if you can identify the two or three things you absolutely 'must do' to get to your destination, and can manage to put the majority of your effort into accomplishing those 'must dos', you will be amazed at what you will be able to achieve from the concentrated power of that 'must do' focus. The advantage of *Destination Planning* is the orientation it provides to guide you like a compass to the most important things you must do to achieve your goal. 'Must do' items should probably include the three or four customer-centric objectives from your *Success Dashboard*.

Alignment up front

Knowing that getting to a destination will require the concerted effort and brain power of a range of internal and external constituencies, it is important to involve them from the beginning in the *Destination Planning* session. A shared approach will not only help you establish your *Success Dashboard* inclusive of a transformational goal and an enhanced customer value proposition, but the involvement of the key constituencies will also ensure that the goal and your value proposition are aligned with your core competences upstream and deliverable objectives downstream. Remember that what makes this exponential is how you create momentum by capturing all of the growth power within the organization.

The actual *Destination Planning* session can usually be handled in a day, but you should do it away from the regular ebb and flow of the business. Go off site. Start by asking the participants to think about situations and businesses unrelated to their own. By initially thinking about other businesses, they can begin to look at the concept of *Destination Planning* with a more open mind about what it is and what it can accomplish. After a warm-up relating to other types of businesses (such as examples of ones who leap ahead, or catch up to establish the concept of getting to someplace that matters) begin to dig into the evolving needs of your own customers. What value would you need to provide in order to acquire and sustain new customers?

It all starts at the end

It is critically important to establish your destination first – where it is you want to be – and only then analyze the current situation. Whether you utilize a SWOT (Strengths, Weaknesses, Opportunities and Threats) analysis, or even the more comprehensive *Value Diagnostics* step that we will talk about in the following chapter, you can do so with the focus on new opportunities and their importance in achieving your ultimate destination. You will also be able to better identify any potential barriers that may stand in the way of where you want to be. You know the end game and this will stimulate your thinking and the thinking of all of the constituencies involved in growing your business.

In the *Success Dashboard*, these four interrelated elements – goal, objectives, core competences and the customer value proposition – may seem obvious, and you may feel like you already know and are focused on all four drivers. But are you really? And are they integrated into a single, *Success Dashboard* that everyone in the organization can see and understand?

The examples of a regional airline, a telephone company, or a supermarket chain may seem very different, but it is important that you recognize that *Destination Planning* relates to what you 'must do' if you want to be successful, regardless of what industry you are in. You need to know from the very beginning, where you want to want to be in the end, and it will be that focus on what you 'must do' to get there that will move mountains. So, now that you know how important it is to focus your organization on a shared destination, and on the need to concentrate your energy on the 'must dos', let's move to the next step – determining those opportunities and barriers that are standing between you and your destination. The *Value Diagnostics* step will help you identify those absolutely 'must dos' to stimulate the strategies needed to achieve success!

Building a *Success Dashboard* – INTERSPORT

By Gábor Bródi

*Gábor is a consultant at the Garrison Group where he covers a broad range of business including pharma, telecom and retail. He is a native of Hungary.**

Businesses in the retail sector have especially close relationships with their customers. Having customers regularly 'come into your facility' looking for assistance and asking you questions about your products is a luxury most sectors do not enjoy. Consequently, I find it strange that marketers from the fast moving consumer goods (FMCG) side of life are usually seen as the cutting-edge marketing experts when it is the retail guys who usually have the most intimate relationships with their customers. In a sense, the retail sales floor can be seen as an ongoing focus group – observing customer behavior that may or may not correspond with actual purchase decisions. Because the sales floor is easily viewed by management, the connection between the competences of the retail staff and their corresponding effect on the delivery or non-delivery of the value platform is more readily apparent. It is this direct linkage between staff, product and customers that makes INTERSPORT – a sporting goods (clothing, equipment and accessories) retailer – a clear example of how interconnected a *Success Dashboard* should be.

The first three steps of constructing a *Success Dashboard* for INTERSPORT are:

1. Define its *core competence*.
2. Formulate its *customer value proposition*.
3. Establish its *overall business goal*.

INTERSPORT is a company with over 5000 stores in almost 40 countries primarily (but not exclusively) in Europe. On visiting the stores, their commonalities are easy to spot:

- All stores are very well equipped and stocked: they have a diverse selection of sporting goods for a vast number of sports.
- The stores are interactive to a great extent – INTERSPORT makes it easy to try various pieces of sports equipment. In fact, most of the products on the shelves are not in their packaging so it is easy for customers to try them out.
- The sales staff is exceptionally well informed about sports and is highly skilled at giving expert advice to potential customers about sporting apparel and equipment. Hungarians need only travel to neighboring Austria to see INTERSPORT stores in the very heart of large skiing areas, often just a few meters from the slopes. These stores obviously specialize in winter sports equipment and the staff is capable

---

* Gábor can be contacted at gabor@garrisongroup.eu

of giving almost the same level of help and advice to skiers and snow-boarders as a personal ski/snowboard instructor.

It is this width and depth of sporting products, and the interaction with those productss linked with a very experienced and knowledgeable staff that defines INTERSPORT's core competence.

This is what INTERSPORT does. More important is what INTERSPORT does for customers, which thus becomes a meaningful and deliverable value proposition. Having this level of choice (allowing customers not to have to make multiple trips to multiple stores to fulfill their needs), this level of interaction, and this level of expertise at the customers' disposal, we can say that what INTERSPORT offers as a value proposition is a *hands-on, one-stop sports shop powered by expert consultation*.

As for defining the overall business goal – let's say hitting a profitability amount of X million within five years.

Once the core competence the value proposition and the overall business goal have been defined, we then need to fill the *Success Dashboard* with the customer-centric objectives that link them all together. Knowing so many things about customers – how many pass by the store daily, how many actually enter the premises, how much time they spend in the shop, do they seek assistance from the sales force, how much time they take (consideration period) before they make a purchase decision, how many return on a regular basis and how often, etc. – makes it easy to demonstrate how many different kinds of clear and measurable business objectives are possible in a typical retail business. But what are the three or four that absolutely must be achieved if the overall profit goal is to be realized?

First things first! Visitors are key. Unless INTERSPORT can actually attract visitors into the store (or onto its website), it will find it very difficult to sell them anything. So attracting visitors is its first customer-centric business objective. We can count the number of visitors that go into the store – is it enough or do we want more? By delivering strongly on the value proposition based on INTERSPORT's core competence, we can expect to significantly increase the number of potential customers.

The second important customer-centric objective is to convert as many visitors as possible into actual customers. The conversion rate can also be significantly increased by all three attributes that come from the value platform:

1. The wide variety in stock helps potential customers find something for themselves and convinces them to actually buy it.
2. The interactive experience can also help drive the conversion rate; we all know that people are much more likely to buy something if they've had a chance to try it out.

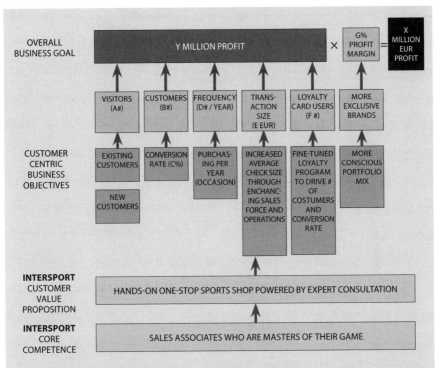

3. Expert advice is again something that can drive conversion, especially in cases where a store visitor is looking for a piece of equipment that is quite expensive (e.g., running shoes over 100) but does not appear to be a connoisseur of the sport. In such cases, when the involvement level is high because of the price, but low because of insecurity concerning the category, expert reassurance can be the conversion driver.

The third objective is about getting customers to return more often to the store and buy more sporting-related stuff – frequency. Purchase frequency is again; driven by making the store interactive – people will know that if there is a new product on the market, they can simply go to INTERSPORT to see it and try it without any hassle. Also, frequency can be significantly increased by adding a more personal touch to the relationship between sales staff and customers. It's easy to understand why somebody would come back to a store where they can meet with somebody whose opinion they can trust. This customer-engagement approach can be enhanced by providing a loyalty program (e.g., a card for people who have purchased on multiple occasions) that not only ensures price discounts, but also value-added services and experiences related to the value platform (e.g., interactive premier trial of innovative products, expert consultation for hardcore customers).

The last customer-centric objective for INTERSPORT relates to transaction size which refers to the average amount of money customers spend on a visit to the store. This can also be increased based on INTERSPORT's value proposition. The combination of a wide variety of available goods and a sales staff willing and able to give competent advice on how to effectively and efficiently combine different pieces of sporting equipment and accessories is an excellent way to promote cross-selling opportunities – and drive transaction size accordingly.

This is an important priority for 'farming existing customer relationships'. It obviously makes much more sense to sell an additional item to a person who has already decided to visit the store and to purchase something than to focus on people who aren't even sure they want to visit the store and purchase sporting goods in the first place. But if it is so obvious, why do so many businesses spend a majority of their marketing trying to 'hunt' new customers rather than 'farming' existing customer relationships? Not having a *Success Dashboard* on hand with a clear understanding of how different and corresponding objectives can deliver an overall profit goal makes it easier to make that expensive mistake.

These four consumer-centric objectives all relate to increasing overall revenue – top-line business growth. The other important factor of the overall business objective – achieving X billion annual profit – is the profit driver. There are the classical ways of trying to improve this key indicator, such as aiming for better deals with suppliers, cutting costs on HR spending, etc. But having a powerful value platform such as the *hands-on, one-stop sports shop powered by expert consultation,* offers INTERSPORT other, more customer-oriented possibilities to improve its profit margin.

INTERSPORT, apart from carrying the top global brands, also sells its own exclusive brands (Pro Touch, McKinley, etc.). By enabling people to try these products in an interactive way and giving them professional advice, INTERSPORT stands a much better chance of selling these brands than a 'regular' retailer would. The challenge that most exclusive and private label brands face is that they are usually considered lower quality than the global brand products. If customers are given the chance to try these products first-hand and are told by 'expert' sales consultants whom they trust that they are just as good as the big brands, then they are likely to feel more comfortable about giving these exclusive brands a try. The profit on these products is obviously much higher. Without the hands-on experience and the expertise of the sales staff as reassurance, other retailers cannot increase the proportion of exclusive products within their overall sales, so INTERSPORT actually has a customer-centric means of increasing its profitability because of a core-competency-driven value proposition that truly drives its overall business goal via a limited set of measurable customer-centric objectives.

It is easy to see how these customer-centric objectives help connect the value platform to the overall business goal. If we were discussing a different retailer with a different core competence, and thus a different value platform, we would have to go about defining these customer-centric objectives in a very different way. Every *Success Dashboard* is unique to the organization it serves with the purpose of creating a roadmap of the journey that lies ahead in order to achieve that overall business goal.

CASE STUDY

The transformation of Real Madrid
– *Destination Planning* at work

By Roberto Garcia

Roberto is a former consumer insights analyst for the Garrison Group. He is currently working as a financial analyst in Budapest. Roberto is a native of Mexico.[*]

Editor's note: The true measure of good Destination Planning is looking back after a few years to see how far you have come and whether you are heading in the right direction. This case study about Real Madrid appeared in the first edition of Exponential Marketing *in 2006. Football fans will be very aware that Real Madrid did outstanding things – both sportswise and businesswise – in the years following the publication of that chapter. Real Madrid won La Liga (The Spanish Championship) in 2006/2007 and again in 2007/2008. In summer 2009, it announced a spending spree on new, iconic players in the range of €300 million. It has already signed Kaká, Xabi Alonso and Cristiano Ronaldo (the latter breaking all previous transfer records when leaving Manchester United for a whopping €94 million).*

This means not only is Real Madrid likely to do outstandingly on the pitch, it is also likely to continue to grow as an outstanding business franchise. It seems like Real Madrid continues to have the right destination and is moving ahead full steam.

The business of sports

Despite its sometimes up and down performance on the pitch in recent years, Real Madrid stays at the top of the league in business performance. According to Deloitte's Football Money League, which measures the income of football teams, Real Madrid is the world champion – overtaking long-time ruler,

---

[*] Roberto can be contacted at roberto@garrisongroup.eu

Manchester United. However, as recently as 2000, Real Madrid was in financial distress – its expenditure was significantly higher than its revenue. What was the cause of this turnaround? Did Real Madrid focus its thinking on reducing costs – sell its expensive marquee players, or sell and lease back its stadium as many financially ailing teams have done in the past to restore profitability? Not at all. In fact, Real did exactly the opposite. Starting with the acquisition of Luis Figo for €61.7 million, the turnaround strategy focused on the acquisition of one mega-player each year. The next addition was Zinedine Zidane, a transaction that became the most expensive transaction in football history. Ronaldo joined the team after the 2002 World Cup, and yet another jewel in the crown, David Beckham in 2003. Moreover, the Santiago Bernabeu stadium was expensively renovated to provide greater comfort for the fans.

Rather than reducing costs to drive the bottom line, Real Madrid has focused on the top line – increasing revenue. It has rigorously integrated marketing into the team's business model. In addition to the two traditional revenue sources – TV rights fees and match-day income – Real Madrid accelerated into €148 million of new commercial revenues from merchandising, sponsorship, and licensing. Shifting from the floodlights to the spotlights, Madrid players are now appearing in more advertisements than many movie stars.

It started with leadership

In 2000, Lorenzo Sanz, then club president, was confident. The club had just conquered its eighth Champions League title. It could now boast two European Champions Cups, one Spanish League title, one Spanish Super-Champions Cup and one Intercontinental Cup. Understandably, Sanz felt so certain that he was going to be re-elected by the members (shareholders) that he decided to call an election that summer. However, to his surprise, the voting members turned out to be not only dedicated football fans, but concerned owners as well. The members took a hard look at the numbers and saw that since Sanz had taken over management of the club, the already alarming debt that Mendoza (the previous president) had left behind had in fact grown to four times the size – to over half a billion euro. The greatest soccer club of the century, as certificated by FIFA, was in financial distress.

A contender for Sanz in the elections was Florentino Perez, a successful businessman whom at a first glance appeared less than formidable because of his unsuccessful 1995 challenge of Mendoza. But Florentino had an ace in the hole: his business reputation for making money. Florentino could see that his time had come to set Real Madrid straight and he intended to prove his case to the members in the election. Florentino devoted his campaign to attacking the sustainability of Sanz's financial planning and promised to get the club into an optimal financial position – one that would also allow him to buy the best players in the world. The vision Florentino articulated was to bring truly world-class players to the club to drive his financially sustainable international *Golden Team* concept. The destination Florentino had in mind was to create the first truly international team – not merely in terms of on-the-pitch success (which many before had perused), but more importantly, he believed, in the hearts of football fans around the world. To many it seemed contradictory to eventually make more money by spending more money to acquire the high-priced talent Florentino needed to achieve his goal, but in a closely run election, Florentino beat Sanz to the finish and became the new president of Real Madrid.

Taking aim at the goal – the *Golden Team* destination

After winning the election, Florentino went straight to work in building the *Golden Team* by quickly 'stealing' Barcelona's biggest star Luis Figo. But Florentino knew it was just the start; his *Golden Team* had to spread Real Madrid's prestige all around the world and attract a legion of young fans. Florentino's destination of becoming the most popular team in the world was indeed transformational because in order to achieve it, every way in which the club was doing business had to change. Based on a clearly articulated value platform (international superstar players – the *Golden Team*), Florentino could set clear and measurable objectives that would create the conditions for a new vision of a successful football club – both in terms of athletic as well as financial measurements.

Real Madrid's fundamental values (its core competences) are rooted in its history of excellence – success, effort, competitiveness and honor. Florentino's strategy was to build on this foundation of customer value to get worldwide football fans to believe that when they bought Real Madrid merchandise, they were acquiring a model of sporting excellence represented by superstar players such as Figo, Beckham, Raúl, Ronaldo, Carlos or Zidane. The fans would feel that by wearing their favorite players' t-shirts, they would be part of an unrepeatable moment in history where some of the best players of the world fight together in pursuit of football excellence. What Florentino's Real Madrid *Golden Team* would represent was not only the best football team, but also the standard of sporting excellence through those fundamental Real Madrid beliefs and attitudes. Supporting this higher ideal was the club's history of beneficiary games, its active charity foundation, and its players acting as sport ambassadors.

Scoring a goal: The objectives

The bridge between the value platform and the destination was in the measurable objectives that Florentino established for Real Madrid. As the traditional Spanish saying goes: 'to make chicken soup, the first thing that you need is chicken.' Consequently, the first objective for Real Madrid was to bring in one of the best players on the planet to the team each year. To afford such acquisitions, Florentino established financial objectives on the team's real estate holdings that resulted in the sale of the training fields at Ciudad Deportiva and then the purchase of Ciudad de las Rosas – a huge property near the airport on the outskirts of Madrid. This transaction instantly reported a profit of €425 million, which eliminated the debts, and created a better training facility than before.

Florentino next asked his marketing and sales departments to boost the sales of t-shirts and other 'star' merchandise items by more than four times to exploit the new appeal of the recent acquisitions. This merchandise objective not only created more revenue from the merchandising, but also had a knock-on effect on team sponsor revenue from the greater exposure of their brands. Other objectives, including increasing the income of friendly matches, football schools, licensing, increased TV rights, etc., were all driven by the value platform Florentino had established.

What business are you really in? From the pitch to Hollywood

Normally, presidents of soccer teams will say that they are in the sports industry. Florentino redefined the business because he realized that if more than 350 million people worldwide are watching your games, you are actually in the entertainment business. Moreover, if several of your players are considered to be among the sexiest men on Earth, your football team should be promoted more as a weekly movie serial where the audience is able to see their 'stars' in action every weekend. Florentino's value platform attracted much more than football fans; it expanded to teenage girls with posters of David Beckham on their walls, or wives that declared Raúl to be the perfect husband. Player-stars with incredible market value would help Madrid to sell its famous white shirts in every corner of the world – stars that happened to play football. David Beckham is the face of Gillette, the legs of Adidas, the eyes of Police sunglasses, and the ears of Vodafone mobiles. He had led the way for all stars – movie, music and sports – into beauty products as an integral part of a modern man's world, and the personification of the term 'metrosexual'. World tours have expanded Real Madrid's brand to reach a huge Asian market and reinforced sales in the important US market, which has its share of other superstars. In 2005, Real Madrid literally went into the movie business and released worldwide *Real: the Movie* showing Real Madrid values personified by the players and sustained by inspirational stories.

The rise of a new Galaxy: Increasing income and profits

The first four years of Florentino's leadership were magnificent; two Spanish League titles, one European Champions Cup, one Intercontinental Cup, two Spanish Supercups, one European Supercup, and growing revenues in 2000, 2001, 2002 and 2003. Many of the players were recognized for great accomplishments in their respective national teams and clubs – Figo, Zidane and Ronaldo earned outstanding individual awards, the Golden Ball or the FIFA best player award. The Spanish press went beyond golden, and baptized the players as *the galactics*, because they were considered to be out of this world.

By 2003, Florentino also had a new nickname – the *Midas King* of football with a string a successes to match:

– Real Madrid's Asian tour reported about €40 million in revenue.
– New agreements to create soccer football schools with Real´s name generated €6 million.
– The income reported from the image rights of its players (the club owns half of such rights) added up to approximately €36 million.
– The lead sponsors – Siemens and IC Mobile – provided €12 million each.
– Additional sponsorships with Adidas, Pepsi, Mahou, Rexona, Electrolux and Viceroy accounted for approximately €20 million.
– And the sale of t-shirts with David Beckham's name and number brought in €625,000 in a single day.

From 2001 to 2005, revenue doubled and Real Madrid conquered the top of another competition, the *Money League*. Unfortunately, Florentino Pérez was not there to pick up the trophy he most deserved. Still a true sportsman, he had quit one month before because of his team's poor performance on the pitch – two years without a single cup. Thanks to Florentino's leadership and his legacy, Real Madrid is now truly a global brand and has the financial strength to not only sustain Florentino's winning *Golden Team* value platform with worldwide fans, but the means to do everything it must to put the team at the top of the athletic game with a steady flow of new on-pitch talent – superstar talent.

CHAPTER THREE

Value Diagnostics

Imagine the new manager of a Formula One team. His goal has been predetermined with extreme clarity: 'Win the Formula One within three years.' Because he comes from a business background, he pulls out the tried and true SWOT analysis form (Strengths, Weaknesses, Opportunities, and Threats) and begins to fill it out. If he is like most managers who use the SWOT analysis, he will occasionally succumb to the mirror-image trap: the strengths of the competitor show up in his weaknesses column and any opportunities he lists will automatically show up as threats considering that the competitor might try them first. But even if he doesn't fall into the mirror-image SWOT trap, at the end of the day all he really has with his SWOT analysis is a concise competitive assessment document. Has he dug into other important areas to determine all of the factors that can contribute to, or hinder, his team's capability to win the Formula One within three years? Where would he put funding issues and sponsor-related activities on the SWOT analysis – strengths and opportunities, or weaknesses and threats? How about new drivers coming up in the next two years, or new tracks to be added to the series? Clearly, those are threats, right? Has he included an assessment of potential new technologies from tire manufacturers and fuel experts? How about learning from other related fields? Is there anything in NASCAR racing or with motorcycles that could be applied to his situation? And how about really digging into his team's performance?

You get the point. Even in a field that has very clear competitors and a very clear goal, the SWOT analysis can come up short. No matter how rigorously you apply it, it's limited. How well do you think SWOT works when you have to consider various customer targets, a complex value chain, and a competitive set that includes not only the usual suspects, but also a range of products and services that could be viewed as substitutes for your product from the customer's perspective?

If you are going to fully determine the key opportunities to reach your destination, as well as identifying any existing or potential barriers that may stand in your way, you need something more than SWOT.

Let's go back to Formula One and modify the assessment process instead of attempting to impose our tried (and found wanting) SWOT analysis. The key word is *diagnostics*. In motor racing, they perform diagnostics on a wide range of factors that affect the performance of the team. In Formula One, speed is paramount. In business, customer value is paramount. Just as the best team in Formula One is consistently the fastest, the best team in business is the one that consistently provides the best value for its customers. And again, best value is not necessarily the best price, but rather the best customer-delivered value for the price – *more for more and worth it*.

So instead of SWOT, let's use a more appropriate analytical tool – *Value Diagnostics*. The focus, as it should be, is on value. What is your brand and/or company doing, or not doing, to provide value to your customers and correspondingly, better value to your shareholders? Exactly who are your existing and potential customers, and what do they consider value to be? How good has your performance been up to now in delivering value to your customers in an efficient manner? Who are your competitors, from

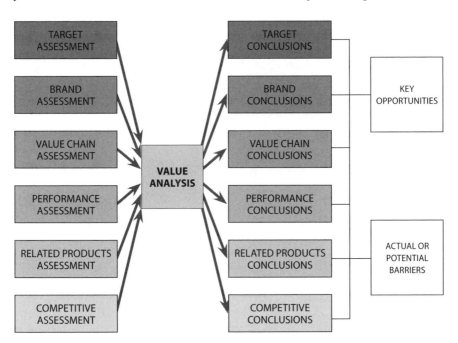

Figure 10: *Value Diagnostics*

your customers' perspective (i.e., available alternatives or substitutes)? What are they doing now, or what might they do in the future, to provide greater value for themselves as they correspondingly decrease the value of your product? What can you learn from related fields that can be potentially applied to your business?

Figure 10 shows the six areas that a typical business would need to assess in its *Value Diagnostics* to determine the key opportunities in achieving its destination, as well as to identify barriers standing in its way. These are, however, only the six most common areas in need of diagnostic work. Your business may require several others, or a completely different set for each group of customers or trade partners. The point is that *Value Diagnostics* is about taking a comprehensive 360-degree look around your business and your customers to determine what value is and how your company can provide it in a more meaningful way than any other.

Exploring the relevant

As you can see, there is a lot that you can explore and learn from – almost too much. So how do you keep from drowning in data as you struggle to complete this analysis? The answer is… relevance. You don't need lots of data; you only need relevant data. Relevance is determined by what will contribute, or hinder value delivery to your customer. That isn't to say that this *Value Diagnostics* step in the strategic planning process is simple and easily achieved – it isn't. Take your time and dig deep to get the real answers, not just what is easily found lying about on the surface.

The most difficult of all the diagnostics work you will need to do is to develop a deep understanding of your customers' functional and emotional needs relative to what your brand can deliver, and the value it can provide. Your understanding of your customers' needs will allow you to discover most of what you must know so that you can craft a purchase-motivating strategy for your brand. It will also provide you with the lifestyle and 'state of mind' data that will help you reach your customers with the right messages, at the right time, at the right place.

By looking comprehensively at your company's performance in delivering customer value, you will discover how important it is that everyone, from production to sales to customer service, understands their special role in delivering value to the customer. By looking at your competitors from your customers' perception of viable alternatives and substitutes, rather than from your own perspective of the competitive set, you might come to realize that your real competition is much different from what you originally thought. The business you are in may also be different than you previously imagined. For example, is a ski area in the skiing business, or is it in the family-bonding business? Or, depending on what type of customer we are talking about, maybe it is in the memory collection business, or the adventure business. It's the same ski area, but how its benefits are perceived can vary, depending on who is likely to come and spend money there. The value equation for each customer segment and the available alternatives differ a great deal.

The biggest problem most people have when they set out to assess the current business situation is that they lose their way in the doing. They can't see the forest from the trees. Whether it be analyzing potential competitors, establishing priority customer segments, or trying to figure out what has been working and what has not, an objective view is essential.

Whenever I start a new position or a new assignment, I always ask for the available information relating to what we are setting out to do. What I want is good customer data: a tight review of the competitive situation with an emphasis on how the customer views the field of alternatives. I take a look at current KBIs (Key Business Indicators) that show us how we are doing on a trend basis. What I usually get is a data dump of anything and everything. The good news about the advent of electronic filing is that everything is available at the touch of a button; the bad news is that you literally get everything because it is now so easy to produce.

Once the material has arrived and is cluttering my desk and every flat surface in sight, I start to wade through the jungle of information. I try to separate the meaningful from the meaningless. In the event you ever find yourself in a real jungle, you will quickly discover that the most useful things to bring along are a compass and a machete – the compass to keep you oriented toward your destination and the machete to slash a path through the morass. Getting through a data dump requires a machete mindset. Because you have started your business plan process with a destination (that includes your basic value platform, an overall goal and the most important objectives to get you there) you are way ahead of the game – you know where you want to be. As you slash your way through the jungle of data, it is important that you quickly identify the relevant from the irrelevant. Keep in mind what you intend to do with any gems of information you are about to discover. How do you intend to apply the information you find? If it doesn't help you develop your thinking in any of the following four strategic areas, slash it out of the way with your machete and keep moving.

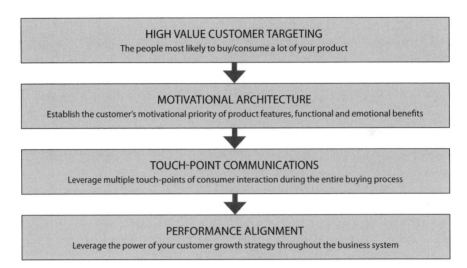

Figure 11: The *Exponential Marketing* process.

Some data are specifically related to building a more motivating brand architecture, such as which features and benefits are the most meaningful and provide the best usage to focus on going forward. Segmenting customers on the basis of how they approach and interact with your product category is also important. How different customer segments perceive and value different functional and emotional benefits is even more important.

As you begin to understand the motivations of different customer segments based on lifestyles and values, you will need to also look for information on how they move through their world in order to gauge their moods and state of mind from one potential usage occasion to the next. Understanding your customer's state of mind is crucial to developing an occasion-based sales plan, as well as helping you target the most effective communication touch-points.

Customer target assessment

Right from the beginning you need to break out of the demographic habit that is practiced by most marketers when segmenting potential customers. Like most bad habits, it's a case of doing the easier wrong rather than the more difficult right. It is much easier to segment your customers based on demographic data such as age, sex, income size, family size, or where they live. That sort of data is readily available and fairly easy to validate for accuracy. The problem is that demographic data have only a tangential effect on what customers actually do, and consequently, on the types of products and brands they buy to do it.

Your customer assessment must break through this old demographic segmentation habit and come to understand customers as belonging to distinct lifestyle communities, interests groups, and cohorts. It would be nice to be able to target customers as individuals, but short of that perfect marketing world, wouldn't it be much more effective to segment them, based on shared values and lifestyles, rather than on what city they live in or what their level of education happens to be?

Brand assessment

Brand assessment is the process of determining the current value assigned by customers to the benefits a particular brand provides. The best place to start your search for brand data is internally. Most companies have done some sort of customer research in the past and that is the first place you should look. If useful research is available, it may not be necessary to spend the time and money to 're-invent the wheel'. It's often possible to simply revisit existing data with a fresh perspective, or to filter the database through a lifestyle-relevant data-mining filter that sheds more light on customer attitudes and values as well as on their buying and consumption behavior. Depending on the industry, however, anything over three years old is usually not very helpful in gauging current brand value and customer behavior.

Larger companies typically have U&A (Usage and Attitude) studies that can help establish which benefits are more meaningful to various customer groups. The problem with most U&A studies is that they focus almost entirely on functional benefits and often break customers into demographic segments, such as age, or where they live, rather than lifestyle. As a result, you have some good brand information about how and when people use your products, but you still won't know who they really are, and consequently, why they are buying or not buying your product. It could be valuable data that will later help you build the functional benefit side of your brand architecture and help establish the broad demographic areas that you want to delve deeper into with psychographics segmentation (lifestyle, values and attitudes).

But if yours is a smaller company, you may not have much in the way of brand or customer data. You probably have limited resources to go out and conduct some of the more substantial types of research we get into in the next chapter. One benefit of a small company over a large one is that management is usually in closer contact with the customer – often on a daily basis. Consider a restaurant: the manager and wait staff are conducting almost a hundred focus groups every day. They've tried new product launches and seen how individuals and groups react first hand. They also have a lot of what researchers call *ethnographic data* – they observe customers in the environment interacting with the product. That stuff is valuable and very expensive for a big company to create in a realistic format. Sure, restaurants are obvious, but just think about it. If you are managing a bank, a car dealership, any sort of retail shop, or a small to mid-size B-to-B (Business to Business), you have regular customer contact and a wealth of brand data just waiting to be scooped up. The problem is how to pull it together and assess it properly. Enter the *Orbiter*.

The *Orbiter*

The *Orbiter* is basically an internal focus group that lasts about two to three hours. Its purpose is to assess the various components of your business in order to determine core competences as they relate to customer value. Your *Orbiter* session group should comprise a range of people who work with the company and have intimate knowledge of the product and the customer. If it is a restaurant, include the manager, a couple of the more insightful waiters, the chef, and the cashier. For a bank, bring in a couple of branch managers, some customer service managers, a cashier and maybe even the guard who spends all day just watching the place. You get the idea. You now have a diverse group of insiders who have considerable experience with your product/brand and the people who buy and use it.

To prepare for an *Orbiter* session, all you need is an empty room with a lot of empty wall space, a bunch of yellow sticky pads, and red and green marker pens.

The first step is a free-for-all – have everyone write short statements (two to five words max.) identifying something about the company (what it does), the product (what it provides for customers), the brand (what it means – its core essence), and the overall experience of buying and using the product/ brand from the company. Statements such as 'have to climb a lot of steps to enter the store', or 'good aroma' are a couple of examples. At this point you are not listing the statements either as positive or negative – that will come soon enough, which is why you brought along the red (negative attribute) and green (positive attribute) markers. For now, you just want to 'go nuts' and get everything up on the wall (Figure 12). Your team can do this individually or together. The idea is to get it all up as spontaneously as possible. Deeper thought will follow.

Figure 12: First step – a free for all

There is a range of questions your moderator can ask to stimulate some thinking about what the brand is and how customers perceive it:

– What do the people **think** about _____?
– What do the people **feel** about _____?
– Is this different between current and past customers? Why don't your past customers buy from you anymore?
– If _____ was a neighbor, building, animal, celebrity, how would you describe it? What would it be like?
– Please describe what a **greeting** of _____ feels like? Why?
– Please describe what a **kiss** of _____ feels like? Why?
– How would your company look like if it was a **building**? Why?
– What is your the brand, package or logo **color**? What does it mean? Why?
– What does the **logo** say, explain, offer, illustrate?
– What does the **name** say, explain, offer, illustrate?
– What is your brand **personality**? Why?
– What is your company **culture**? How is it best articulated?
– What other brands in the portfolio affect the perception of _____?
– What current and past associations does _____ have with time, places, activities, events, personalities, organisations?
– Is there a geographic orientation to the brand? What is it?

– When and where is a _____ moment? What does it tell about you? Why?

– What do you communicate? What does it say about the brand?

– Past advertsing that lingers in customers memory – what does it say?

– What do you say about the company and its people by the media you choose? On your website? Why?

– What would your neighbors think about you? Why?

– Company leadership or types of employees – is anything communicated?

– Company trucks and cars – describe the logos and graphics, condition, type of driving etc.

– Why do people buy _____?

– What are the some key characteristics of the _____ customers?

– What do the different packages communicate about the brand?

– Are there any historical roots to the brand?

– Is there anything unique about the manufacturing process? What does it communicate?

– Are there any brand extensions? Why? How do they add/detract from the brand?

– How is _____ different from other category brands?

– What are its pros? What are its cons?

– What does _____ **look** like?

– What does _____ **sound** like?

– What does _____ **smell** like?

– What does _____ **feel** like?

– What does _____ **taste** like?

In about 30 minutes you will have anywhere from 100 to 300 short statements that will probably capture just about everything your business does relative to the customer experience. Have everyone take a close look at all the comments on the wall and take another five minutes to add anything that may have been missed.

The next step is to look over all the notes on the wall and identify some common areas. What you will quickly recognize is that the many of the statements relate to each other. So, pull them and stick them up again where you think they should be (Figure 13). A discussion about what relates to what and which statement goes where will ensure that you have explored a full range of perspectives. That's good – it's all part of the process to determine just what it is that your business does and what it does for customers.

Figure 13: Identifying common areas

The next step is to simply name these different elements or activities, such as flavor selection, check out, administrative/paperwork, after-sales service, and so on. Figure 14 is an example of the different functional areas for amazon.com.

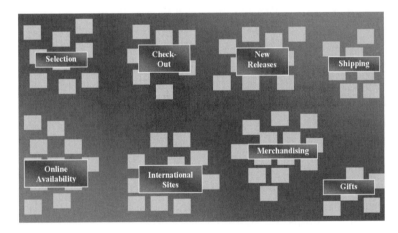

Figure 14: An *Orbiter* for amazon.com

Figure 14 lists just some of what amazon.com does. The last step is to translate what you do into what you do for customers. In other words, change the features of what you do into customer benefits. Some of your sticky pad statements may apply to more than one area. No problem; simply write the statement on a second or third sticky pad and place it where you think it also fits. Figure 15 shows what customers ultimately value from amazon.com.

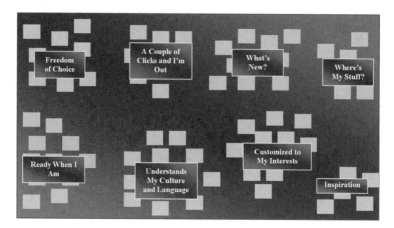

Figure 15: Translating what amazon.com does into what amazon.com does for customers

The reason this analytical model is called an *Orbiter* is pretty obvious at this point. Around each value (sun), you have all the details (the planets and moons) that define what your brand or business does that adds to, or detracts from, providing value to your customer. This is the point where you circle each statement with a red or green marker to establish whether that assessment statement is positive (green – a brand value opportunity) or negative (red – a brand value barrier). Several discussions and debates will most likely ensue about various factors, and consequently, what can be done to exploit opportunities or overcome barriers. This is a good thing. You are having a discussion about customer value in relation to specific activities and functions within your business.

The *Orbiter* isn't a scientific process with reams of validated customer research, but it's a pretty good 90% solution to quickly assess your brand's value by utilizing the knowledge of the people in your organization who are in close contact with your customers. And that's pretty good.

The next step is to prioritize these value areas into functional and emotional areas, but that will come later when we get into brand strategy.

Related products assessment

It is often helpful to look beyond your particular industry to see what other people are doing that can be applied to your business. When taking a broader look around, think of the Australian dog, the Dingo. It runs as fast as it can through the high brush, but every so often, it will leap high up into the air for a quick look around. Look for best practices and good ideas, wherever they are, while you move as fast as possible to your destination. We could use a little bit of Dingo in all of us.

An excellent Dingo example is how Ryan Air assesses train travel. By looking at the motivations of train travelers between London and Paris, Ryan Air can more effectively sell plane tickets for weekend getaways. It rightly understands that its customers are buying the destination – not necessarily the vehicle.

When looking at best practices in another field, it is important to understand not just what works, but why it works. With a bit of analysis and some common sense, you will find that only some elements will apply to your category and your brand situation, while others will not. That's fine – pick and choose. The important thing is that you are starting to *think outside the box* that is your own industry.

Competition assessment

When you are trying to figure out where to take your business, or to establish your current value proposition, it is a pretty safe assumption to say that the answer is not with the competitor; unless, of course, your business is based on simply being a cheaper knock-off of the category leader. Assuming you want to establish your own brand value, the answer lies with the customer and what you are doing to add to or detract from the value your brand provides.

While it is certainly true that there is a competing product in the market and the customer can potentially substitute that product for yours, you should think of what you can do to make your product their first choice. Let the competitor deal with being an alternative.

Because you are customer-focused instead of competitor-focused, you are not looking first at your competitor to establish your value proposition relative to them, but rather are linking customer needs with your core competences. Consequently, the most important thing to do in the competitive assessment step is to try and anticipate the competitor's reaction to any new customer-driven initiative you are considering so that you can make your initiative defendable as well as meaningful. Your competitor's subsequent actions can affect your brand's value and you have to be ready with a range of options to protect or restore this value. Assessing the value customers place on competitive products, and how that will change as a result of what you may do, is good practice. It is also a good idea to understand how your principle competitors make decisions and how fast they can react. Remember, you should be setting the pace and controlling the competitive environment by consistently making your brand so close to your customers' needs that there is no room for the other guy.

As competitive people, we often go out of our way to strike out at the competition, when the reality may be that they are not standing in our way at all – at least not standing directly between us and a potential customer. It's fun to hit the competition; we're programmed to do that almost from birth with sibling rivalry and organized sports programs in school. After university, I was recruited by Procter & Gamble, who were specifically targeting student athletes to capture a heightened competitive spirit – and they got it in spades. The competitive environment that resulted from the P&G recruitment practice in those years accomplished a lot of good things, but it also manifested itself in an inward competition that had one Procter soap brand directly competing in its advertising with a rival Procter soap brand.

At Coca-Cola, we also got sideways with our competitive attitudes. We had a practice of never referring to the competition by its name (Pepsi). Instead we called it 'the imitator'. It was ridiculous. It also created a scenario whereby we were either too arrogant when we were doing well in terms of market share to appreciate new thinking in the industry, or too obsessively focused on the competition during the cycles when it was gaining market share. It took New Coke for the company to finally realize that Coca-Cola is all about a special relationship with customers, not about the Pepsi Challenge that drove us to modify its 100-year-old formula to make it sweeter and less carbonated – like Pepsi! More often than not, what the competitor is doing with his challenges and comparison claims is just a side-show. Keep your eye on your customer!

In college, I was a lousy ski racer. I certainly was motivated to race and I worked hard at it. Unfortunately I had a problem: I liked hitting the gates too much. There are a lot of great experiences in life, but for me one of the best is to crash through the gates on a steep, hard-packed slalom course at 60km/hour. It is like Kung Fu at warp speed. The adrenalin, the crashing sound of the gates on the plastic pads on your forearms, shins and helmet, the near misses, and then the surge across the finish line. Incredible! Unfortunately, I got so caught up in smashing those gates that I often went out of my way to hit one that really wasn't standing between me and the finish line. Last time I checked, the winner of a ski race is the one who gets from the start to the finish fastest, not the one who hits the most gates or the one who hits them louder and harder than anyone else. It was good that I got this gate-smashing mentality out of my system in college rather than carrying it into business.

There can be a certain joy in smashing the competitor, whether it be hitting back at the guy who builds the restaurant across from yours, or even the other person in line for a promotion. The reality is that in more cases than not, the competitor you want to take out is probably irrelevant to what you really want to achieve. The other guy is only in your way if he is standing directly between you and your objective. If not, forget about him and stay focused on the customer – your real objective.

This may seem obvious; yet, as competitive people we have a very difficult time avoiding a head-to-head fight. Many of us feel that we can't really determine what we are made of unless we go toe to toe with the competition. Get a hobby. Take up tennis. But stay out of a costly competitive fight unless you absolutely have to; unless you know for certain that the competitor is actually standing directly between you and your customer.

When you do have to fight, pick the battlefield (and the weapons) to your best advantage. As General George S. Patton famously said to his troops: 'The objective is not to die for your country, but to let the other poor bastard die for his.' See your competitor through the eyes of your customers rather than through your own biased vision – that is your secret weapon. Fight only when you absolutely must and then only so that you remove him from any proximity to the customer. Establishing where and how to fight is the real value of competitive assessment.

In order to make an important symbolic point to your troops that it is the customer, not the competitor, who drives your business strategy, insist that working hours be devoted to customer-value discussions – talking about the competition is best left to after-hours. I used to tell my team at Coca-Cola that it was okay to think about Pepsi, just as long as we did it after five o'clock. What the competitor is doing is almost always interesting to you (you're competitive after all), but the truth is that it is only important if the customer says so. Don't worry about what the competitor is doing unless the customer considers it meaningful and the competitor is, consequently, a threat to your relationship. Keep the focus where it needs to be – on your customers and on their emotional and functional perceptions of the value your product/ brand provides.

It is usually smarter and much more efficient to simply sidestep a competitive thrust and get to the customer first with a more meaningful value proposition. The entire *Value Diagnostics* process will help you do just that. The competitive piece of it is no more than getting your back-up plan ready so you can react quicker in the event the competitor actually gets between you and your customers.

Silesia City Center – Putting the *Orbiter* to work

By Milena Dyankova

*Milena is a consultant at the Garrison Group where she works primarily on brand strategy in the banking and real estate sector. She is a native of Bulgaria.**

In November 2005, the big news in the city of Katowice, Poland, was the opening of Silesia City Center, the first world-class shopping mall to open in the region. Spread over a retail area of 66,000 m², the mall is the largest multifunctional commercial development in south-west Poland and comprises some 220 shops, a wide range of food and beverage outlets, a multiplex movie theatre, and a modern hypermarket. For the first time, the citizens of Katowice were given direct access to such world-famous brands as Zara, Mango, Benetton, Sisley, Hugo Boss,  Pierre Cardin, Mexx, Timberland, Max Mara, Nike, Adidas, and many more.

Silesia City Center was built by the TriGranit Development Corporation, which develops and manages commercial and residential properties throughout Eastern Europe and Russia. True to its corporate mission to create connections and meeting points that enrich  local communities, TriGranit took the extra step of incorporating into its architectural design a coal mining tower as a symbol of the region's past, and a small chapel just outside the main entrance as a connection to the deep faith common to the people of the area. Currently, Silesia City Center is owned by Nowe Centrum, part of the Austrian real estate corporation IMMOEAST AG.

Katowice is the main city in Upper Silesia (Gorni Śląsk), an important industrial region in south-west Poland bordering Slovakia and the Czech Republic. Known mainly for its mining and heavy industry, the region is nowadays striving to transform into a modern multifunctional Polish and European region. Besides being a commercial and administrative center, Katowice is a major educational hub, with seven local universities.

---

* Milena can be contacted at milena@garrisongroup.eu

The opening of the shopping center was carefully prepared. A marketing campaign was launched with the slogan *Let's meet* to introduce the Silesia City Center brand to the public. This campaign also reflected the philosophy of the TriGranit Corporation that the shopping centers it builds are lively places that bring people together for recreation  and socializing, as well as for shopping. The opening turned out to be a major event in the city, by far surpassing the expectations of the organizers.

Although the early days of operation proved to be quite successful, producing good numbers, the Silesia City Center management team was not satisfied. Experience gained in other markets had taught the team that competition would follow sooner rather than later, and so, in order to establish a solid foundation for long-term growth, it understood the need for creating a more meaningful positioning for the mall to customers; a positioning that was both *deliverable* and *defendable* by the Silesia City Center brand. Dariusz Rudzinski, the managing director, and Marek Ciszewski, the marketing and leasing manager, saw they had to define a clear customer target for their marketing investment – the people who would not only be most likely to visit the Center, but who would also have the potential to produce the highest business impact – coming to the Center frequently and spending a lot on each visit. It was also essential to build a lasting relationship with their customers so that the high-value targets would remain loyal, even when other competitors began to appear on the market.

Which segments are good customers for a shopping center?

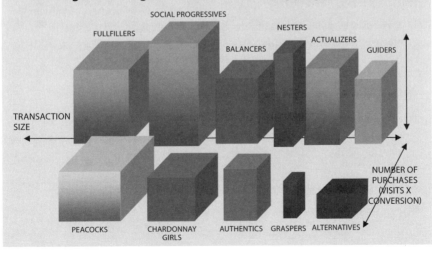

The customer segment identified as the highest-value was called *Social Progressives* due to a combination of purchases and transaction sizes that could be expected to stay loyal over a longer period of time. Confident and success-oriented, *Social Progressives* want to make the most out of their lives. They are typically young professionals or students who are optimistic and forward-looking – they want to be on top of what's happening. They are very much interested in foreign cultures, social and cultural events, technology trends, and yet they keep the connection with their families, which provide the stable point, the balance, in their fast-moving lives. Seeking a modern lifestyle and yet wanting to maintain traditional values are not mutually exclusive to people in the Silesia region.

After the key customer target was selected and agreed upon, the next step was to develop the brand strategy, which would enable a stronger and more

meaningful connection today and sustain itself well into the future. However, the two mall managers faced a dilemma: how could they develop a single-minded positioning for such a complex brand as Silesia City Center? How could they uncover all the relevant benefits of a shopping, entertainment and cultural complex that had so many dimensions and then prioritize the appropriate benefits to drive communication focus? What they needed was an effective and efficient tool to help them analyze the brand and lay down all product features, functional and emotional benefits and any other related factors. They found the solution in the brand inventory assessment tool called the *Orbiter*.

The *Orbiter*

The *Orbiter* for Silesia City Center was developed during a half-day session conducted on the mall premises. Key staff members who were knowledgeable about the Center from a marketing, sales, and operations standpoint were invited.

The first step in any *Orbiter* session is to search out and uncover all the features, attributes, values and benefits each brand has by putting together single thoughts – short sentences and statements – on small sticky notes that characterize various aspects of the brand. These can be anything from the related products and services, to packaging, and ambiance, or even how long it takes to access the brand, and how. Think in terms of a 360-degree customer involvement with the brand touching all the senses (taste, sight, sound, touch, even smell), all within the usage occasions associated with the brand. What is crucial in this stage of the *Orbiter* session is to walk in the customer's

shoes – see the brand, all the communications and interactions, and the experience the brand creates through the customer's perspective.

For Silesia City Center this assessment of attributes and benefits resulted in more than 200 Post-It™ notes stuck up on the wall. The notes included statements such as: 'long, wide, sunny corridors', 'beautiful fountain', 'a lot of natural light', 'roof garden', 'good transport connections', 'long opening hours', 'large,

guarded parking', 'top brands', all of which represented the various attributes of the Silesia City Center. Other statements were included from previous research and mall intercepts with consumers such as: 'no need to travel to get good clothes', 'feels like abroad', 'lively energy', 'inclusive', 'stay current on trends', and 'fulfilling many needs quickly'.

What followed was a process of re-arranging about 200 Post-Its™ into common areas and themes, and attaching a brief title to the different orbit groups. The Silesia notes were organized into 15 orbits along the themes of 'Architecture', 'Environment and nature', 'Adjacent services', 'Access', 'Ease of use', 'One-stop shop', 'Key attractions', 'Fashion trends', 'Ours', etc. They formed the smallest orbits of the big solar system.

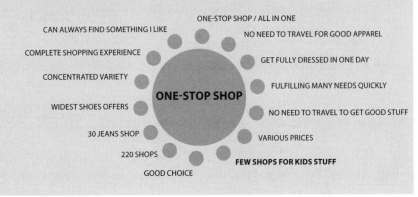

ONE-STOP SHOP / ALL IN ONE
CAN ALWAYS FIND SOMETHING I LIKE
NO NEED TO TRAVEL FOR GOOD APPAREL
COMPLETE SHOPPING EXPERIENCE
GET FULLY DRESSED IN ONE DAY
CONCENTRATED VARIETY
FULFILLING MANY NEEDS QUICKLY
ONE-STOP SHOP
WIDEST SHOES OFFERS
NO NEED TO TRAVEL TO GET GOOD STUFF
30 JEANS SHOP
VARIOUS PRICES
220 SHOPS
FEW SHOPS FOR KIDS STUFF
GOOD CHOICE

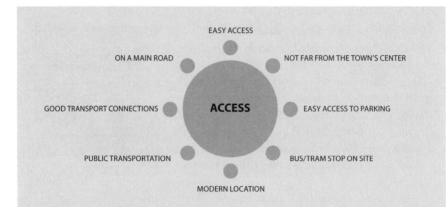

Putting all the pieces together

The final step in the *Orbiter* session required putting on the customer's hat once again and transforming the various group headings from *what it is* (features), into *what it does for customers* (benefits). Sometimes smaller orbits could be grouped at this stage into a higher level of benefits (a 'solar system' so to speak), which the Silesia City Center team found very useful as it began to prioritize these orbits for brand strategy development. In this manner 'One-stop shop' and 'Adjacent services' were transformed into 'Convenient shopping solution' and 'Helps me out' to form another orbit around the theme of 'Smart shopping'. The end result of the *Orbiter* for the Silesia City Center demonstrates how lower-level benefits were organized and grouped.

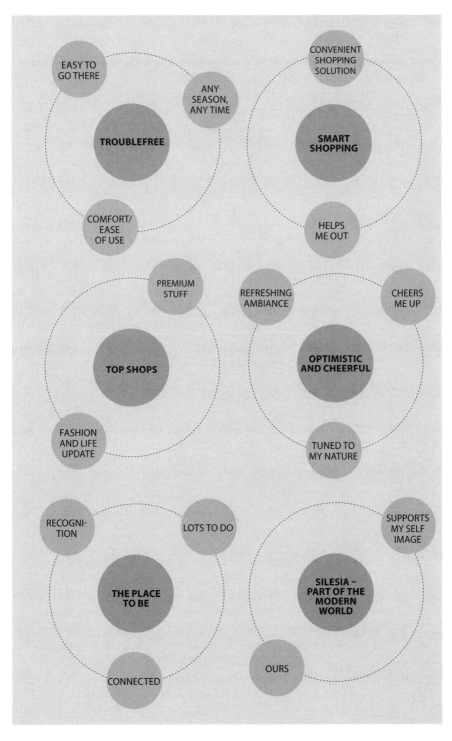

The brand strategy

With the help of the *Orbiter*, the Silesia City Center team created a comprehensive assessment and resulting graphic map of the brand's benefits. Developing the brand strategy required looking at the map from the perspective of the selected leading customer target – the *Social Progressives* – and prioritizing the features and benefits into a motivational hierarchy building from *Cost of Entry Features and Benefits*, to *Differentiating Benefits* and finally, to *Crucial Experience* – the most compelling aspect of Silesia City Center for *Social Progressives*.

The *Crucial Experience* for this high-value customer group was articulated as *We (Silesia) are part of the modern world* with two very important benefit categories supporting the *Social Progressives'* self-image and being part of the community.

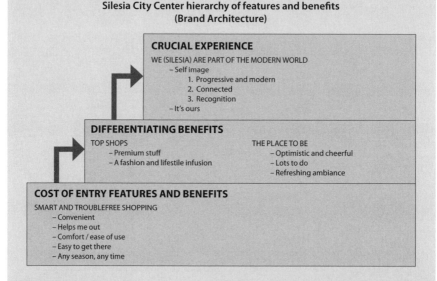

Silesia City Center hierarchy of features and benefits
(Brand Architecture)

CRUCIAL EXPERIENCE
WE (SILESIA) ARE PART OF THE MODERN WORLD
– Self image
  1. Progressive and modern
  2. Connected
  3. Recognition
– It's ours

DIFFERENTIATING BENEFITS
TOP SHOPS
– Premium stuff
– A fashion and lifestile infusion

THE PLACE TO BE
– Optimistic and cheerful
– Lots to do
– Refreshing ambiance

COST OF ENTRY FEATURES AND BENEFITS
SMART AND TROUBLEFREE SHOPPING
– Convenient
– Helps me out
– Comfort / ease of use
– Easy to get there
– Any season, any time

Next steps

Now that a more meaningful, deliverable and defendable brand strategy had been established targeting the highest-value customer segment, the Silesia City Center team could move on to developing a communication strategy that would leverage important inside- and outside-the-mall customer touch-points using a variety of mediums. The new brand architecture would enable them to develop the right message, which could then be combined with a communication strategy focused on key touch-points to deliver that message at the right time and at the right place to create those strong brand connections that fuel exponential business growth today and in the foreseeable future.

CHAPTER FOUR

Understanding your Customers

Capturing timely and insightful customer information is one of the key elements of the *Value Diagnostics* step. As a matter of fact, *Value Diagnostics* only makes sense if you manage to see all of the other business elements of distribution, packaging, communication, and even the competition, through the eyes of your customers. A thorough understanding of your customers' needs and alternatives as seen through their eyes is the only sure way of avoiding the trap of trying to sell what you have instead of what they actually want to buy. This internal focus on what you can produce rather than an external focus on what your customers actually want continues to be the greatest obstacle to sustained business growth (Figure 16). Your customers have lots of choices these days and vote on their preferences with every purchase.

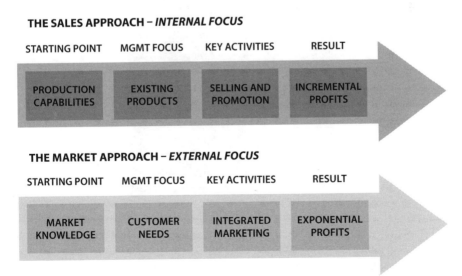

Figure 16: Are you selling or marketing?

It is natural for you, as a business person, to love your product. Maybe you have an idea for a new feature that no other competitor has, and you can't wait to get it out on the market and tell everyone about it. But is this new feature what your customer actually wants and needs, or just something you can do that the competitor cannot? Competitive advantage is not the point – customer advantage is.

A Hungarian Tourism ad from a couple of years ago is one my favorite examples of this internal focus problem. You may not be a tourism expert, but if you drive around Budapest, it is pretty apparent which customer target is the greatest opportunity for current and future tourism growth – Germans. If you ask Hungarian Tourism officials, they will agree with this, and will go on to point out that it is specifically Germans aged 55–70 who are the core demographic target. Now go one step further and think about who typically makes the purchase decision in such a German household. That's it, you got it. It's the wife – Frau Schmidt. Now try to see the world through Frau Schmidt's eyes and try to predict her reaction to this Hungarian Tourism ad inviting her to come to Hungary on vacation this year (Figure 17).

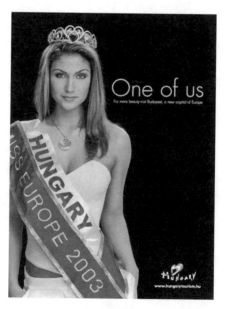

Figure 17: Hungarian Tourism ad

We actually have the unique marketing phenomenon in this example whereby the Hungarian Tourism Department (MTrt) is actually spending advertising money to convince the core target <u>not</u> to come to Budapest. You can easily imagine Frau Schmidt muttering to herself, as she thinks about her husband ogling all the beautiful Hungarian girls that walk by the café on the Duna Corso: 'We will go anywhere this summer – except Hungary!'

And this internal focus doesn't stop here. Just about everything Hungarian Tourism does in terms of advertising is focused on a perspective of what Hungary has, as opposed to connecting to the hearts and minds of potential customers and offering something specifically meaningful to what those tourists want. I once asked the director of Hungarian Tourism why he didn't utilize the incredible panorama of the Chain Bridge crossing the Danube with the castle above with perhaps some sort of Frau-appealing tag line about how beautiful the sunsets are in Budapest as you sip a relaxing coffee along the Duna Corso? He replied: 'I'm tired of that.' Maybe he is, and maybe he would prefer sitting on the Duna Corso looking at beautiful girls, but of course, he's not the target.

An internal focus is natural; it may be difficult for you to get out of your own head and into that of your customer. You must come to the realization that what you have, or what you can produce, is merely interesting. What is important is what your customer actually wants to buy. There are two fundamental questions about the target customer that you need to consider:

1. Who really is the target – i.e., those people most likely to buy your product.
2. What does the purchase decision process look and feel like from the target's perspective?

Customer segmentation

Customer research can be an excellent tool to help you predict future customer behavior, and to make assumptions about probable reactions to product development, communication, or a new positioning. You need, of course, to talk to the right people – the people most likely to buy. Segmenting customers based solely on demographic factors (age, race, sex or education) makes little sense when you think about the obvious truth that you – and virtually everybody else on the planet – don't buy things because of *what* you are. You buy based on *who* you are and what you are interested in relative to your values, lifestyle and attitudes. Understanding and segmenting customers based on these factors is called *psychographics*.

Good marketers want a holistic picture of their customers. They understand that demographic factors provide only a one-dimensional reflection of a person. Getting a firm grasp of the customers' lifestyle, way of thinking, attitude about the world, desires, and fears, is essential to building a more meaningful brand. Who the customers are and how they relate their sense of being to your brand will crucially influence their preferences and buying behavior.

The role of customer is just one of the many roles people play in their everyday relationships and interactions with others. At any given moment, they are also dads, moms, brothers, sisters, sportsmen, travelers, bosses, and outdoor enthusiasts – you get the picture. That's right; the perception of *who* they are can change with the years, the seasons, or even during the time of day and is crucially important in determining which interests or needs you intend to appeal to with your brand.

Unfortunately, when making a decision about who to target, it is very easy to come up with a demographic description – something like 40–60-year-old married women. Although you can make some pretty reasonable assumptions about how Frau Schmidt, as a 55–70-year-old German housewife (demographic), will react to the Hungarian Tourism ad, you will need to know a lot more about her if you intend to move Budapest to the top of her vacation list. Is she more likely to imagine herself relaxing on the Duna Corso having a pleasant café conversation with her usually busy husband, or will she be more motivated to find unique little antique or porcelain buys along Vaci street because the kids are grown and gone, and she can finally decorate her home for herself? Maybe she is adventurous and has a passion for discovering new things and would be interested in the Turkish influence on Hungarian history and the architecture that she can explore while enjoying many of the Turkish-inspired thermal baths. I don't know which is more appealing, but attitudinal and lifestyle research will get you a lot closer to Frau Schmidt than simply knowing her age and where she is from.

For examples of great tourism marketing, check out Croatia and Austria. They know exactly who their target is and how best to appeal to them. One Croatian Tourism ad emphasized the combination of discovery and collecting new memories: the ad literally shows incredible pictures you can capture and collect while on vacation in Croatia. Look at how effective Austria is in exploiting the personal touch you get with predominantly family-owned inns along the Danube, and in the Alps. For further proof of their strategic effectiveness, check out the size of Croatia and Austria's tourism business compared to others in the region… including Hungary. Austria and Croatia have built sustainable customer value through a deeper understanding of both the functional and emotional needs of their customers. Demographics help you with the functional needs; psychographics are absolutely necessary to understand emotional needs.

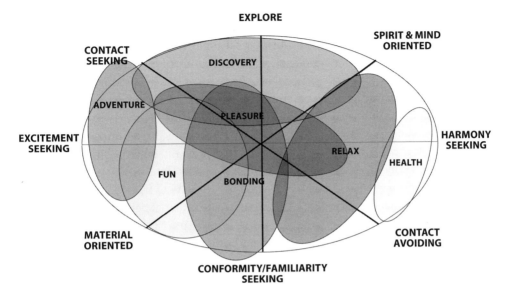

Figure 18: Grouping Western European tourist experiences (© The Garrison Group)

None of us like being classified by one-dimensional measurements such as age, sex, marital status or income level, yet we all suffer from the contradictory habit of putting strangers into such a one-dimensional box based on *what* they are rather than *who* they are.

There is no question that it is harder to get at the underlying interests and motivations of people than it is to put potential customers into convenient little demographic boxes. Resist the temptation and it will be well worth the effort to delve deeper and identify lifestyle, psychological and social characteristics that will most probably cut across several demographic groups. Look at it this way: imagine your competitor will stay stuck on demographics while you actually break through to communicate meaningful brand benefits to real people.

Psychographics customer segmentation gets to the heart of why customers are who they are and do what they do. This includes why they buy or don't buy your product. Psychographics are holistic and look beneath the surface – they describe, for example, affluent committed women who focus equally on their careers and their private lives; they enjoy making decisions for themselves; are health conscious; and live a complex and active lifestyle. Perhaps they drive – or aspire to drive – an Alfa Romeo, crave more free time, and absolutely hate household chores.

Two people may belong to the same demographic segment, yet one is a successful career woman living in an 'emancipated' marriage and the other is a happy housewife living in a traditional family model, completely fulfilled in spending 100% of her time caring for her family, doing the housework and dedicating her life to providing physical comfort and emotional support to those around her. It is the combination of sociological and psychological inputs that makes us who and what we are today. Just because you are 20 doesn't mean you like rap music and go out drinking three nights a week, no more than when you turn 62, you will automatically love classical music and favor a good book over a wild night out on the town.

The better we understand our customers in terms of their full lives, the easier it is to understand both the functional and emotional benefits our brand may acquire in their eyes. It is much more likely we will come up with real insights that will power a successful brand positioning, which will be rewarded with increased sales and profits.

You are who you are as a result of a variety of cultural, social, familial and peer group associations. Who you are also depends on your changing moods and other environmental factors that affect your current state of mind. You are not one type of person all the time; you change significantly relative to your wants and needs over your lifetime, the year, the month, and even throughout the day. Likewise, your brand will appeal to a certain group of customers if properly targeted relative to their psychographics and lifestyle needs at a particular moment (their state of mind) with much greater accuracy and appeal than any demographic qualifier could ever provide (Figure 19).

Psychographics targets lifestyle segments. The emancipated, career-oriented woman and the traditional housewife will differ significantly in their attitude to brands, simply because their aspirations, their desires and their fears are different. Talking to them and establishing a meaningful brand relationship will help define an emotional benefit for one that will differ from the other.

Depending on whether your product requires a high-involvement customer purchase decision (cars, computers, appliances, etc.) or a low-involvement purchase decision (bread, coffee, snacks, soap, etc.), the time your customer spends on each stage of the buying process can go from a matter of months, to a matter of seconds. It is not just about how much time is involved in each step, but what the factors are that pull the customer to one product category, or shift them from one brand to another.

Let's look at a parent life-stage psychographics group we will call *Balancers*. *Balancers* are typically slightly older parents who began having children later

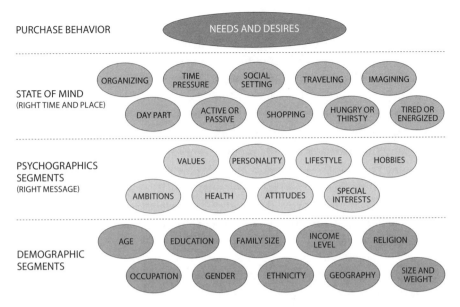

Figure 19: Psychographics and demographic segmentation

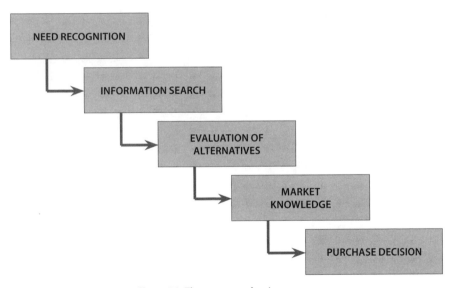

Figure 20: The consumer buying process

because both parents are career driven. Now that they have kids, they are both trying valiantly to balance a thriving career with being good parents. *Balancer* parents will take the morning off to attend their nine-year-old daughter's first play at school one week, and then spend four nights out of town the next week on a business trip. In the ice-cream category, the *Balancer's* decision to go down that frozen aisle is driven by conflicting feelings of guilt that perhaps they should indulge their children at dinner to make up for the nights they were out of town on business, and the conflicting guilt of not eating enough healthy food. In both cases, they are struggling to be good parents and worrying that they are falling short of the high expectations they have imposed on themselves. Nestlé recognized this emotional struggle within *Balancer* parents (who have a lot of buying power) early in the buying process. Consequently, it communicated the message 'Go ahead, spoil them' at the entrance to the ice-cream aisle. It hit the heart of the emotional tug-of-war going on in the *Balancers'* hearts and minds during those crucial seconds and gave them a meaningful reason to enter the category – the ice-cream aisle.

Figure 21: Nestlé's message at the ice-cream aisle

Next comes the actual brand purchase decision. Nestlé recognized that flavor variety is very important to the rather up-scale B*alancer* customers. It entices them with a 'variety' strategy that offers at least one new flavor every time they go into the store. It is not uncommon in the ice-cream category for customers to make a category decision in three seconds, a brand decision in two, and then to spend three or four minutes deciding on flavor.

It is the excitement of something new that drives growth and market share in the European ice-cream business, and both of the top players – Nestlé and Unilever – have a deep understanding of the ice-cream customer-decision process – particularly the conflicting emotions of one of their most important customer segments.

The hidden psychology of customer decision-making

While more and more marketers agree that it is crucial to understand how customers both think and feel, we have only begun in practice to delve into the area of buyer psychology and related emotional drivers. Even if we do break through and look at people based on lifestyle and attitudes, we still jump from one rut in the road to another when we fall into the trap of making assumptions about the way people are supposed to think and feel rather than figuring out how they actually do.

The most common fallacy is that the customer thinks in a rational, logical, and linear fashion. Traditional marketing logic assumes that customers make purchase decisions after carefully evaluating and weighing the attributes of each individual alternative; they then process this data to arrive at a rational value determination. For some products that process takes days or weeks, while for others, merely seconds. Although well-reasoned, rational, and step-by-step decision-making processes do take place in some cases, psychologists consider rational decision-making as the exception rather than the rule, and instead see customers as thrifty perceivers – people who pick and choose information based on their predisposition toward an over-arching emotional motivator.

Cognitive processes are very costly in terms of brainpower expended. There is a limit to our free brain capacity since our mind is preoccupied carrying out what we perceive as more important, or at least more urgent tasks immediately at hand than remembering and processing new information and brand impressions. Everyday decision-making is influenced simultaneously by several rational and non-rational factors, both conscious and unconscious, from a wide range of emotions, habits, and social norms. As a result, people tend to gravitate toward a decision, rather than moving toward it in a straight line.

Reason and emotion are often confusingly intertwined. They jointly influence behavior in thinking about, remembering, and recognizing personal emotional and functional benefits. Emotions and habits tend to make the decision-making process non-linear. In the abstract, the process seems illogical, distorted and perhaps more simplified compared to the linear and computational model you, as product manufacturers or brand managers, would like the customer to think and act upon. If however, you want to work with a model that describes the complicated nature of decision-making, a model which can explain and predict consumer behavior better, you need to develop an alternative process to assess and gauge how a potential customer moves through the buying process to arrive at a combined emotional and rational decision.

The 'gravitational mapping' of the decision process

Before you can construct an actionable, customer decision-making model for a specific brand, and a particular customer segment, you need to identify some gravitational factors that may affect that purchase decision process. First, you must understand what triggers the process to begin with. The widely used term 'problem recognition' suggests a rational and conscious detection of a problem, which in many cases could not be farther from the truth. Impulse purchasers, of items such as snacks and beverages, often mask the real need behind the purchase. In most cases we don't even know whether or not a rational explanation is simply an emotional decision in disguise. Often it all happens at lightning speed. Just think of buying the pair of shoes that you just fell in love with, or that extra tennis racket you've just spotted. Now think of all those rational reasons you use to justify spending the money. You rationalize that you need the shoes or the racket, but inside your gut the 'gotta have it' emotion is really driving your decision. A better term than 'problem recognition' would be 'need perception', because we do experience an urge, but is it a need to solve a problem or to satisfy a desire? When you bought the new tennis racket, were you buying it to solve a problem (your old one was lousy with drop shots), or because you simply had to have the latest thing (satisfy a desire)? The very first task in gravitational mapping is therefore to connect what is typically the nature of the need perception with a particular product category.

In recognizing an underlying need, you can develop a clearer understanding of the evaluation process going forward. Once customers have perceived a need, they enter into a consideration phase. They will consider not only the alternatives, but also the perceived costs and benefits of the alternative choices. This consideration may happen all at once, in a matter of seconds based purely on habits or pre-established emotions, or it may formulate over a considerable period of time within a more involved purchase decision process for items such as a computer or a new car. In many cases we cannot separate the evaluation of alternatives based solely on benefits. At times the consideration may include perceived costs – such as the time spent in line at the cashier, or the sudden drop in price of a viable alternative.

A brand decision may happen simultaneously with the consideration of alternative categories. The decision-making process is seldom as simple as 'evaluation of alternatives', then 'evaluation of brands' and so on. You need to research the process for your specific brand and product category relative to your different customer targets. Ask yourself how much customer involvement your brand or product category stimulates. What are the simultaneous and/or linear phases of consideration relative to your product and the target group?

No doubt, you can identify rational factors that influence the decision each step of the way, but rather than believing that your customer is consciously and rationally evaluating alternatives, explore the motivational factors at work in pulling the decision-makers toward buying your brand, or pushing them away with variable intensity – all at the same time.

Getting inside your customer's head, heart and gut as he passes through the decision process is the key to understanding what you are doing, or could be doing better, to attract more customers.

The Nestlé 'spoil them' POP (Point-of-Purchase) poster at the entrance to the ice-cream section illustrates the value of understanding a gravitational pull on *Balancer* customers' thoughts and emotions. Only when the Nestlé marketing people realized that there was a strong feeling of healthy-eating guilt pulling people away before they even entered the ice-cream section, were they able to counteract any negative purchasing emotional pull with a meaningful *Balancer* customer message that was meant to help customers overcome that one emotion (healthy-eating guilt) and compensate it with another (indulgence) – *go ahead and spoil them.*

Memory matters

Memory is important to us marketing guys because we would like our targets to store the brand message and brand experience in their memories to create positive *purchase intent*; we want to have a special desire pop up in the minds of our potential customers and influence them when they actually enter into the purchasing environment. Consequently, it is worth a few minutes of your time to get acquainted with the way memory works.

Not only is your decision-making strongly influenced by emotion, but the non-computational nature of the brain strongly influences memory as well. Your customer's brain is not a camera that can capture and store an adequate and non-fading picture that can be fully and accurately accessed anytime and anywhere. On the contrary; remembering things is a far more creative process than we would logically suppose. The mind has to reconstruct the images, feelings, and facts again and again with each recall command. Moreover, when we recall an event, we not only remember the facts, but also the emotions we experienced when we participated in the event. Brain scans prove that parts of the brain responsible for processing emotions are activated both when learning new things, and when trying to remember them after the experience as well.

Thousands of impulses bombard you every morning during your drive into the office – the number of cars in one lane or the other (the other one always seems faster), the dirt on the windshield, the timing of the traffic lights, the seemingly contradictory road signs, the provocative billboard, and so on. Some of this information is highly relevant to your journey – the traffic lights, the directional signs, and the speed of the car in front of you. Your brain needs to process this information so that you can react adequately – alternately push the brake or accelerator in order to make your way safely through traffic to the office. These pieces of information, however, only get to the 'working memory' storage. Once you have passed the traffic light, its color becomes irrelevant and it is instantly erased from your memory. In case the information stays relevant for longer than a few minutes, it is placed into the 'short-term memory' storage, the scope of which is not seconds, but could be a couple of hours or days. One example of short-term memory is remembering a phone number that you need to call. If the line is busy, and you have to try it again and again, you will probably notice after the third time dialing that you remembered the number automatically. However, after the call is finally completed, the information becomes irrelevant and quickly fades – automatic delete function. Or, if you need to buy a pair of shoes and you check out five different stores in the shopping mall, you may remember where you found the different choices only until you have made a purchase.

This short-term storage is also considered the gateway to 'long-term memory' storage; psychologists suppose that it is only by accessing through this storage that durable memory traces can be created. When something really important happens to you, it has an effect on your life, be it marvelous or shocking; you think of it again and again. You tend to talk about it to friends and relatives, and make an effort to integrate it into your perception of the world, your attitudes and stereotypes.

Your brain naturally makes an efficient attempt to minimize processing costs, and because modifying your existing stereotypes is a very expensive process for your brain, only a very limited number of impressions get through the long-term memory gateway. Those impulses that do not fit into your preconceived expectations (stereotypes) get discarded right away. You simply, and usually subconsciously, choose not believe them. Those that build on your existing views and impressions have a greater chance of getting through the gate if they reach you at an appropriate time and place when you are open to new impulses. If a guy that you think is a jerk starts to behave in a very attentive and kind manner toward you, you will probably not change your mind about him being a jerk; instead you will start to look for reasons to explain this change of behavior, reasons that fit with your pre-existing attitude or feelings – perhaps he is trying to manipulate you. You simply cannot afford the brain-time to re-evaluate people around you based on a single instance, because that would create a chaotic and very unstable inner world for you, resulting in a lack of continuity, and therefore, a reduced sense of security.

Look at political elections. Notice how people who gravitate toward the Left tend to look for and absorb only that information which makes the Right appear extreme. People who gravitate to the Right are equally likely to accept only information that confirms their perceptions of the Left. Accordingly (and many would say unfortunately), politicians and their handlers recognize this behavior and focus their campaigns on defining the other guy negatively in terms of stereotypes.

Whether you are a politician trying to get elected to actually try and make a positive impact, or simply a guy who wants to sell a few more boxes of soap in the market, it is fundamentally important that you understand how people think, feel and consequently come to form attitudes and opinions that will affect what you would like them to do.

CASE STUDY

A new approach to customer needs assessment in real estate development

By Milán Herczku

*Milán is a consultant at the Garrison Group where he works primarily in the telco, and pharma sector. He is a native of Hungary.**

A deeper knowledge of your customers can offer a fresh perspective on your business and open up yet unknown sources of growth regardless of the product or industry. There are industries which have embraced the idea of building business strategies and brands around customers, but there are others where the importance of who the customer is and what they genuinely need surprisingly remain relatively minor elements in the overall go-to-market equation.

---

* Milán can be contacted at milan@garrisongroup.eu

Unfortunately, the real estate business in rapidly developing markets typically falls into the latter group – especially in markets like Russia, where during recent years the dynamics of the economy provided extensive freedom to developers, investors and architects to build almost wherever they wanted to and to construct whatever they wanted based on their own internal notion or perspective of what the market wanted or needed. In most cases they were granted the luxury of not having to concern themselves too much about who would purchase the house, flat or office space and why – the immense demand continuously swallowed the supply.

Despite the fact that this 'build it and they will come' approach to development was successful for many real estate entrepreneurs in the past, post-crisis growth will likely require a more customer-centric alternative for establishing go-to-market strategies for real estate developments.

BUSINESS AS USUAL
'BUILD IT AND THEY WILL COME'

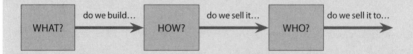

CUSTOMER CENTRIC
'FIND OUT WHO YOU'RE BUILDING FOR AND THE REST WILL COME'

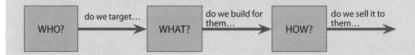

Business as usual

Developers, like everyone, can fall in love with their own ideas. This is especially easy to do in real estate development when these ideas have the power to literally change the face of a city or region, as they so often do in emerging markets. This can result in placing the actual people who will purchase and use the properties and facilities at some point at the bottom of the priority list. Higher on the list are the expectations of investors, shareholders, other developers and the architects – all centric to the developers' focus on 'what do we build?' This is also more likely in real estate projects whereby the initial investors often 'flip' (sell) the investment to a new group of investors and therefore never have to come face-to-face with actual end-users two or three years down the line. In practical terms, business as usual means first building the idea and then, much later, contemplating how to market it to end-user customers. Perhaps at that later point someone comes up with the idea of hiring a research company to help identify just who the customer is.

A customer-centric approach

The customer-centric logic of *Exponential Marketing* in contrast claims that, similar to any other industry or product category, you significantly increase your chances of financial success if you examine key dimensions such as location, product portfolio (of the development), pricing, timing, competitors, proposition and integrated communications within the context of who the customers are and what they want. Adjusting the major *Exponential Marketing* steps to a real estate development project incorporates the following phases:

- *Who do we target? – high-value targeting and needs sssessment – based on:*
  - **Segmentation**
    Combined lifestyle data which gives a better insight into people's attitudes, values and motivations with category-related needs. This allows us to see who individuals are as people and as customers specific to the product.
  - **Financial planning (ROI, IRR)**
    The defining guideline of the whole project must be profit-oriented, of course. Sounds simple enough, but what you build should generate the optimal ROI relative to the number of customers and what they will be willing to spend. Financial planning, just like marketing, should be customer-centric because without the top-line drivers (customer demand), the bottom line won't happen.
  - **Supply demand modeling**
    Analyzing the market broken down into customer catchments zones – overlaying the statistical data with the motivations and expectations of various customer segment targets.
- *What do we build for them? – motivational brand strategy – based on:*
  - **Orbiter tool**
    The *Orbiter* is a valuable feature-and-benefit inventory tool which helps distill the real estate development project into its core elements and then visually organizes these elements into various benefit levels to evaluate the customer merit of concepts. Later on, it serves as a valuable framework, guide, and reference point in managing, understanding, communicating and nurturing those high-value customer targets.

- **Competitive assessment**

  Knowing what the other real estate developers are doing tells you which consumer needs are being catered to and which are not. It identifies important needs gaps from the customer's perspective and allows you the ability to chart a development course that will better meet customer needs. The goal isn't to beat the competition, but rather to be the most meaningful to the customer – that's the win.

- **Portfolio strategy**

  Enabling synergy between different business areas within the development (if there are several) and among high-value segments to generate profit. A good retailer doesn't try and attract different customers to each department in his store. He maximizes his cross-selling opportunities by designing the layout of his store, as well as the product mix in each department, to fit the needs of his best customers overall. This doesn't mean that secondary targets don't count, but that the value of any customer target should be understood not just on the basis of how and why they will buy in a certain area, but also on their willingness and motivation to shop in other areas so that ROI is maximized. This is very important in mixed-use real estate developments as well.

- **Motivational brand architecture**

  Structuring and establishing the functional and emotional benefits of specific high-value targets into a persuasion hierarchy for the overall development, as well as aligning this overall *Motivational Architecture* with separate architectures for each area that will need to be developed.

- *How do we sell it to them? – Integrated Touch-Point Communication Strategy*

  Developing the right touch-points enables you to 'engage' the targeted customer with the right message delivered at the right time and at the right place to ensure the right state of mind so that they will seriously consider the proposition.

Defining your high-value customers

Let's look at the targeting challenges encountered during a multi-use project in Russia. The investors dreamed of establishing an entire city of approximately 30,000 people on the outskirts of a regional capital which would eventually offer a complex portfolio of both residential and non-residential facilities (from restaurants, stores, sports and medical facilities to schools). It would provide its residents and visitors with a progressive living space that was above any currently available on the Russian market. The site was located on a hill just outside a dynamically growing city; it spread through 200ha with some parts having a great view of the city. When we were developing the marketing strategy, the site was a clean slate: almost 100% untouched green area. This project had a unique advantage from a marketing perspective: it could be positioned in almost any way to consumers because there were few existing perceptions of the development.

In the case of established brands and existing products, it is usual to filter and rank the customer segments based on how lucrative they are through their own consumption and through inspiring others to buy/consume and so define the highest-value segments. In the case of a new real estate development that has yet to be constructed, this process is much more complex. Targeting and needs assessment at such an early stage can influence not only eventual marketing communications, but more importantly – influence and guide product development and the overall proposition of the project.

The lifestyle and category-based (needs assessment, need states) filtering comes together to guarantee a more precise and successful targeting.

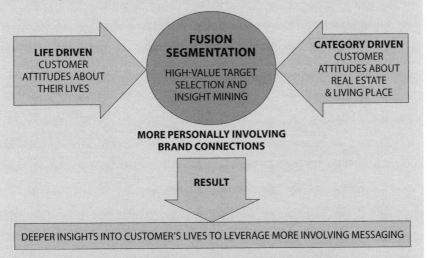

Lifestyle-driven segmentation – filtering for customers

To find the most valuable segment(s) for the Russian project, we looked at the customer not only from a demographic and geographical standpoint, but also from a lifestyle point of view; we examined their attitudes, values and consumption related to various propositions.

Filtering customer segments to identify potential customers, good customers and ideal customers gradually narrowed down the number of segments which qualified as high-value target(s):

1. To screen *Potential* customer segments, we analyzed several base criteria factors. *Potential* customers are more likely to be able to afford to purchase

a new home. They have stated their intention to move to a new dwelling within 12 months and are willing to turn to mortgage if needed. They are also over-represented within the catchment area of the development. By cross-tabulating these factors we found those segments that were serious about and capable of purchasing a new home and also living near enough to the area to realisticly consider moving there.

2. *Good* customers are defined as being receptive to cross-selling opportunities in other business areas (such as retail, office, education, sports, culture, etc.). These are the people who spend a lot on premium shopping, dining, sports and cultural events etc., and furthermore, would be willing to pay extra for additional residence/office/education services which will likely be found onsite. This part of the filtering process is the **Lifestyle fit criteria**.

3. The most valuable *Ideal* customers for the business are the people who can influence the largest number of customers to move to the site. In other words, they have an impact on people's decisions on the subject of real estate and living space. By finding the positioning for the brand which appeals to them the most, we could maximize our business results.

WHO ARE THE HIGH-VALUE TARGETS FOR THE SITE?
PUTTING TOGETHER ALL THE SELECTION CRITERIA…

WHAT MAKES A GOOD CUSTOMER?
IS RECEPTIVE TO ALL THE CROSS-SELLING OPPORTUNITIES (RETAIL, OFFICE, EDUCATION, SPORTS, CULTURE, ETC…)

FULFILLERS (P)
CHARDONNAY GIRLS (E)
MAÑANAS E
PEACOCKS (E)
BALANCERS (P)
ALTERNATIVES (E)
HEDONISTS (E)
ACTUALIZERS (P)
BEGIN-AGAINERS (S)
BREAKOUTS (E)
OLD GUARDS (S)
REVITALIZERS (P)
NESTERS (E)
SOPHISTICATED (S)
SHARERS (P)
NOSTALGICS (E)
GUIDERS (P)
PROVIDERS (S)
MAT. WANNABES (P)
MAT. WANNABES (S)
COMFORT PROVIDERS (P)
GUIDERS (S)
LAGGARDS (S)

WHAT MAKES A POTENTIAL CUSTOMER? WANTS TO MOVE TO A NEW PLACE AND CAN (AFFORD TO) MOVE TO A NEW PLACE

LIFESTYLE PARAMETERS

BASE CRITERIA

By combining the ranking of the different psychographics segments for the *Potential* and *Good* filtering, we found our high-value targets. Two segments – the *Fulfillers* (more self-focused, highly educated, materialistic, career-driven, quality-seeking parents) and *Balancers* (more value-driven parents segment striving to be the best parents possible while still excelling in their careers, also highly educated and quality seeking) – scored consistently high for the criteria set for *Potential* customers (*base criteria*). They showed a high intention to purchase a new home and they possessed the money to do so. In addition, they were both over-represented in their numbers in the catchments area. When screening with the *Good* customers (*lifestyle criteria*) we found that although they ranked relatively high on the charts referring to the cross-selling business opportunities, they clearly would not be the leading segments in all non-residential business fields (the non-residential targeting is not elaborated in this case study). However, the ideal (highest-value) segment would determine the atmosphere of the site (residential) and serve as a guideline as to how to best 'shape' complementary services and other business areas.

Fulfillers were the top segment when it came to combining the base criteria for targeting with the lifestyle parameters which revealed the overall cross-selling opportunities. The *Balancers* came second in a very tight race. By finally filtering with the ideal customer criteria and looking at their influencing capabilities in the category, *Fulfillers* were the absolute winners. This was the segment which could guarantee the highest business impact by positioning the site's residential brand according to its lifestyle, values and attitudes.

Once we had identified the ideal customer segment(s) that made it through all levels of filtering, we needed to deep-dive to expose their genuine motives in the 'living space' category to gain further insights for the subsequent brand-positioning phase.

What future customers will look for

Based on learning from the lifestyle-driven targeting and during the needs assessment, the primary focus became the *Fulfillers* and the *Balancers*. Exposing why they wished to purchase, seeing behind the functional needs they brought up related to the topic, and digging down to the core emotional needs behind those that would influence their decision was indispensable for finding the 'hot buttons' for the these high-value segments. Hot buttons told us the exact emotional benefits the product or products should communicate if we wished to convert them to customers. Accordingly, we could examine the needs relevant for the specific category (living space) via focus groups conducted among individuals, including people who belonged to the *Fulfiller* and *Balancer* segments. The participants were a mix of recent and prospective real estate buyers.

A PARTIAL LIST OF TOPICS COVERED DURING FOCUS GROUP SESSIONS

PRE-PURCHASE AND DECISION MAKING PROCESS	SOURCES OF INFORMATION	CURRENT OR PREVIOUS HOUSING CONDITIONS	REASON TO BUY AND REQUIRED FEATURES, BENEFITS	FINANCIAL MEANS, MORTGAGE	THE IDEAL HOME

The needs and benefits revealed during the sessions were then categorized into three groups depending on how dominantly they were mentioned by the participants: (1) Sporadic Reference; (2) Average; (3) Dominant. By comparing the oft-mentioned topics of the focus groups with the descriptions of the relevant psychographics segments, we were able to combine the category-related need states with the personality dimensions that define the psychographics segments (Adler's map).

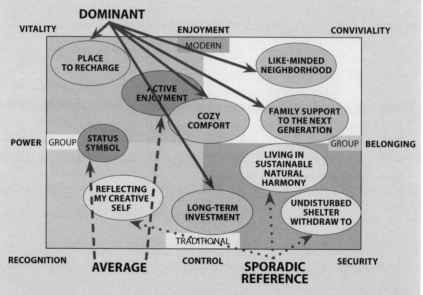

By combining the knowledge of their general lifestyle and values with what we knew about their attitudes and usage toward the category, we were able not only to identify who these people were, but also target them with personally involving messages: a far more lucrative way to understand, reach and influence these customers.

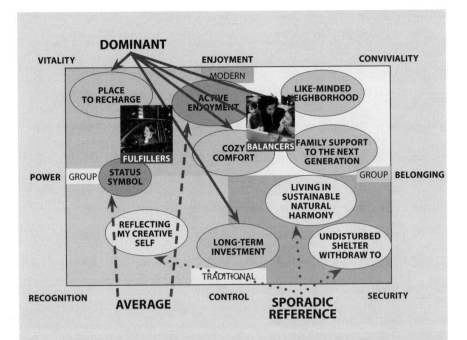

Balancers and Fulfillers may have had similar demographics, but their values, attitudes and lifestyle differed and this was inevitably reflected in their expectations and desires toward the category. *Fulfillers* sought a place to recharge after work where they had all the facilities to help them accomplish those recharging objectives and at the same time keep the family occupied. Most important of all, every aspect of the property and its additional services needed to communicate their success to the outside word. *Balancers* sought equally high levels of quality, but on the other hand, a house for them needed to be a cozy and comfortable home where they would have the opportunity to actively engage the family and socialize with people who shared their lifestyle and values.

These differences – beyond determining the many aspects of communication from messages to training the real estate sales force – could have practical implications for how the homes and services were to be developed. (i.e., a *Fulfiller's* garden was more like a display for others to be impressed by, lacking functionality, small in size; a *Balancer's* garden needed to be a genuine playground for the kids and a place to hang out with friends and family where functionality was appreciated).

Moreover, in the case of the current project, the two most valuable target segments – taking into consideration the *Destination Planning* of the site, along with the trajectory of the Russian post-Soviet society – triggered a two-phase overall site development concept as well.

Staying ahead of the game

It was critically important that the site development concept took today's needs into consideration, but also that it could evolve to cater to the changing needs of tomorrow. In the end, such a large-scale development project became a complex site offering products in the following categories: residential, office, retail, education, sport and recreation, culture and entertainment and other basic, public facilities. It was capable of functioning almost like an independent city, located right beside one of the most dynamically growing cities in the region.

Within the market circumstances of the Russian project, residential units were to have an overwhelming majority within the overall product and services portfolio. Other uses may have promised a higher return per square meter, but the development plan elected not to put them in a dominating position for the overall project for two reasons:

1. The residential units offered the highest market potential. At the time there was over-demand for new dwelling spaces.
2. If the overall plan was to turn the development into a city, it was fundamentally important to ensure steady supply of residents who could define the character of the site and provide a secure flow of consumers for all the other business areas.

During the high-value targeting of the residential area, two psychographics segments ranked high in almost all the relevant filters applied to define the most valuable target group: *Fulfillers* scored highest with *Balancers* following closely behind. This, combined with the knowledge gained from trend-spotting tools, allowed us to develop a concept that broke down the site's evolution into two phases: the first one targeting *Fulfillers*, the second one focusing primarily on *Balancers*. Because of the nature of the Russian market, the self-focused and hard-working *Fulfillers* were the drivers both economically as well as within the perception of who leads a successful life overall. *Balancers* would most probably take over the role of being the trendsetters from *Fulfillers* in the perception of most people relative to having a successful life with a greater balance between family and work – but today it was all about the *Fullfillers*. Also important, specifically for the Russian market, is that segments capable of leading a modern lifestyle while still embodying traditional values would be the role models for the majority of the population in most areas of life. *Balancers*, with their stronger family and community values are seen to rise in prominence as this cross-over between modern lifestyle and tradional values continues to grow in Putin's Russia.

The development project that plans to build and sell units for at least the next five to ten years cannot afford to only take the next two to three years into consideration when defining high-value segments and the resulting value proposition and communication tools. Any concept chosen to determine the future of the site must be expandable chronologically to make sure the development not only stays relevant to the changing times, but also has an opportunity to leap ahead relative to forecasting dominant lifestyle trends.

EVOLUTION SETS THINGS IN MOTION...

AS SHOWN BY THE THE ' KWASNIEWSKI CURVE'

AS SHOWN BY MACROECONOMIC (TIMELINE) DATABASES

AS SHOWN BY LOCAL MARKET CHANGES AND CONSUMER DYNAMICS

TO MAKE SURE THE HIGHEST VALUE SEGMENTS ALWAYS FIND THE IDEAL PROPOSITION AT OUR SITE

SEGMENTS ARE EVOLVING

RUSSIA IS EVOLVING

THE NEARBY CITY IS EVOLVING

OUR SITE'S DEVELOPMENT CONCEPT NEEDS TO EVOLVE

This shift would naturally change the core proposition behind the site and also affect the communication channels and touch-points.

PHASE 2

THE SMART PLACE TO LIVE

PRIMARY TARGET:

• CORE VALUES:
– HARMONY
– EQUILIBRIUM
– SELF-ACTUALIZATION
– HOLISTIC & WHOLESOME

BALANCERS

PHASE 1

THE PLACE TO LIVE

PRIMARY TARGET:

• CORE VALUES:
– PRESTIGE
– THE PLACE | DESERVE
– CUTTING-EDGE

FULFILLERS

AS THE SITE BECOMES MORE DEVELOPED, IT WILL HAVE THE LIFESTYLE IMPACT TO FURTHER STRENGTHEN THE NEARBY BOOMING CITY AND HELP PEOPLE (*BALANCERS* PRIMARILY) DISCOVER 'A SMARTER WAY OF LIVING'

In the first phase, the site would benefit from the dynamic development of the nearby city and offer a new, prestige-oriented living space aimed at *Fulfillers: THE place to live*. The second phase would turn the site into a holistic bubble offering harmony and self-actualization for *Balancers*, creating *the SMART place to live*.

This concept takes into account the likely changes in the dominant trends within society and is thus capable of leaping ahead of current trends and shaping them. It makes it possible for the development to 'outgrow' the nearby city and turn into a destination in its own right, actually improving the near-by host city's reputation and positioning.

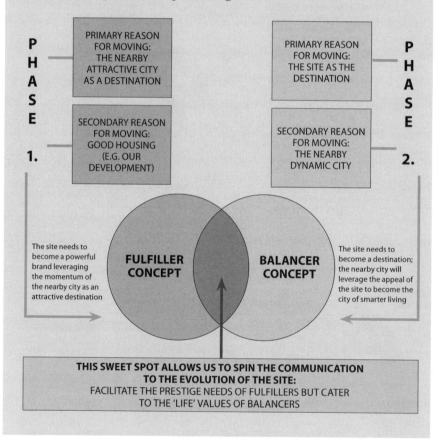

CHAPTER FIVE

Integrated Strategic Targeting

Getting the customer on the CEO's agenda

In a successful business, you must integrate your business goals and objectives with the driver that makes it all possible – increased customer value. Financial objectives are certainly important, but there must be an understanding that specific customer actions drive the overall financial results of the business. Of course, most successful executives would agree wholeheartedly with that. But if the focus is truly on the customer and we agree that our core strategies are meant to drive specific customer actions that ultimately drive superior financial performance and shareholder value, then how much do we really know about our customers so that we can optimize the interconnected results?

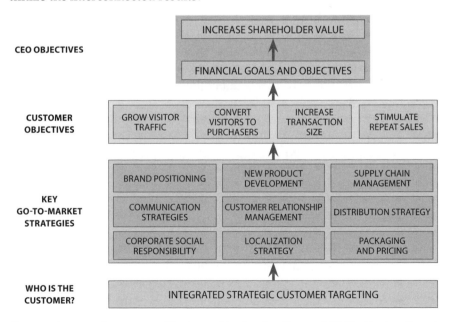

Figure 22: Integrated customer and business objectives (retail example)(© The Garrison Group)

While you may be very busy developing a lot of strategies to drive customer results, the truth is that you probably don't have enough data about who your best customers are, or could be; the chances that your strategies will fully impact your customers are severely marginalized. Most of us simply do not have the customer information we need to guide all of our core business-growth strategies. We have bits and pieces, such as some lifestyle segmentation that we hope increases the efficiency of our media strategies, and perhaps some current customer sales data that can help guide our CRM (Customer Relationship Management) program, but do we really have the customer data to drive all of our 'customer-based' strategies? The answer is… probably not.

What do you want customer segmentation to do?

Most current segmentation models that you could use will simply run out of gas before you're able to reach your destination – in-depth customer understanding that can guide all of your go-to-market growth strategies. Before you move into a more versatile form of segmentation – *Integrated Strategic Targeting* – perhaps you should first identify what it is exactly that you want to use customer segmentation for in the first place. Like many new marketing tools that require a lot of resources and a new level of complexity in how you go to market, it is easy to get so lost on the journey that you lose sight of the destination – remember how technology applications overwhelmed the original repeat and cross-selling intent of CRM? When you are up to your neck in alligators, it is hard to remember that your original intention was to drain the swamp.

Figure 22 listed several go-to market strategic areas where an enhanced level of customer segmentation can significantly help target the strategy with greater precision and thereby achieve much stronger results – attract more visitors who convert to purchasing customers who buy a lot, for more money, more often! The following are just a few examples of how more effective customer segmentation, and the better targeting that results, can drive some key go to market strategies:

1. **Brand positioning.** This is the most obvious place to put your segmentation to work. To develop a more involving brand-positioning strategy that connects at both the functional and emotional level that you will need, category U&A data will help you identify the functional drivers of purchase and consumption; but you will also need broader lifestyle

data to uncover the crucial emotional levers that you will need if you are going to move beyond merely satisfied customers to brand advocates – the highest level of customer brand involvement.

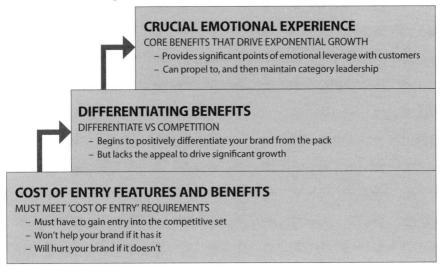

CRUCIAL EMOTIONAL EXPERIENCE
CORE BENEFITS THAT DRIVE EXPONENTIAL GROWTH
   – Provides significant points of emotional leverage with customers
   – Can propel to, and then maintain category leadership

DIFFERENTIATING BENEFITS
DIFFERENTIATE VS COMPETITION
   – Begins to positively differentiate your brand from the pack
   – But lacks the appeal to drive significant growth

COST OF ENTRY FEATURES AND BENEFITS
MUST MEET 'COST OF ENTRY' REQUIREMENTS
   – Must have to gain entry into the competitive set
   – Won't help your brand if it has it
   – Will hurt your brand if it doesn't

Figure 23: Effective consumer research can establish the motivational hierarchy of the brand
(Source: Zyman Marketing)

2. **Localization strategies.** This is basically an extension of the brand positioning strategy, but deserves a separate point because this global/local brand-relevance debate is still a difficult balancing act with most multinational companies. Global brands need consistency in how they go to market from one country to the next, but they must also have some local relevance. To achieve this crucial balance, marketers are very much in need of insights both from the category and the customer's life in general. Category data can help you connect the global product and usage imagery elements to ensure your brand is consistently communicating and delivering on the key features and benefits across multiple markets.

But for the brand to truly take hold in any market, it must have some sort of relevance to local customers' lives and what they do; otherwise they simply won't buy and will instead buy another brand that offers more relevance and meaning to their lives. This relevance takes form primarily with user imagery (are the other users like me, or who I aspire to be) and comes to life with the connections your brand has and can build with other prominent brands in the local market (retailers, promotions, sponsorships, events and activities) – *associative imagery.*

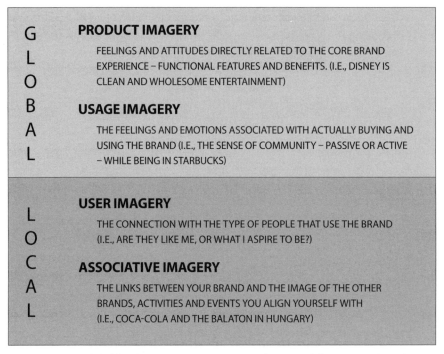

Figure 24: Global/local optimization (© Zyman Marketing and the Garrison Group)

3. **Communication strategies.** To create a more engaging communication strategy that can deliver a stronger brand message at the right time and place, you need to know when your best customer prospects are more likely to want to engage with the category and with your brand. Again, category-driven data will tell you when, how and even partly why they purchase/consume, but this data will not look at their lives in a broad-enough context to tell you how they move through their days and nights, the media they use, the networks they are increasingly connecting to, and most importantly, the advice and powerful word-of-mouth recommendations they receive from social and business networks.

Retailers need to create better in-store communication and store layouts that enable customers to become more involved during a visit, thus driving both purchase conversion and increased transaction size. Producers also need to create more involving packaging designs and a range of availability options that have greater application to how customers use the product. Both require insights from a deeper understanding that reflects the broader lives of their customers as well category usage for their existing and potential customers.

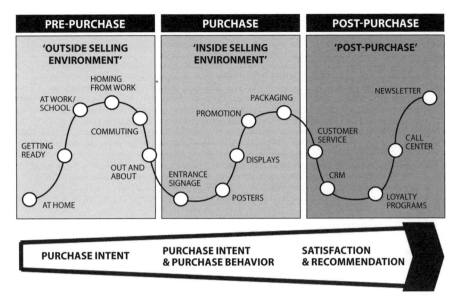

Figure 25: Target the right message to the right people at the right time
and at the right place (© The Garrison Group)

4. **Product development.** The product development process for new goods and services must have the ability to anticipate new demand and reflect the role of the brand/products in providing a wider and/or deeper value to the customer. Figure 26. illustrates some breakthrough product innovations that would have been very difficult to conceive without a deeper understanding of customers' lives as well as a more thorough understanding of the nuances of the category, the brand, and the business system as part of a more customer-integrated ideation process.

The explosion of the SUV category 15 years ago wasn't driven by insights from the category usage of pre-existing outdoor enthusiasts; otherwise Jeep would have continued to offer such predictable added-value benefits such as free 5000lb wenches and CB radios. The importance of new suburban mom customers wanting to feel in control (they sit higher) and safe (all-wheel drive) was a key lifestyle driver for a potential new group of Jeep customers that would never have been recognized if someone at Jeep in the early 1990s had not had the imagination to look broader than its pre-existing category data for new product and positioning ideas. The same sort of dynamic is now happening with the rapid demise of SUVs in favor of hybrids; this also reflects a much deeper sociological issue than just rising gas prices.

IDEATION AREA	PURPOSE	BREAKTHROUGH EXAMPLE
1. CORE COMPETENCE?	What is the fundamental purpose/ benefit of this product or service? What business are you really in?	Club Med discovers that it is really in the escape and rejuvenation business – the 'The antidote for civilization' and the practice of no money required onsite.
2. FOR WHOM?	What customer target is most likely to buy this product or service? What do they really care about in their heads, hearts and guts relative to this type of product or service?	Porsche's loyal 'sports car' fanatics don't buy often enough. Porsche shifts target to prestige-oriented customers who are more likely to buy every two years with Cayenne and the now more luxurious 911.
3. INSTEAD OF WHAT?	What can this product replace? What other uses does it have that have not been considered, or what category can it potentially compete against? A wider look at alternatives.	Vail adds simple metal brackets on the back of chairlifts to hold mountain bikes; creates huge summer sports business with under-utilized winter assets that can now attract repeat as well as new customers.
4. DIFFERENT? BETTER? SPECIAL?	What can the product do that is different, better and more special than anybody has done before in that area of business based on what we have discovered in the earlier steps?	IKEA's room-design layout allows it to motivate more sophisticated customers to come to IKEA first for new ideas – from low-price furniture positioning to a much more involving 'inspiration' positioning.
5. VALUE CHAIN	How can a customer value idea be leveraged into the business system? How can the sales, distribution and production resources be leveraged for maximum effectiveness and efficiency?	McDonald's leverages its real estate presence in Europe to launch the McCafé concept to dominate the neighborhood 'third place' coffee market prior to Starbucks entry into most European countries.

Figure 26: Customer-insight-driven innovation (© The Garrison Group)

5. **Corporate social responsibility (CSR).** This strategic area is getting more attention globally as well as locally in Eastern Europe, but the problem is that it is often connected to phrases like 'corporate citizenship' and about 'doing the right thing' – i.e., acting responsibly. As such, it basically becomes a 'gold star' collection effort by the company and its executives to better protect them in the event something goes wrong. This is a 'the cup is half-empty rather than half-full' mentality. I prefer the upside approach reflected by naming these 'Corporate Social Optimization (CSO)' initiatives because fundamentally what the intention should be is to optimize business results through a better understanding of what is happening in society as a whole, both globally and locally, and then acting on that knowledge for the benefit of the business. So it

only stands to reason that you need some broader insights into what is happening in the market beyond the interaction customers have with your product. CSO connects to local customer values, but isn't just about global warming and ethical corporate behavior. For example, if you are a business that requires a steady inflow of relatively unskilled workers, yet the local homogenous population is experiencing declining birthrates, perhaps a viable CSO strategy could be through better accessing a growing immigrant population – as is the case in many Western European markets as well as, say, in the city of Moscow. You would need to not only recognize this important societal change but also perhaps determine how you can maintain growth by developing employee cohesion programs that better integrate local and immigrant employees, as well as educating customers on the benefits this approach can mean for them.

The limitations of current customer segmentation models

Customer segmentation is a hot topic in marketing globally and has been widely debated over the years. Daniel Yankelovich introduced the idea of moving beyond simple demographic segmentation over 40 years ago; he argues that segmentation has more recently moved too far into 'nebulousness' with an over-focus on segmenting customers on the basis of their lifestyle rather than sticking closer to category perceptions and attitudes that he and others argue are more closely aligned with met and unmet product needs. He's right.

On the other hand, the practitioners of lifestyle-oriented segmentation argue that if you segment customers only on the basis of category involvement such as what yogurt marketer Danone has called 'Late Night Snackers' or 'Early Morning Nurturers', where exactly would you find these customers in the real world? It's not like these customers go to the store as strictly yogurt consumers, and they certainly don't engage in various forms of media with yogurt solely on their mind and a cup in their hand. It is their lives that we must understand better if we are going to find them and convince them to buy more yogurt. This counter argument is also right.

So what are the commonly used segmentation models and what can they do?

1. **Category-based segmentation.** Most large marketing-driven companies have U&A data that relates primarily to their category and have segmented their customers accordingly – such as what Coca-Cola has done for years with its 'Drinks and Drinkers' studies around the world. As a result, these companies have good insights into how customers specifically

interact with their brands and with those of their competitors, as well as some relevant current customer relationship data which they can mine. These insights can be very helpful in developing new packaging options, competitive pricing strategies and seasonal promotional programs. The problem with this category-based segmentation lies in attracting new customers to the category; this segmentation model doesn't know enough about the customers' overall lives and so it is difficult to create relevance where it doesn't currently exist. Also, because it is so tightly focused on category U&A rather than on the overall lives of potential customers, it becomes difficult to determine where to find these customers to communicate with them when they are not directly in the purchase/consumption environment. For this we need to know how and where they move, who they associate with, and how they interact with different forms of media. Also, in terms of emerging markets, it is typically the case that strong category usage data isn't available because your brand, or many of your potential competitors' brands, may not be present in the market, or have only been available for a very short period of time. Consequently what is currently in the market and the perceptions of that reality may be very different from what it will be in the future – which is, of course, where all your sales growth will be coming from.

2. *Lifestyle-based segmentation.* The companies that have gone wholeheartedly into VAL (Value and Lifestyle) research have become frustrated because although they have excellent lifestyle behavior and attitudinal data that have proven useful in creating more customer-involving advertising materials, the data fall short on providing actionable insights that could help those marketers develop better products and services because it is lacking the insights on how these VAL segments specifically interact with the brand or category.

3. *Price/quality-based segmentation.* This is the last of the major segmentation methods offered by the likes of BCG (Boston Consulting Group) and McKinsey that seeks to differentiate between six or seven different customer groups driven almost purely by price at one end to premium quality driven at the other (Figure 27).

This price/quality segmentation is especially popular these days among FMCG marketers because it tends to confirm their world view that today's customers are looking only at two intersecting factors – quality and price. Their stay-awake-at-night fear is that retailers recognize the same version of reality and are rapidly grabbing more market share by introducing retailer brands with increasingly higher quality levels that increases their appeal from what has been primarily lower demographic groups necessarily gravitating toward price as the key differentiator, to higher end customers who are driven on the basis of quality – *more for more and worth it.* As a result, it is these higher-end consumers who are starting to suspect that brand value is less about quality and more about an 'advertising facade' which they are less inclined to buy into – literally as well as figuratively.

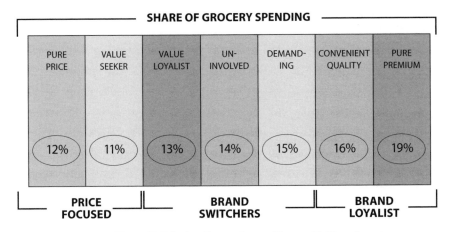

SHARE OF GROCERY SPENDING

PURE PRICE	VALUE SEEKER	VALUE LOYALIST	UN-INVOLVED	DEMAND-ING	CONVENIENT QUALITY	PURE PREMIUM
12%	11%	13%	14%	15%	16%	19%

PRICE FOCUSED — **BRAND SWITCHERS** — **BRAND LOYALIST**

Figure 27: Price/quality continuum (Source: McKinsey)

The fact that the price/quality segmentation method has gained popularity with marketers such as Procter & Gamble and Tesco demonstrates the frustration many marketers feel about the limitations of the first two forms of psychographics-based segmentation (lifestyle or category-driven). In essence, they have basically retreated to an old-fashioned form of demographic segmentation that is only peripherally disguised as attitudinal.

4. **Demographic-based segmentation.** With the most experienced of marketers divided into one of these first three camps, less sophisticated marketers are avoiding any form of psychographics and instead find themselves sticking with fact-based demographic factors such as age, sex and income. Although banks, retailers and white goods manufacturers who predominately use this most basic form of segmentation find it convenient and easy to access from existing customer data, they are increasingly coming to the realization that it lacks the customer insights needed to create better products, to develop a stronger brand proposition, or to execute a more efficient and impactful communication strategy.

MOST COMMONLY USED CUSTOMER SEGMENTATION MODELS

KEY GO-TO-MARKET GROWTH STRATEGIES	LIFESTYLE-BASED SEGMENTATION	BRAND/CATEGORY USAGE AND ATTITUDES-BASED SEGMENTATION	PRICE/ VALUE-BASED SEGMENTATION	DEMOGRAPHIC-BASED SEGMENTATION
BRAND POSITIONING	YES	YES	NO	NO
COMMUNICATION STRATEGIES	YES	PARTLY	NO	PARTLY
CORPORATE SOCIAL RESPONSIBILITY	YES	YES	NO	NO
NEW PRODUCT DEVELOPMENT	YES	YES	PARTLY	PARTLY
CUSTOMER RELATIONSHIP MANAGEMENT	YES	YES	YES	PARTLY
LOCALIZATION STRATEGY	YES	YES	NO	PARTLY
SUPPLY CHAIN MANAGEMENT	PARTLY	YES	YES	YES
AVAILABILITY STRATEGIES	YES	YES	YES	YES
PACKAGING AND PRICING	YES	YES	YES	YES

Figure 28: Linking customer strategies with existing customer segmentation methods

Integrated Strategic Targeting, as the name implies, doesn't attempt to favor one form or the other of current segmentation models previously discussed in terms of what is most important. The breakthrough comes from developing much stronger growth strategies by integrating multiple forms of customer data (demographics, lifestyle, category usage and price sensitivity) into a single segmentation and customer-targeting tool. This tool then enables you to go to market with products that are more *meaningful* within customers' lives, *deliverable* relative to existing brand and category usage and expectations, and *defendable* because your brand has added value that can better resist purely price-driven competition.

Looking for love in all the wrong places

This *Integrated Strategic Targeting* method was inspired by an unlikely source – MTV's *Room Raiders* program. This show is a modern adaptation of the classic *Dating Game* that was aired in various forms around the world in the 1970s and 1980s under various local names. The original show was basically a focus group on dating. A young woman would ask three men sitting on the other side of a room-divider a series of category questions. The three bachelor respondents would typically answer in a way that most marketers are all too familiar with, and the main reason why their focus groups so often go wrong. The young bachelors on the *Dating Game* would usually answer the given question such as 'do you believe in kissing on the first date' or 'what is your favorite first-date activity' based on one of three primary intentions, rather than on what he really believed:

1. What he wants the girl to believe about him.
2. What he wants the audience to believe about him.
3. What he wants the other two guys sitting next to him to believe about him.

When the girl finally picks bachelor number two, you groan and say she got it all wrong. From your perspective (as the audience, you enjoyed a broader context than she could because you were able to see and read facial expressions, could see what he was dressed like, how he interacted with his peers, and so forth – all of which led you to believe that you had better insights into who was the better date choice for the girl beyond the stated answers.

MTV's newer *Room Raiders* went deeper and revealed much better insights about the three bachelors than you or the girl were ever able to get within the old *Dating Game* format. In *Room Raiders*, the girl visits each prospective date's home while they are away before she ever gets around to asking them questions in person – the questions then become more of a validation exercise based on what she has already discovered in their kitchen, bathroom, bedroom and closets. Because there is now an even larger perspective on the lives of the three date candidates, we find that we almost always agree with her final decision as being the right choice for her. She could see if their bed was up in a frame or lying on the floor, what clothes they really wore based on wear and tear, and what was in their cupboards, refrigerators, or medicine cabinets. She could discover their favorite sites on the Internet, what magazines or books they read, and even see the mail they received. She got lifestyle context that she could later fuse with category data so that when she asked her potential dates her questions, she could fit that within a broader understanding of who they really were – what their lives, motivations and aspirations were really about.

MTV's *Room Raiders* illustrated in a very fundamental way that we need a more integrated (category and life) model of segmentation and customer understanding.

The solution is hiding in plain sight

So, how do we get this broader data in a timely and cost-efficient manner? After all, who can afford to execute a thousand *Room Raider* scenarios in a market? The answer is that there is typically a broad, single-source database available in almost any market in the world that large research companies have developed over the years to efficiently research hundreds of categories and then sell this essentially category and brand data on a piecemeal basis to individual brands and their agencies. One of the best known research is TGI – a single-source database that has primarily been used by a wide range of brands from soft drinks, automobile manufacturers, mobile phone operators, and retailers to better understand how their customers and their competitor's customers interact with media. To answer the media question, TGI goes into incredible detail on not only what media customers interact with, but also how they move about in their daily lives so that media planners can identify new media opportunities. This huge lifestyle insight opportunity exists within this single source because the data cover so many individual categories; it becomes possible to look at the sum of the parts as a composite picture to determine who people are based on a wider selection of brand, product, media and leisure choices. All of the lifestyle choices represented within a single-source database offer much deeper insights if the database, which has typically been used on a micro category level rather than on a macro lifestyle level, is properly processed and analyzed.

TGI and several other single-source databases go well beyond *room raiding* and into *life raiding* because they cover a lot more about what people do than simply what happens within their homes. It tracks where they go on vacation, how often they go out each week and where they go. You can determine if people watch television primarily for escape and release or for information and discovery by checking the programs they watch. This sort of viewing information says a lot about people. These databases are much larger than what most companies could afford on their own – there are 36,000 respondents for TGI in Russia, for example. Because it is conducted quarterly in most markets, you can even dig into the data with the right tools to determine who is the first to buy a new product in a category – *the valuable early adopter.*

We all know that the key factor in movie marketing is to reach those people who watch movies the opening weekend because they are the influencers who make it their job to tell the rest of us which movies to watch and which ones to avoid. But how does this differ for an action movie, a romance, or a family movie? Lifestyle segments (i.e., *Actualizer* parents) layered on top of category segmentation (i.e., *First Weekend Movie Goers*) are crucial in answering the important influencer question. You need to know who these people are specifically and what else are they buying and using so that you can better understand their lives from a much more holistic standpoint (Figure 29).

Figure 29: *Integrated Strategic Targeting* **inputs process**

How it works for IKEA

We have developed a methodology to utilize these large, single-source data-bases, combine them with other existing category data available within most companies to create this new integrated segmentation process. The first step in developing the *Integrated Strategic Targeting* process is to create a mathematical model that enables us to take the entire TGI database and filter it through a personality mapping model. We prefer Adler's personal-ity dimensions (Figure 30) as a base model because it is widely used in re-search circles and so utilizing it within our process not only accesses one of the best means of identifying personality types, but also increases the cross-correlation capabilities with other research; this becomes important later on in the process as we layer on additional primary research studies for a particular brand or company. Again, what we are seeking to do is to build upon best practices in an evolutionary fashion rather than trying to reinvent the wheel.

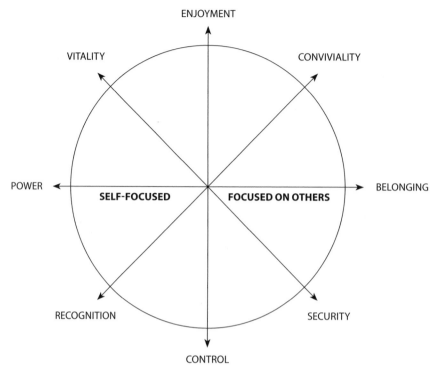

Figure 30: Adler's personality dimensions serve as the basis of
the *Integrated Strategic Targeting* 'life' segmentation

What happens in the initial filtering process is that the thousands of respondents begin to cluster on the basis of similar purchasing behavior, lifestyle
choices, and attitudinal statements included in the TGI survey that reflect
shared values, attitudes and behavior. In each market there is a multitude of
brands that are highly indicative of lifestyle values and attitudes. Choices in
automobiles, mobile phones, cigarettes and alcoholic beverages are the most
obvious lifestyle indicators, but in the case of Hungary we found one particularly revealing brand/lifestyle indicator within 100% juice brands. HohesC
and Granini are two high-end juice brands that reflect very different values.
Granini, as the name and beautiful designer package would indicate, is all
about style. In contrast, HohesC, as the name and very scientific-looking
package would indicate, is much more about substance. It is basically the
same product – 100% orange juice, but the type of mom who puts HohesC on
the table is very different to the mom who puts Granini on the table. Within the database, there are literally hundreds of brand choices that indicate a
very distinct lifestyle story based on a range of lifestyle choices as reflected in

brand purchase decisions and across a wide range of entertainment and activity choices.

As a second step, we dig into the new clusters to better understand the core characteristics of each cluster. We can also filter it on the basis of some demographic characteristics such as where they live, how much they earn, family status, etc., to create a separate lifestyle segmentation that may be more appropriate for a soft drink (teens), a real estate developer (geography) or bank (income levels). IKEA has used life-stage demographic criteria because understanding this factor is so important in separating home-living circumstances. The three life stages IKEA uses in the segmentation are early (18+ pre-kids), parents, and seniors. Figure 31 is an example of parents' life-stage segmentation for Russia.

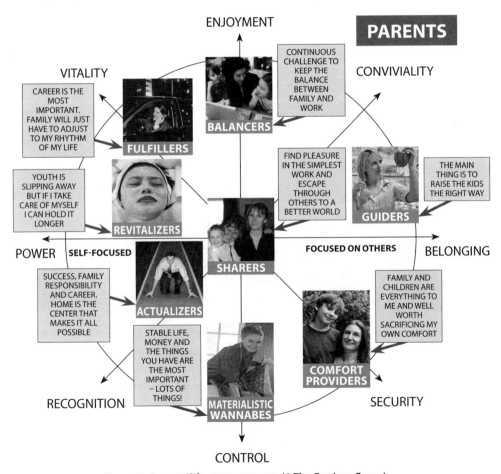

Figure 31: Parents' life-stage segments (© The Garrison Group)

From the demographic aspects of the database, we know that *Fulfillers, Balancers* and *Guiders* are among the highest income segments. However, the way they live their lives is remarkably different, and, consequently, how and why they shop at IKEA is also strikingly different. And that is what IKEA must know if it intends to increase the percentage of visits, visit frequency, purchase conversion rates on each visit, and of course, transaction size – the four most important business success drivers for IKEA.

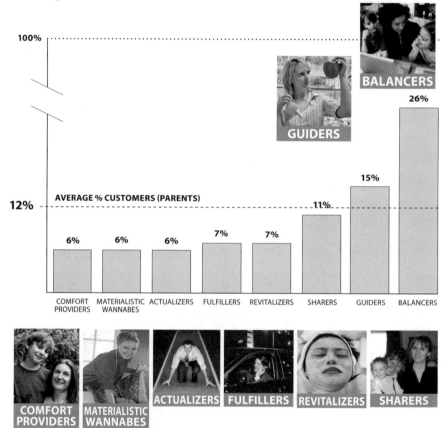

Figure 32: IKEA's customer penetration for Parents' life stage (© The Garrison Group)

Balancers is a segment name that represents a widely recognized lifestyle in the West. They exist in Russia, as well as throughout Eastern Europe, but what and how they balance is somewhat different. Russian *Balancers* are incredibly guilt-driven due to the fact that they desperately want to provide a better life for their families than their own parents could offer them in previous times, yet they also want to be a tight-knit family unit like it was in the old days when they were children before the political changes. Add to that the enormous number of opportunities available in Russia today that offer one lifestyle advantage, but take from the other, and you begin to understand the guilt picture. Because they don't feel that they spend enough time at work or at home and feel badly about it in both places, they tend to over-compensate in bursts of spontaneity that reflects their 'home living' category usage. Like other Russian parent segments, *Balancers* spend a lot on their children, but they are more likely to edge toward spoiling their children with race-car-themed bedroom sets and big home entertainment centers equipped with the latest gadgets. Unlike another parental group, *Fulfillers*, who live close to their work, *Balancers* will commute several hours a day so that their children can live in green areas and afford bigger homes that enable their kids to have their own bedrooms.

Guiders are another high-value segment in IKEA's parent life-stage segmentation and again, relative to demographics such as income and educational level, they are similar to *Fulfillers* and *Balancers*. The difference is that they do not feel guilty about the time spent at work because they have a well-focused plan. They may live in the suburbs or in the center – the deciding factor is typically the quality of local schools. Their children may have computers and other gadgets, but the focus is less on spoiling than on preparation. The category hot-button for them is a living room that is connected to the kitchen so that they can cook and interact with the family at the same time. Unlike cocoon-driven *Fulfillers*, bedrooms are much less important for *Guiders* and they like them to be in close proximity to the children's room, all of which are typically centered on the family room/kitchen.

Fulfillers are one of the most self-focused of the segments. *Fulfillers* would tell you that the 16-hour days and extensive business traveling and other engagements are for the sake of their families and for the better life that such hard work and success will provide for them. But the reality is that they are doing it because they have a consuming obsession of living up to their own expectations and the expectations of others around them. It is about them. They were expected to be the most successful after graduating university and they have been wholly focused for quite some time on proving that assessment correct. Or perhaps they were even underestimated in school (the Russian equivalent of Bill Gates), but the point is that they are still obsessed with fulfilling expectations – hence the name we gave them. They shop at IKEA at a rate of about half the life-stage average but their focus, more than any other segment, is on bedrooms. They spend disproportionately on big comfortable beds and the reason has much to do with their lifestyle. They are 'on' all the time and the most treasured moment they have is to retreat into the secure cocoon of their warm and soothing bedroom. We also know that in the living room and kitchen areas they are more concerned about style rather than substance, but it is in bedrooms that IKEA is able to really capture them emotionally.

Just to close the loop from an earlier point about juice customers in Eastern Europe, *Guiders* are the HohesC juice customers and Granini is all about *Fulfillers*.

The early life-stage segments are even more distinct from the parent life stage not only in how they live their lives, but also in how and why they shop at IKEA (Figure 33).

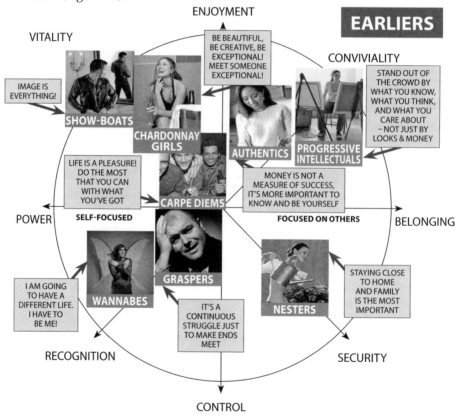

Figure 33: Earliers' life-stage segments (© The Garrison Group)

The two highest-value segments (potential to shop at IKEA) could not be any more different from a lifestyle standpoint, but demographically they are very similar as both are well educated and financially relatively well off compared to their peers. They also shop a lot at IKEA, but it is here that the difference is most striking and it is directly related to who they are as people from a more

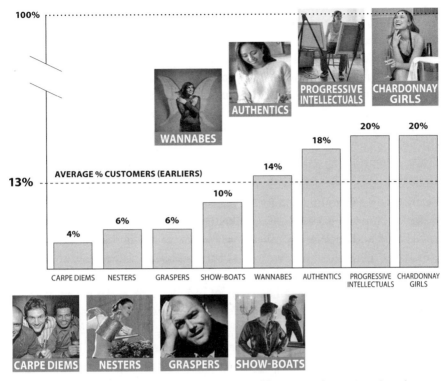

Figure 34: IKEA's customer penetration for Early life stage (© The Garrison Group)

holistic standpoint. *Chardonnay Girls* are basically the *Sex in the City* TV show characters – Russian style. Like their New York counterparts they have a problem finding 'Mister Right' because they typically go for single Russian *Peacocks* or married *Fulfillers*. Style is more important than substance, which is reflected in their dating choice as well as much of their social and fashion choices. However, they yearn for something more and this tension between what they have versus what they really want particularly defines them and their interaction with many product categories, including home furnishings. Small studio living settings with lots of mirrors (confidence builders) and matching accessories are major hot-buttons for them. The internal IKEA merchandising group that puts together those living areas on the upper floor are well aware of this because they have been fully briefed on the particulars including segment 'day in the life – and day in the store' training videos that IKEA has produced so that when a *Chardonnay Girl* walks by one of the settings targeting her, she immediately feels 'this is me'. Pull-out sofas are also important for visiting family and friends from the countryside (a lot of *Chardonnay Girls* are small-city girls attracted to the fuzz and buzz of Moscow) and for those 'girls only' nights spent commiserating over the latest boyfriend break-up.

Progressive Intellectuals is a group that IKEA was surprised to find it attracted in such numbers – the highest percentage of IKEA shoppers in the entire life stage, neck and neck with the *Chardonnay Girls*. Unlike their Western counterparts, whom we would call *Alternatives*, the nearest Russian equivalent, *Progressive Intellectuals,* are less green and typically work for multinationals or local big companies just as the *Chardonnay Girls* do. But their lifestyle and resulting purchasing patterns differ dramatically. *Progressive Intellectuals* don't really like the perfectly appointed room settings so common at IKEA. They are much too eclectic to find comfort in sofas, tables, chairs and curtains that all match. Where *Chardonnay Girls* are likely to place a mirror, a *Progressive Intellectuals* will add another bookshelf (their source of intellectual confidence). So why then do they go to IKEA at a rate of almost twice the life-stage average? It is to visit and shop in IKEA's famous Market Hall on the ground floor. IKEA's Market Hall has a wonderful assortment of knick knacks, fabrics and accessories that allows the *Progressive Intellectuals'* uniquely personal style to flourish and be fully realized. And if by chance a *Progressive Intellectual* does wander upstairs for something specific like a bed frame or chair, the IKEA Russia sales people can quickly spot the type based on the training they have received and will know to ask style questions to stimulate additional purchases rather than to suggest matching items as they would with a *Chardonnay Girl*.

Time spent in the store is also dramatically different as we have learned by combining the traditional category and brand U&A studies used by IKEA with the broader segmentation the TGI data provides. *Chardonnay Girls* tend to spend between 2.5 to 3 hours on an IKEA visit that happens about once per month. *Progressive Intellectuals* only visit about every six weeks and stay only about an hour in the store. Furthermore, *Chardonnay Girls* are more likely to fall into the sweet temptation of all the ad-on sales placed around the room settings (even before arriving to the Market Hall), whereas *Progressive Intellectuals* have more conscious and planned purchases and are less likely to be driven by impulse.

The ability to combine the data from IKEA's U&A studies within the broader *Integrated Strategic Targeting* process is possible by finding the attitudinal statement that overlaps between the two databases and then using this as a 'data doorway' to either bring in broader information into the IKEA-customized research findings available in its U&A studies, or vice versa by taking very precise brand usage and behavioral data into the broader lifestyle segmentation.

Who are the 'bell cows'?

The final benefit this *Integrated Strategic Targeting* process offers to marketers is the ability to determine which segments are more likely to influence other segments and why. As individuals living in a society, we all recognize that we routinely look to certain people we know to help us with information and knowledge that we believe they possess; information that for some reason or another, we ourselves lack. By digging into purchasing patterns of a very broad and very deep database in *Integrated Strategic Targeting* we can identify certain characteristics that help us determine who these influencers are. In general terms, we use the broader lifestyle data to separate influencers from the influencees based on a variety of attitudinal statements contained in the database that indicate whether one person is more likely to seek out opinions from others or to offer their opinion. This is interesting. But what is important to marketers who have specific products and services to sell, is the ability to understand who the influencers are relative to specific categories.

We know from the Russian segmentation that *Chardonnay Girls* are influential establishing fashion trends (Figure 35), but depending on the style, *Progressive Intellectuals* can also be quite influential, but for different segments.

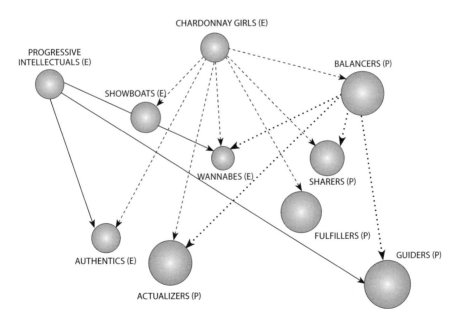

Figure 35: Fashion category influencers (© The Garrison Group)

Chardonnay Girls and *Progressive Intellectuals* are both trendsetters in fashion – but through very different styles. In contrast, the role hierarchy of influence changes significantly when we look at the travel and tourism category (Figure 36).

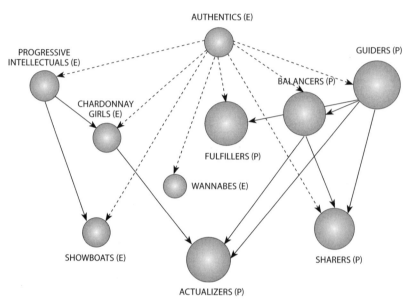

Figure 36: Tourism and travel – Authentics are the alphas that trigger travel destination popularity; they are the influencers (© The Garrison Group)

To determine the business impact of lifestyle-segment influencing patterns, as well as the nuances you would need to make in positioning your brand within a product category for different high-value targets, take the case of a family-oriented wellness hotel (Figure 37).

Wellness hotels are a rapidly growing category in Eastern Europe and Russia, but almost all are positioned with benefits and packaging that target *Fulfillers*. The reason for this is interesting: we discovered in our research that most wellness hotel owners are themselves *Fulfillers* and consequently are caught in the self-limiting trap of thinking they themselves are typical of their customers. Consequently, they are in effect marketing to themselves. They have the *Fulfiller* segment well understood but it is a significantly smaller market than they could enjoy when you take into account other segments that could potentially be influenced by the lead segment if they had a better understanding of who their best potential customers could be and what their much different needs are.

LEAD CONSUMER TARGET			
	FULFILLERS	BALANCERS	GUIDERS
(% OF THE POPULATION)	12%	12%	16%

WELLNESS HOTEL CATEGORY NEED STATE			
	RELAXATION FOR MYSELF AND FUN FOR MY KIDS	FAMILY BONDING ENJOYING AND SPOILING	FAMILY BONDING WITH A PURPOSE
NUMBER OF INFLUENCED CONSUMERS (% OF THE POPULATION)	10%	15%	23%
TOTAL CONSUMER IMPACT (% OF THE POPULATION)	22%	27%	39%

Figure 37: Segment positioning business impact – measuring the business impact for a new wellness hotel concept linking the specific category need state for each lifestyle target (© The Garrison Group)

Bolt-on capability

The key to the impact of this *Integrated Strategic Targeting* process is that it does not attempt to rank one particular model of segmentation over another, but seeks to combine the unique benefits of each so that you can see a fuller picture of your brand's appeal and your competitor's appeal all within the context of the customers' overall lives. While it is certainly a leap-ahead methodology, it is more evolutionary rather than revolutionary in application. This should be comforting to you because it does not require throwing out everything you have expensively done previously, but builds on to where you are by adding a new and broader database combined with a new form of segmentation modeling. As a final example of how one builds on the other, take the McKinsey price/quality model that we discussed earlier; a model that keeps the FMCG marketers awake at night. What we found by overlaying our lifestyle segmentation on the price/quality model is that in general there are no surprises – the higher-income lifestyle segments fit predictably where you would expect them to on the price/quality continuum.

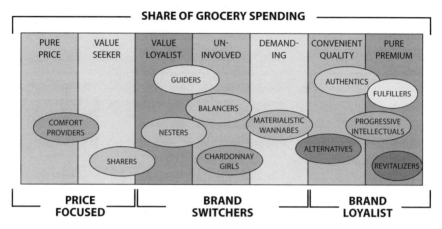

Figure 38: Lifestyle segment integration within price/quality continuum
(Source: McKinsey and the Garrison Group)

But Procter& Gamble and Unilever are not selling grocery products in general; they are selling specific brands in specific product categories. In Figures 39–41 we see that the various segments fall onto the price/quality model differently depending on the grocery category. Logically, because of the lower instances of brands delivering on emotional benefits in the washing soap category, most customer segments are clustered in the price-oriented end of the model.

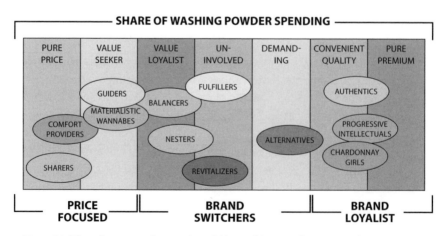

Figure 39: Lifestyle segment integration within washing powder price/quality continuum
(Source: McKinsey and the Garrison Group)

But if you move into soft drinks or hair care, where customer lifestyles are better connected through more involving emotional benefits that are harder for retailer brands to match, there are very specific customer segments moving toward the quality end of the spectrum.

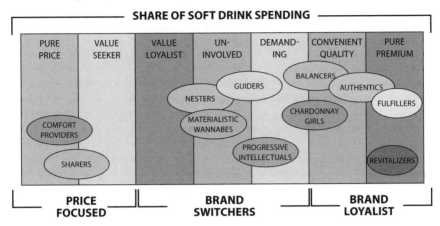

Figure 40: Lifestyle segment integration within soft drink price/quality continuum
(Source: McKinsey and the Garrison Group)

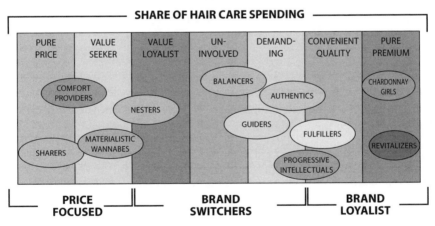

Figure 41: Lifestyle segment integration within hair care price/quality continuum
(Source: McKinsey and the Garrison Group)

So where to from here?

It is time for marketers to get back on their the CEO's agenda by better clarifying why deeper customer understanding needs to be developed and how that enhanced understanding can be best utilized to drive better shareholder value through better customer value. Before you start down the complicated and often expensive path of customer segmentation, you must first assess what it is that you need the segmentation to do for you (brand positioning, communication strategies, distribution activities, etc.) and how these strategies will drive specific customer actions and the impact these actions will have on the overall financial results of the business. Customer understanding and how that links to core business growth strategies is 'too important to leave to the marketing guys'. It must be integrated into every aspect of the business that impacts your company's customer value proposition and therefore deserves to be high on the CEO's agenda.

It isn't enough to know how customers interact with your brand. It's important, but it's not enough. It is also important to know how customers view your brand relative to your competitors as well as within the category drivers of satisfaction. This is also important because it will help you determine the functional benefits that your brand must provide to capture additional sales and market share. But unless you can understand how factors such as brand attitudes and category usage are reflected in the broader lives of customers, you will find it very difficult to emotionally connect with those customers. And when you have the ability to truly connect emotionally as well as functionally with your customers, as IKEA has been able to do in Russia and elsewhere, where it has employed the *Integrated Strategic Targeting* model, you will find it enables a greatly enhanced ability to target your best customer prospects with the right products communicated at the right time and place to optimize your marketing impact and efficiencies. It is no accident that this model was developed in Eastern Europe where, once again, necessity has proven to be the 'mother of invention'. It is well accepted that the customer is changing at an unprecedented rate in these markets and that this rapid change is reflected in both their brand usage as well as within their evolving lifestyles. And because marketing budgets are often more restricted in Eastern Europe, it was imperative that we not only find a method to access better customer knowledge more cost efficiently, but also that the marketing strategies and tactics that result from this new segmentation would allow us to ensure that limited marketing budgets are truly targeting the right people at the right time. The goal of the *Integrated Strategic Targeting* approach is to achieve the seemingly impossible result of increasing marketing's impact while simultaneously decreasing its cost in absolute terms.

Psychographics segmentation for Subway

By Ildikó Kókai

*Ildikó is a former Garrison Group consultant who is now the marketing manager for NetAcademia, an online learning resourse. She has long been active on environmental issues facing emerging markets. Ildikó is a native of Hungary.**

In 2010, the Subway chain entered its 45th year of operation. It is the world's largest sandwich chain, and the world's fastest-growing franchise. The company currently has 25,702 franchised restaurants in 84 countries.

Many restaurant analysts attribute Subway's fast growth to the growing health concerns of its customers, a trend that Subway has taken advantage of in its marketing. Subway uses the advertising slogan *Eat Fresh* to explain how every sandwich is made with fresh ingredients on freshly baked bread without high-calorie additives – all assembled right in front of the customer according to their exact specifications.

In addition to traditional restaurants, Subway also operates in many non-traditional locations, which also contributes to its success and fast expansion.

Attract more customers to the Hungarian Subway restaurants

Subway opened its first store in Hungary in 2004. Today, there are 12 restaurants in Budapest alone, with more planned.

In order to attract more people to the restaurants and be more focused in its marketing activities, Subway wanted to identify its most important target groups and decided to create a segmentation of the Hungarian market. It believed that this sort of study could help fine-tune the operations and activities of the existing restaurants and could provide expansion guidelines in terms of finding the best locations for future stores.

Subway already had extensive demographic data on Budapest and used that information to determine the locations of current stores according to the age and incomes of nearby residents. Unlike Western markets, however, where neighborhoods are more narrowly defined, Subway found a very mixed demographic composition in virtually all of Budapest's 23 districts. In a single block of flats, there could be a full range of the population from an affluent young professional making 800,000 forints per month, to a pensioner taking home 65,000. Obviously one could more readily afford to eat at Subway than the other, but looking deeper, the affluent professionals could be attracted to Subway's fresh-food proposition to a greater or lesser degree according to their lifestyles. It was decided that the segmentation Subway needed going

---

* Ildikó can be contacted at ildiko@garrisongroup.eu

forward would be one based on psychographics, something that would give insights into areas such as customer values, attitudes, consumption behavior, leisure activities, and media usage to help focus future communications plans.

The segmentation method

Subway mostly attracts younger people, and this is likely to remain the same in the near future. Its particular focus is on the urban population between 18 and 35. The database used for the segmentation was a nationally representative omnibus study, containing a wealth of information about Budapest residents and their lives. In addition to tracking actual consumption behavior (which says a lot about a person), this study included statements reflecting what people think about their lives; what they find important; and what they think about certain topics related to daily life.

With an abundance of data now readily available, Subway needed some sort of filter to process the data and separate thousands of individual respondents into more manageable groups based on similar values, attitudes and lifestyles – *psychographics*. The solution to this filtering problem was found in the famous psychologist Alfred Adler's eight personality dimensions: *enjoyment, conviviality, belonging, security, control, recognition, power* and *vitality*. The vast number of statements in the database could be connected to one of these dimensions, so by filtering (technically called 'factoring analysis'), the selected statements and consumption behaviors of similar personality types would pass through into common segments.

As a result of this process, the Budapest population between 18 and 35 was divided into nine psychographics segments. Each segment was named in a way that reflected a core characteristic of that segment. Adler's model was graphically mapped to illustrate the segments' core characteristics relative to each other as an overview of the examined population.

Choosing the right targets

Dividing the population into lifestyle segments is only the first step of the process. More important is the examination of each segment to determine which ones offer the greatest business potential; i.e., interest in going to Subway (*trial*), coming back to Subway (*frequency*) and purchasing a lot each time (*transaction size*). Also, how do the segments influence each other in terms of communication efficiency?

In identifying the most valuable segments – the so-called *high-value segments* – for Subway, the three most important characteristics considered were the size of the segments, the amount of money they spend at quick-serve restaurants, and how often they visit. From the segment descriptions, we also know the average income level of each segment, which Subway has found strongly correlates to the potential transaction size. Rather than looking at fast food habits that in Western terms would mostly include burgers, pizza and an assortment of other food items that could be questioned on the basis of health, Subway broadened the classification into quick-serve, which could be sandwich and salad shops, buffets, and even the Chinese food that is widely available in Budapest. Based on these parameters for selecting high-value targets – those customer segments most likely to buy – Subway was able to map the business potential. The Subway high-value charts are presented below, where the size of the bubbles represents the size of the segments. The high-value segments fall into the shaded triangle, where both *income* and *potential frequency* are high.

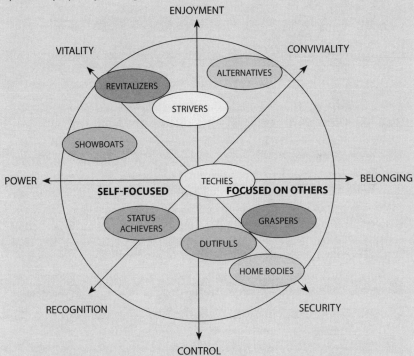

The highest-value segment are *Strivers*, who balance their career and private life, and strive to succeed in both; *Alternatives*, who avoid following mainstream trends but would appreciate the freshness of the Subway offerings; *Revitalizers*, who are concerned about their bodies and what they eat; and *Techies*, who basically live their lives from behind computer screens.

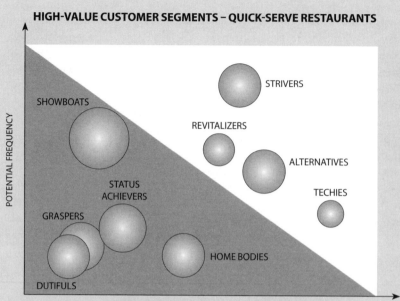

HIGH-VALUE CUSTOMER SEGMENTS – QUICK-SERVE RESTAURANTS

POTENTIAL FREQUENCY

STRIVERS

SHOWBOATS

REVITALIZERS

ALTERNATIVES

STATUS
ACHIEVERS

TECHIES

GRASPERS

HOME BODIES

DUTIFULS

POTENTIAL TRANSACTION SIZE (INCOME LEVEL)

The main difference between the two charts is that *Strivers* tend to spend the most time in the quick-serve restaurants – they are very busy people.

To be able to pick the best possible choice, Subway also needed to consider how the segments influenced each other – finding the 'alphas'. Targeting one segment could have a positive effect on another. For example, a large number of *Showboat* customers would keep *Alternatives* away, but conversely a large number of *Alternatives* could be a healthy endorsement for *Revitalizers*. Also, the degree and direction of positive influence of one segment on another is an important factor in choosing the alpha target. Like fish in the sea, you want to be as high on the 'food chain' as possible.

Determining influence patterns and identifying the alpha customers was a complex process that required extensive insight mining from the data of each segment. Eating at Subway can represent something more than just having something to eat, so it was worth taking a look at the influence from a broader array of factors. Subway examined three areas:

1. Fashion trends. A restaurant choice for younger people can be a question of style.
2. Foreign culture. Subway also represents part of the American culture, but with some food items that reflect other cultures as well.
3. Success. Subway is not a cheap place to eat, so going there demonstrates a certain financial success in life.

INFLUENCE PATTERNS CONCERNING FASHION TRENDS

INFLUENCE PATTERN CONCERNING FOREIGN CULTURES

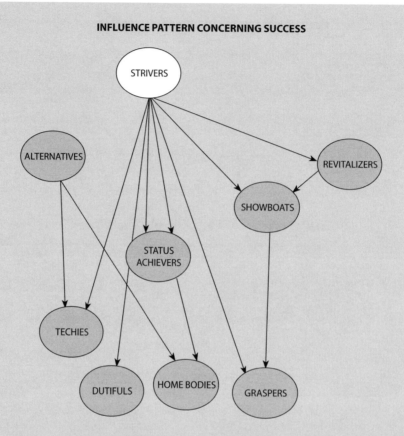

INFLUENCE PATTERN CONCERNING SUCCESS

In the three influence patterns we can see that *Strivers* and *Alternatives* seem to be the two most influential segments – the alphas – among their peers. Considering that *Alternatives* have a decidedly non-American outlook toward food choices, and *Strivers* spend the most time and money in quick-serve restaurants, the best choice for Subway was to choose *Strivers* as its alpha customers.

Next steps for Subway

Now that Subway has identified its core target, it can fine-tune its position-ing and adjust its marketing communications both inside and outside the restaurants to address *Strivers'* needs and desires more effectively. This depth of lifestyle information will help Subway to come up with not only the best message for its target, but will also help ensure that it reaches its target with that more meaningful message at the right time and at the right place – and in the right state of mind.

CASE STUDY

How to leverage doctors as key influencers in the pharmaceutical industry

By Daniel Arnold

*Daniel is a consultant at the Garrison Group and the general manager of its creative unit – 7Field Communications. Prior to the Garrison Group, Daniel held a variety of brand and trade marketing positions at Procter & Gamble in Germany and in Geneva at P&G's European headquarters. Daniel is a native of Germany.**

Why targeting *influencers* matters

In my opinion, there exists only one real computer brand worldwide. Apple manages to communicate with its key target in a way that builds advocacy for its brand. A core group of influential Apple enthusiasts do most of the communication with the wider target group. Surely this does not happen incidentally? All of Apple's communication is optimized in message, medium and occasion to reach its core influencer groups when and where they are interested in the specific Apple message, or even better, desperately waiting for it. Apple has made clear choices about whom it wants to talk to...or not. But even more, it has made a clear decision about what its brand stands for...or doesn't. By consistently making the right choices over many years, Apple has become the most distinguished and sharply differentiated computer brand moving toward an exponential future. If a potential consumer happens to talk to Apple enthusiasts, or just observes certain well-placed and well-promoted Apple users, there is a good chance they will start to consider themselves as future Apple users. An option they might have never thought about moves into their close range of purchase options. And all this with very little direct marketing expense spent to achieve this enviable position. Apple values marketing intellect over marketing muscle and the use of influencers is central to that advanced level of marketing thinking.

Influencers – who are they?

Leaving the world of computers aside, who are the influencers that consumers of other product categories listen to willingly; who do they listen to more than advertising when making purchase decisions? All of us can be influencers – and we often are without noticing it. Just think of when you where last asked by one of your friends for your opinion on a purchase decision. It might have been for anything: a car, computer, cosmetics, skies, detergent, music CD, a contraceptive, etc. You were asked for advice because your friend

---

* Daniel can be contacted at daniel@garrisongroup.eu

or colleague sees you as an expert, or at least more experienced in this category – and consequently, you influenced their purchase decision. Who is perceived as an influencer depends strongly on the category we are looking at. You might ask a techie friend for his opinion on the latest tech toys; a close girlfriend's opinion on the best contraception method; or a colleague who you know to be a car enthusiast for input on the purchase of a new sports car. Consumers do this naturally in the same way they appreciate an opinion from the hairstylist on the best shampoo against dandruff or their dentist's opinion on which electrical toothbrush he would recommend. On the other hand, people themselves like to be asked for their opinions, specifically if it concerns a field of interest in which they have special knowledge. The question is how can we as marketers bring these influencers and influencees together, measure the impact and use it systematically to build our brand to ultimately grow our sales?

How can we identify influencers in specific categories?

The first step in leveraging this understanding is to identify the relevant influencers in your category. This is done by analyzing interconnections and dependencies in relation to a specific category between the different consumer segments. Simply spoken, the more we know about the different consumer segments, the easier it is to spot the few heavy influencer segments who most of the other segments tend to follow relative to a certain product or service category. There exist lead segments for each product in any given category and – as has often been empirically proven – we can see a Pareto principle for most of the categories: about 20% of your target influences 80% of your potential consumers.

Influencers in the pharmaceutical industry

Next to consumer segments influencing other consumer segments, there are also other groups who more obviously influence our target; for example, certain professional groups. Using a contraceptive brand which specifically targets young mothers as an example, we can see that there are several different influencers during pregnancy and after giving birth.

Within the pharmaceutical category, doctors and pharmacists are key influencers for many purchase decisions, specifically for prescription drugs. Heavy, legal limitations often restrict the possibilities for marketing communication. A key question for any pharmaceutical marketing director or brand manager is where to focus their communications budget – on expert (doctors and pharmacists) or on end-consumer communication. No matter

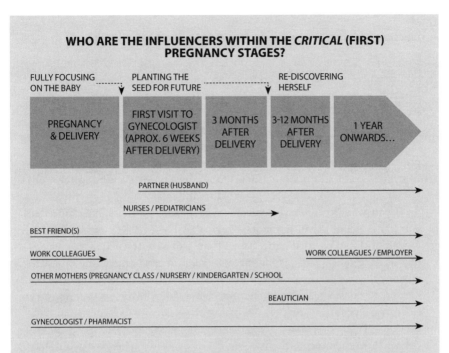

WHO ARE THE INFLUENCERS WITHIN THE *CRITICAL* (FIRST) PREGNANCY STAGES?

where they decide to focus the budget, sustainable wins are only possible if they have a clear understanding of who they want to talk to, at which occasion, through what media, and what the relevant message is at that right time and place. For a pharmaceutical company that wants to target *Actualizers*, it makes most sense to follow a push-and-pull strategy. Interconnected with the end-consumer communication (not the particular focus of this case study), which creates a pull for the prescription, is the expert-targeted communication necessary to create a push for the brand from the doctor's side.

REACH YOUR DOCTORS AS INFLUENCERS VIA A PUSH-AND-PULL STRATEGY

Doctors are doctors – why do we need to segment them?

How does communication with doctors traditionally work? By analyzing best practices and widely used tools, we identified a repeating scheme: scientific arguments with massive facts and figures are accumulated and deployed to doctors in the form of PR events, DTCMs (direct to consumer mailings), brochures, PR articles, etc. There is a traditional and widely used way of segmenting doctors or pharmacists measured in their sales numbers or prescriptions. As a result, doctors are often overwhelmed by mostly irrelevant mass communication and tend to ignore it, thus sticking to the well-known and traditionally recommended treatments.

If you want to convince someone to take some sort of action, the more you know about them, the more likely it is that you will say something meaningful and motivating to them. They will take the action you would like them to take – such as buying, using and/or recommending others to buy or use your product. Often in the pharmaceutical industry, many of the managers, salesmen and marketers are themselves doctors so they are very close to the problem – that of convincing other doctors to recommend their products. They often take their understanding of the target for granted, forgetting that other doctors are parents, friends, family members – people like them. They tend to underestimate how lifestyles and values strongly differentiate different types of doctors. Doctors are not different just because they have different specialties, but also because they approach their work and their patients very differently. Pharmaceutical companies regularly fail to understand their key influencers as human beings and to support them with information that would be highly relevant to them – behavioral data as a basis for doctor segmentation. It is hardly a surprise that our analyses revealed that most doctors were strongly convinced that the pharmaceutical industry looks only at sales figures regardless of a patient's 'real needs' – this is code for 'the doctors' real needs in supporting their patients' needs'.

Psychographics segmentation

To increase the power of communications with doctors we needed to think differently. We need to look at doctors, the key influencers for prescription drugs like contraceptives, from an entirely new angle: doctors as human beings.By basing a segmentation on psychographics data including lifestyles and values, we would be able to reach them in a more personally relevant way which breaks through the clutter of visits from sales reps and 'yet another statistic-driven product launch'. Naturally, there was no existing useful data that we could use for such an in-depth segmentation, so we had to go out and get it ourselves. Face-to-face interviews, mystery visits and fill-in questionnaires were the main tools used to build the base for analysis. As our project was in the contraception category, our focus was on gynecologists with detailed focus on contraception topics fused with the psychographics filters. Within the research, we looked at three main factors concerning their work as doctors:

1. The relationship between doctors and patients.
2. Their attitude toward contraceptive methods.
3. The overall impression of the consulting relationship with their patients.

We learned specifically that in various CEE countries, contraception is not a priority for these doctors. Most of the visits to the gynecologist are to 'cure' (a particular disease) rather than to prevent pregnancy. To try and change this, a consumer-centric push strategy from doctors and a pull strategy for end-consumers was developed, which would serve to instigate brand sales simultaneously from two directions.

The resulting six clusters were categorized along four dimensions separating them by their risk adversity, their focus on patients, their openness to change, and their decision-making process with regard to how they involve or do not involve their patients.

It is important to understand that these psychographics segments, the map of doctors as well as the indicators for each segment, vary by area of specialty and by country.

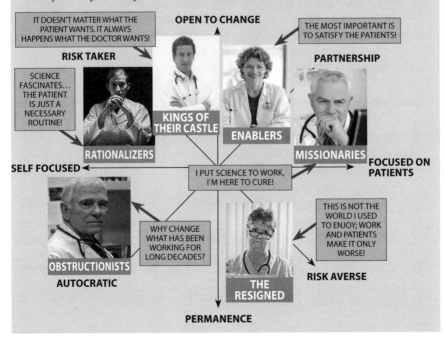

How to grow your business exponentially based on this psychographics influencer segmentation

Based on their psychographics profiles, we named them *Rationalizers, Kings of Their Castle, Enablers, Missionaries, the Resigned* and *Obstructionists*. But, on its own, having this segmentation with detailed knowledge about their attitudes toward work and patients as well as their career goals, lifestyles and beliefs was not enough.

Based on the new brand positioning, we were facing the challenge of adding the lifestyle dimension of the product, which is more relevant to the consumer, into the communication strategy. We needed to transfer a product, which was perceived as a treatment for a patient problem post-motherhood to a lifestyle contraception product for a modern *Actualizer* woman after every child, improving her already very satisfying life. As many features of the contraception product could be interpreted in different ways, we needed to ensure that doctors established an emotional connection with the product so they would be more likely to become involved with its key features and benefits.

To gain actionable and measurable recommendations for the new doctor-focused communication, we needed – similar to what we recommend doing with consumer segments – to identify the high-value targets (HVTs). To do this we used a three-step filtering process:

1. Identify the segments that are in line with traits and values that are important to the product category – contraception.
2. Filter the segments whose traits and values are relevant for our specific brand.
3. Analyze which doctor segments are capable of making an impact on the doctor society.

During the entire filtering process we screened for attitudes and parameters specifically relevant not only to the category, but to contraception in general; we did not want to be limited to oral contraception. Only the segments making it through all three filters would receive the focused attention of the new communication strategy.

Armed with all the data about the segments' attitudes toward our brand, we could now analyze and calculate the chance that each segment would recommend and prescribe our brand.

Enablers, Missionaries and *Kings of Their Castle* were already prone to describe our brand of contraception as medicine. The *Rationalizer* had no objection to recommending the brand as medicine, but tended not to recommend it as contraception. *The Resigned* and *Obstructionists* were more prone to traditional methods and were unlikely to support the brand.

To make sure that the doctor segmentation linked well into the parallel consumer segmentation, we needed to ensure that our HVT doctors interacted well with our HVT consumers. To do this we overlaid the psychographics profiles of the doctors segments onto the consumer segments to understand who was likely to connect with whom.

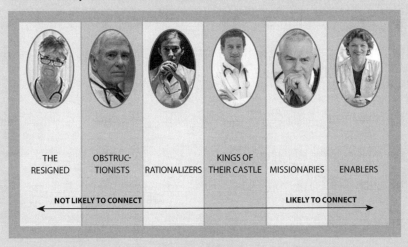

THE RESIGNED	OBSTRUC-TIONISTS	RATIONALIZERS	KINGS OF THEIR CASTLE	MISSIONARIES	ENABLERS

← NOT LIKELY TO CONNECT   LIKELY TO CONNECT →

This and further analysis of the data resulted in a ranking for the strongest sales potential for the brand. Based on this we could strengthen our position with brand supporters and further grow them, but we also knew how to reach those undecided or soft against segments and how to address their specific purchase barriers.

SALES POTENTIAL FOR THE BRAND

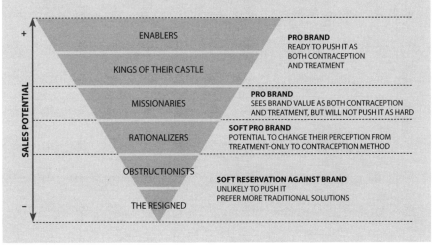

The second filter defined which of the segments had the power to influence within the medical community to create strong goodwill. *Enablers* are next to medical professors, who are perceived as a separate universe, the most powerful influencers in the doctors' community. This is easy to understand, as *Enablers* are generally dynamic, passionate and self-confident. They have a charming and open-minded personality with a positive outlook on life and on being a doctor.

WHICH SEGMENTS COULD BE THE MOST IMPACTFUL WITHIN THE DOCTORS' SOCIETY?

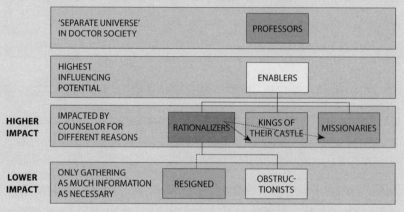

------ Dotted lines indicate a weaker connection

INFLUENCING POTENTIAL FOR THE BRAND

Overlaying the sales potential and the influencing power per segment helped us to identify the HVT doctors on which we should focus our communication: *Enablers*.

SALES POTENTIAL *VS* INFLUENCING POTENTIAL

ENABLERS ARE THE COMMUNICATION FOCUS THAT WILL BRING IN THE FULL SALES POTENTIAL

So who are the *Enablers*? Our data offered insights into our new influencer HVT. Enablers are not only at work to provide medical solutions to patients but to inspire and empower others to be self-confident and successful. They take pleasure in, and respond quickly to, professional challenges and situations where they feel they can add value and have a personal impact. With their open attitudes, *Enablers* are pro-innovation and like to keep themselves up-to-date with the latest professional developments. Not surprisingly, it is mostly because of these personal and professional traits that other doctors look to them for new practices and techniques.

To *Enablers*, career and expertise matter, but they serve the purpose of becoming a better doctor. Within the specifics of contraception, they have their own professional preferences, but always consult with a patient before making a recommendation, and will easily give in to the patient's wishes, provided that there are not conflicting medical conditions; something *Actualizers* tend to especially appreciate. Based on this information and further insights into the *Enablers* psyche, we could develop a much stronger value proposition for the contraception brand and leverage the segmentation by developing laser-focused communication to our influencer HVT to exponentially grow the business with a much more effective and efficient use of marketing resources.

Chapter Six

Effective Customer Research

Searching for insights

Customer understanding is gained primarily through the windows you can find that allow you to determine a person's thoughts or emotions. Insights are the glimpses of customer information that trigger the 'aha' moments we seek in research. Usually insights are just lying about lost among all the data scattered about. As you get good at looking for insights (the aha moments) and gain more experience, you will begin to recognize them more easily. They are the little behavior windows that offer a closer view of what drives people to behave the way they do. Good insight gatherers are excellent people watchers. Why people say or do things fascinates them, especially those little nuances that set some people apart from other groups of people. They have an innate curiosity about why people do what they do. Remember the secret handshakes when you were a kid? That handshake you and your friends had was meant to differentiate you from everyone else. Its self-identifying behavior is instinctive, and as adults we consciously and unconsciously offer up these indicators that identify who we are.

What people say is often different from what they do. Customer insights are the indicators of what really drives behavior. For example, Hungarians call Lake Balaton simply *the* Balaton. Other lakes in the country are identified as lakes by name, just as they are in other countries and in other languages. If you ask Hungarians why this is so, they will shrug and say that they don't know. It's just that way. Or they will offer up a plausible reason such as it is more than a lake, it is the Hungarian Sea. Right. But if you really start looking at the Balaton experience and how people interact with that rather unique place, you will arrive at the insight that the lake has little to do with the real appeal of the Balaton. One insight about the Balaton is that it is a place to go that offers the authentic Hungarian summer experience whether you are a child, a teenager, a young couple, or grandparents

– each seeking and enjoying a distinct set of functional and emotional benefits. For kids, the experience is three generations of the family coming together for an extended period of time every summer and eating corn on the cob with Grandpa. For teenagers it is breaking away from the parents for the first time, and perhaps getting away with something. Later it becomes the summertime shared-party scene, and around-the-clock periods of intense activity followed by interludes of rest and relaxation. The Balaton is a lot more than a lake; it is a unique association with this one-of-a-kind place so that Hungarians don't call it a lake – it is *the* Balaton. Why it is simply the Balaton is an excellent entry point (or insight) into perceiving Hungarian summertime behavior and attitudes.

Derived *versus* stated importance

The enormous problem in researching your customers' needs is that they might not consciously know what those needs are themselves – and if they do, they may not want to tell you what they are. The truth is that what they do (derived importance) is often only partly explained by what they say (stated importance). Take a look at the following group of musicians (Figure 42).

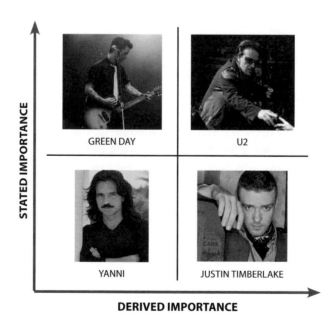

Figure 42: Perceived importance *vs* derived importance

Few adults want to admit that they really like Justin Timberlake. It is much cooler to say that you are a fan of someone more on the edge like Green Day. But if that were really true, why does Justin continue to sell so many more records and CDs than Green Day? After 20 years, U2 has transcended the pop star label. U2's albums sell well to young and old customers alike. It's okay to say you are a U2 fan, and also to buy their music, but poor Yanni is left with neither. He is important to consumers neither in what they say they prefer, nor in what they actually purchase.

How the brand value is established (and maintained through the buying process) in stated as well as derived customer importance is what will make the difference between your brand being Justin, Yanni, Green Day or U2 in your particular business area.

Asking the right questions

Some marketers believe that traditional customer research is prone to massive errors and is too costly compared to the factual information it yields. In a lot of cases, this is probably true. I'll come back to the cost question, but let's first discuss how to get it right with as few errors as possible. Like any tool, you need to make sure research can do the job you intend it to accomplish. You wouldn't use a screwdriver to pound in a nail and you shouldn't use research to try to answer questions that it is not designed for, or is incapable of answering. Some research is qualitative, which means that is has directional insights into customer attitudes and behaviors, rather than being statistically validated (quantitative research). Qualitative research is very helpful in uncovering possibilities, but only possibilities. You should only use this type of research to point the way for further exploration and more thinking. It should not be the final word on a new product or a new communication strategy. Quantitative research is, as the name implies, quantifiable, and if done correctly can actually predict future behavior if statistically representative and if the questions are organized and framed with extreme care.

Getting the questions right is the toughest part in a research project. How you set up and frame the question is of paramount importance to the quality (the validity) of the data you receive. For example, if I were interviewing you for an office job and I asked if you were a morning person or a night person, you might assume that what I was digging for was with how much energy do you start the day – so you answer 'a morning person', of course. Maybe you are, or maybe you aren't. Perhaps I should frame the question differently and in a context that makes it difficult for you to predict what I want to know; perhaps then I will have a better chance of getting the real answer and I can feel more confident that I have the correct answer. So I ask you if you like going to the cinema. You answer yes (almost everybody does) and I follow up by asking you if you usually eat dinner before or after the show. Morning people will typically eat before and night people afterward. Pretty clever, right? But even this shouldn't be taken as absolute. Perhaps you have a partner that you go to the movies with who is a night person and on the once or twice a week you go out (maybe weekends only) you give into your partner's nocturnal instincts. Or maybe you are a Spaniard, or have spent a long time in a Latin country where people habitually eat later. The point is that you need to think about how you ask the questions and you need to take everything you hear with a certain degree of skepticism. In journalism school, they teach young reporters to corroborate important information with at least three sources. Good advice for researchers as well. Come at the question you want answered from different angles to confirm that the insight you have gathered about the target is correct.

Marketing research is like Military Intelligence (MI). MI can tell commanders the lay of the land, estimate enemy troop strength and capabilities – maybe even reveal enemy intentions – but it cannot create the strategy. And when developing the strategy and tactics of an approaching battle, it is extremely important to know that the data are not always accurate. Only a foolish commander would commit troops based solely on a few pieces of intelligence. Instead, he looks at the intelligence gathered to provide insights that can aide him in developing his strategy. Like MI, customer research can only give you directional advice on possible strategies; it should never be the final word. If you do uncover a piece of information from one source that is valuable to you and can be instrumental in developing your strategy, you should utilize another intelligence-gathering tool to corroborate what you have learned. Good research utilizes a combination of methods to check and double-check customer information before it is acted upon and before resources are committed.

Another research trap (one that has a painful correlation to MI and the current events in Iraq) is self-fulfilling research. Design your research with questions and methods to uncover the information that can substantiate your thinking one way or the other. It is one thing to have a hypothesis going in, but you must remain intellectually honest with yourself and allow the research to prove or disprove it. Reserve the right to change your mind. This may sound like common sense, but you would be surprised at how many new product launches are executed on the basis of research that 'led the witness' as lawyers like to say, or only asked questions that confirmed a hypothesis. Be just as rigorous in your research in exploring the null hypothesis.

It is crucial that you have a basic understanding of the different research methods and their applicability to different marketing problems. Customer research methods are grouped into two major areas: qualitative and quantitative. As you will see, they are useful for different reasons in different situations. One can effectively complement the other, but they are not alternatives – one cannot substitute for the other.

Qualitative research

The qualitative approach is useful when you want to understand something in greater depth than strict measurements will likely reveal. Utilize open-ended questions starting with why or how, for example. If you want to explore the emotional and rational attitudes of your target to the product category, you will find qualitative research to be more indicative of customer motivations. Perhaps you would like to collect customer insights to arrive at a more meaningful brand positioning, or to search for product development clues. For these types of questions, qualitative research is an effective tool.

Qualitative research offers profound information about representative members of the target. It can reveal the existence of a variety of consumer attitudes, motivations and influencing factors; in short – insights and directional data. The qualitative researcher utilizes guided, in-depth interviews, focus groups, and observations, none of which provide any pre-set answer choices. The most important point in qualitative research is to avoid influencing the respondent and to stay as open-minded as possible in order to fully uncover the thinking and feeling about the issue in question; in doing so, you will be better positioned to anticipate how the customer is likely to act in the future.

Effective qualitative researchers assemble research guides for the topics or questions they will cover in their interviews; they use these guides as checklists so that they do not forget any important issues, yet still remain flexible enough to follow the respondents' way of thinking, and to observe how they are expressing themselves emotionally. If the qualitative researcher is good and the brief equally so, you end up with valuable insights that can direct your thinking about potential opportunities or barriers in marketing your products.

The problem with focus groups

The most difficult problem in research is getting beyond what people say, to what people do. There are many things people will not say out loud – some things, like emotions, are very hard to verbalize. Sometimes they adapt their true thoughts and feelings to what they perceive the interviewer wants, or what is more socially agreeable to other focus group members. The rational, easy-to-verbalize motivators are sometimes just the tip of the iceberg. A good focus group moderator will know how to probe below the surface to uncover a more important issue. In other instances, responses are disconnected from the real motivations and risk throwing you way off course. To protect yourself against this, it is absolutely essential for the researcher to spot the unspeakable, the irrational, the emotional motivators, as well as the rational ones.

Good researchers can handle conflicting verbal and non-verbal clues to determine what the respondents are really thinking and feeling; they arm themselves with a variety of methods to get around the problem – e.g., projective techniques such as brand personalization, brand party, bubble drawing, and metaphor elicitation. Maybe they should spend more time on these areas. As in all cases of consumer research, it depends on and will require you to think through all the methods and techniques available to you.

So where does this leave us? Qualitative research is supposed to be directional, but does it manage to give clear directions? Is it possible to uncover the hidden part of the consumer motivational iceberg with traditional qualitative research methods – focus groups and interviews? How can a market researcher understand the emotional drivers of a customer in two hours, when it takes many sessions for practiced psychologists to begin to understand the context and underlying motivations of their patients?

One factor that significantly decreases the validity of in-depth interviews and focus groups is that they most often take place in 'laboratory' circumstances, behind a one-way mirror. In spite of the research agency's best efforts to make the facility homey and comfortable, the circumstances will be very detached from real life situations. As a result people may behave quite differently than they would in their natural surroundings. A lot depends on the product, and how disjointed the research situation is from the actual purchase or usage situation.

An alternative to traditional in-depth interviews and focus groups in a controlled environment is the so-called *Street Smarts* approach. More and more, I am moving to the 'on the street' or 'caught in the act' qualitative research techniques that seek to get closer to the customer's state-of-mind during the actual purchase, or usage occasion. The *Street Smarts* approach adapts research methodology to real-world situations by observing and interviewing people in their natural environments, rather than bringing them into an artificial research lab. 'Insider' researchers can watch how customers behave, what environments they live in, check out their surroundings, and talk to them within the occasion or during a particular segment of the decision process. 'Insiders' is a term used to describe the researcher on the basis of their previous involvement with a targeted customer group. Target customers are more likely to feel that the insider interviewer is non-judgmental and accepts them as they are because the researcher is one of them, from a psychographics and lifestyle standpoint. Consequently, they tend to open up within their own environment much sooner and much more deeply than in the controlled environment of the research facility. Insiders encourage interviewees to relate to them in whatever manner they feel comfortable. The purpose is to understand the way in which the customer target sees the world; from there the role the brand has, or could have in their lives is revealed quite naturally.

Regardless of whether you utilize the more traditional qualitative research method of focus groups, or go into more experimental methods such as *Street Smarts*, you are still faced with the fact that you have only uncovered directional insights into customer behavior. Because qualitative research attempts to go deeper into uncovering attitudes and beliefs, it is necessarily conducted within a relatively small sample size. You may need to decide that you want to validate those attitudes and perceptions in a measurable way. In that case, developing a quantitative research brief is your next step.

Quantitative research

When it comes to quantitative research, there is also a wide variety of methods and approaches from which you can choose. In my opinion, there is no such thing as good or bad research methods, only appropriate or inappropriate ones, relative to the nature of the marketing issue to be defined.

The quantitative approach is useful when you want to measure something specific. These are easily measurable answers to questions like, 'How many people use this product?' or 'How often do they use the product?' Quantitative research gives you data about masses of people, and works best with a large number of respondents.

The quantitative researcher employs questionnaires for data collection. To facilitate the tabulation of the data, multiple-choice answers are usually provided for the respondents. Consequently, an important risk of quantitative research is that the researcher might leave out other important answer choices, break them into the wrong sets, or might not think of some important questions when assembling the questionnaire, which can seriously damage the validity of the results.

Many marketers believe in piling up masses of quantifiable research data, and then attempting to compile all the statistics to justify a decision. Numbers can only provide the illusion of security in defense of a marketing decision.

I often hear people mention the example of New Coke to point out the potential inaccuracy of research. They miss the point of New Coke. The problem wasn't that the research was incorrect; in fact it was very accurate. The problem was that we asked the wrong questions. The highest amount of research ever conducted in the history of Coca-Cola was devoted to that project: 340,000 representative blind-taste tests were conducted throughout the whole of the United States to check which taste consumers preferred – the new taste or the old. Research correctly identified a taste that people rated significantly higher than that of the classic Coca-Cola, and importantly, they thought at the time, significantly higher than that of Pepsi. The Coca-Cola formula was changed to suit the taste preference confirmed in the research, and a marketing shipwreck on the scale of the *Titanic* followed. Once New Coke was available and old Coke was not, people became 'irrational' about losing the genuine Coca-Cola they grew up with. Intellectually, the response to New Coke was irrational, but emotionally it should have been anticipated. The emotional connections to Coke could and should have been explored in the research. They were not and that was the failure of the New Coke research – we asked the wrong questions. What we learned too late was that for many consumers, the Coke they had always known was seen as an important and irreplaceable part of their own childhood, of their growing up, and symbolically as the continuity of their perception of American values and traditions.

As a young marketing guy working at Coca-Cola in 1985 in the midst of the uproar over New Coke, I can still remember the moment that the leader of the consumer opposition group actually picked the taste of New Coke in a televised taste test on a major news show. Only briefly embarrassed by his inability to pick the original taste he had been crying so loud about losing, he quickly stated that taste was beside the point. He was absolutely right. It wasn't about taste, it was about values. The question we never fully explored was how consumers would feel if we took the original formula away. Even worse, we, as the marketers of the biggest brand in the world, didn't understand what our brand represented emotionally to consumers. If we would have simply asked the researchers to interview consumers about what Coke represented to them, what emotional meaning it carried, the idea of changing the traditional formula would probably never have seen the light of day. Easy to see in hindsight perhaps, but with a better appreciation of consumer emotional drivers up front, the whole thing could have been avoided. The upside is that we figured it out quickly and went with the consumers' choice by bringing back the original taste. There are skeptics who believe we couldn't have erred as much as we did and believe that we planned the whole thing to get consumers to refocus on what really mattered emotionally after a decade of Pepsi taste challenges. I can only repeat what the president of Coca-Cola – Don Keough – said at the time: 'We are not that smart [to have orchestrated the whole thing], or that dumb [to have knowingly risked such a valuable brand].'

Although New Coke proves that poorly focused research data are worse than no data at all, the lesson isn't to stop doing customer research and just go with your gut. The lesson is to stay objective and look at the customers' perceptions based holistically on emotional as well as functional factors – both matter. Once you have decided that you need to collect information about your customers, the next issue will be to make sure the information you collect reflects real customer thoughts and feelings. This will help you to make solid predictions about future customer behavior. The validity of consumer research is influenced by three major factors:

1. Choosing the appropriate research method.
2. Using appropriate techniques.
3. Asking the right questions.

Cost considerations

Often a financial barrier for most CEE businesses, regardless of their scope of operations, precludes them from spending a large amount of money on research in any one country.

One viable solution that can give you the measurable data you seek within a budget that won't cripple your marketing budget is to subscribe to some omnibus studies that reflect broader attitudes across a very large sample size – typically 10,000–15,000 in each country. These omnibus studies are conducted one or twice a year within virtually all European countries (East and West) and cover a wide range of topics and issues with very large sample sizes. They are especially interesting because not only do they go into incredible detail about what people think about a wide range of issues, they also get into how they feel by measuring what they actually do and what they buy. It is one thing for someone to say they prefer this product or that product (stated importance) and another to see what they actually buy (derived importance).

Another efficient method of gathering both qualitative as well as quantifiable research data is to look around within your industry or within available governmental reports that measure a variety of behaviors and consumption from media and transportation, to vacations and political voting patterns.

Most supermarkets now use scanners to record what people buy, as well as frequent buyer cards that track buying behavior over time. Chains offer this data for a fee with obvious value to FMCGs.

Your advertising agency and media suppliers also have secondary research data that can be helpful in providing insights into what different customer segments are thinking and feeling. In fact, a lot of TV and radio stations subscribe to the TGI data and other omnibus studies (BRAT data in Romania, for example) as a general service available to their clients. The Internet is also a good source of secondary data that can yield insights into your existing or potential customers.

Lastly, look inward at what may have already been done within your company either where you are located, or in another geographical area or division. While the previous research or purchase data may not relate to exactly what you are working on today, what is there is relevant to what you want your customers to think, feel and act about your brand. Look at what has been already been done with fresh eyes.

Whether you take this more efficient approach to quantitative research or whether you decide to field the research on your own, the process still requires that you do some good thinking up front with regard to what you want to know. Then decide if you are using the right tool to do the job and if you are asking the right questions.

Practitioners of the *Exponential Marketing* approach need to look behind the hard numbers and shouldn't be afraid to wander among softer qualitative data to discover insights into customer motivation – the rich texture of the sometimes irrational customer decision. It is the process of 'mining for insights'. Insights are out there; they are sometimes hidden within the quantifiable data, other times in the qualitative work. And still other times again, they are just lying there in the market waiting for you to pick them up. Take time to explore your market personally and just sit back and observe customers doing what they do; living their lives. If you just take the time to look, you will be pleasantly surprised by what you will find.

Deep-dive teen research – Coca-Cola Hungary

By Dénes Tóth

Dénes is the director of Contact – a Belarusian-based creative agency. Prior to his move to Minsk, he was a consumer analyst at the Garrison Group. Dénes is a native of Hungary.*

A need for deeper customer insights

Customer value lies at the heart of *Exponential Marketing*. Consequently, a deep understanding of the target to accurately identify its needs is very importance. The Coca-Cola Company is well known for interactive and innovative youth-marketing activities which require an intuitive knowledge of teen lifestyles and attitudes that can never be fully understood solely on the basis of numbers and statistics. Adding to that complexity is a wide drink portfolio that ranges from iced teas to soft drinks, from waters to juices. The challenge for Coca-Cola Hungary was to acquire a deeper understanding of its core target market in order to align the diversity of its portfolio with the needs and desires of an equally diverse range of consumers.

Coca-Cola Hungary's research team had already completed a psychographics segmentation; this extensive in-house consumer data combined with existing TGI market research grouped consumers based on similar attitudes and lifestyle interests. The team had a lot of useful data and many of the members believed it was enough to align the individual brands with specific user segments – Coca-Cola targeting the most out-going segment known as *Peacocks* and Nestea targeting the more down to earth and inner-connected group known as *Alternatives*. Coca-Cola's marketing director wasn't satisfied that she had enough information. She could see the data written on the pages; data about what the different groups consumed, where they went, and even what media they watched and listened to. But was it deep enough get to the tiny nuances she knew that she needed if she was going to truly connect each of her brands – on both an emotional and functional level – to such a wide range of consumers?

A deep-dive research program was created that became known as the *Insiders Project*. The research strategy was to utilize a new type of research team – a group of *Insiders* who could penetrate and probe for the deeper nuances that defined the needs and desires of a particular segment because the *Insider* would in fact be an actual member of the targeted lifestyle group. Individual consumers from the segments would be more comfortable, and therefore more revealing, because they were being interviewed by a peer.

---

* Dénes can be contacted at denes@garrisongroup.eu

The manner of speaking, style preferences, and what's cool differ from segment to segment. Using *Insiders* not only eased tension, but the questions were also framed in the most appropriate way, using the language particular to a group or subculture.

Knowing that the research standards of objectivity could suffer from the use of what would be have to be young and relatively inexperienced *Insiders*, it was decided that professional researchers would accompany the new recruits. Acting as a camera operator – becoming almost invisible as the actual interviews progressed – the professional researcher could ensure that the *Insider* interviews stayed on track.

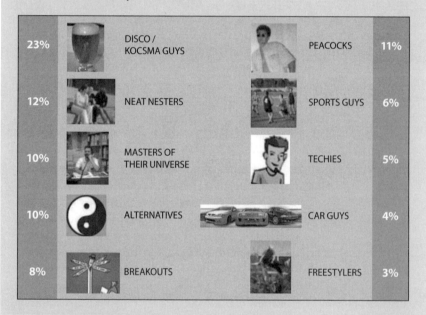

23%	DISCO / KOCSMA GUYS	PEACOCKS	11%
12%	NEAT NESTERS	SPORTS GUYS	6%
10%	MASTERS OF THEIR UNIVERSE	TECHIES	5%
10%	ALTERNATIVES	CAR GUYS	4%
8%	BREAKOUTS	FREESTYLERS	3%

The execution

The basic structure of the plan was to observe, and then interview, the various segments in natural surroundings. The job of the *Insider* was to first gain access in order to screen potential interviewees, and then to select observation and interview sites. The *Insider* would also have an important role in the post-fieldwork phase – to assist in translating slang or interpreting other nuances caught on camera so that the research team could assemble a comprehensive written and video report.

Recruiting *Insiders* for each of the ten teen lifestyle segments was difficult. Beyond ensuring that they were representative of the assigned segment, it was important to select a personality type that was curious and open to exploring what were its own lifestyle and attitude. It was also important that the *Insiders* didn't dominate the interview process so that their own views overpowered the views of the broader segment. Workshops were conducted with the new *Insiders* prior to conducting the fieldwork. The new recruits were taught basic research techniques, and practiced (via role play) the interview situations they would likely encounter.

The fieldwork

The first 'dive' into the lifestyle of a segment was a home visit. Broad conversations were initiated about a wide variety of things, not only connected to the drinks Coca-Cola was naturally interested in, but also deeper into the respondents' lives – sports, family, studying, work – all to fully understand their interests and motivations. Everything they had to say – typically very far from branding or beverages – would later serve Coca-Cola's team well in connecting the personality of the brands with the personality of consumers. Next came the visits to those places most typical for spending leisure time and enjoying social activities. These sessions were conducted across a range of venues from an underground teahouse frequented by *Alternatives*, to the favorite shopping malls and cafés of *Peacocks*. Time with *Freestylers* was often spent in parking garages and the large public squares where they would skateboard and just hang out. *Car Guys* preferred places such as a large parking lot of a McDonald's restaurant in Miskolc, or cruising around the boulevard that rings downtown Budapest. To spend time with *Kocsma Guys* it was off to the countryside.

Capturing the emotional atmosphere of the places where these teens spent a lot of time was very important. How they spoke to each other in their own slang and tone about their activities and motives in everyday life uncovered deep insights into personalities and behaviors. The care with which a *Peacock* took off his branded baseball cap, placed it in a place of prominence on top of a lamp shade, and then carefully made sure his hair was correct captured more in ten seconds than ten pages of research notes. Also revealing was the level of sincerity within the ritual of how one group of friends greeted each other in comparison to another segment. Each of the ten segments was distinctive in appearance and daily consumption habits, as well as in motivations and life aspirations.

The *Insiders* process uncovered a number of oversights in the original segmentation research, just as it validated many previous assumptions. One outcome was that it showed the relatively small amount of time teens spend actually watching TV – especially during the high summer consumption period important to Coca-Cola. They have a lot of other things to do out and about, and when they are home, the TV serves primarily as background noise as they surf the Net, swap sms messages, or browse their favorite magazines. The team could also study the interrelationships between lifestyle groups such as the role that *Freestylers* play in establishing fashion trends for *Techies* and *Car Guys*.

Contrary to their low-key appearance, *Alternatives* do have money; they just spend it differently and less conspicuously than more mainstream segments. Brands are defining in one way or another for most teen segments – even in the deliberate 'lack of clothing brands' for *Alternatives*. As expected, *Nesters* care a great deal about family, and would like to find the perfect relationship that would last forever, but they also relish the idea of stepping out in their one or two items of *Peacock* clothing in those splurge moments when they want to break out.

INFLUENCING POTENTIAL FOR THE BRAND

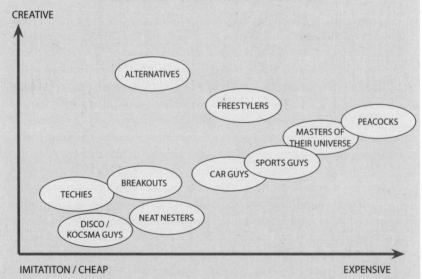

Peacocks – an important segment for Coca-Cola brand – have a very strong interest in appearance. They are very much represented by the brands they are wearing – no less than two or three high-profile brands visible at any given moment when they are out and about (which is almost always). Beyond clothing, the brand of mobile phone, cigarettes, and choice of beverage are crucially important in defining who they are to everybody else. *Peacocks* are very social – life is a party, a good one – and they tend to take it for all its worth. Being seen in trendy places is important – part of the 'fuzz and the buzz'.

Freestylers prefer to live in a more exclusive and closed-off world within their peer group. The extreme extension of their chosen sport (biking, skateboarding, blading or snowboarding) is the center of everything. It defines their clothing, music style, friends and philosophy. Their interactions are also interesting – they state that while performing their stunts, they are only doing it for themselves, but in reality it is the show that counts – think YouTube. The brand message, as well as the media, is crucially important to this group because they discard all form and substance of things they consider to be 'commercial'.

Alternatives are perhaps the easiest to identify walking down the street and that is a result of their 'anti-mainstream' approach to many things, from clothing to clubbing, to entertainment. *Alternatives* have a rich, colorful world of downtown clubs, live mini-concerts, and festivals – all wrapped within a very open and relaxed social circle. Long-standing relationships matter a great deal to them. As expected, they seek a more meaningful and fulfilling life – exploring the world for themselves. Also, as expected, they don't respond well to forced commercial influences, like sponsorships and advertising. Packaging is the brand communication tool that is most influential. Word-of-mouth for their own set of 'cult' brands is the typical manner in which brands rise to prominence within this group. Commercial activities specifically targeting them tend to do more harm than good. Although they will require a very different approach than the other segments, they are intensely loyal and willing to pay premium prices for the products and brands they prefer.

The *Insiders* research provided a number of useful insights in the case of the smaller or less influential segments as well. Although they are not the trendsetters, they serve an important role in providing the commercial mass needed to sustain a brand over the long term. Understanding how these less influential segments interact with higher-profile segments – how, when, and why they adopt trends – was an important piece of learning from the *Insiders* process. Even though these lower-profile segments are highly influenced by activities targeting the upstream groups, it was clear that there are important subtleties that Coca-Cola needed to understand about their specific characteristics as well.

Techies follow many *Freestyler* trends, especially in clothing. In many cases they dress like skaters, which is why *Freestylers* typically look down on them calling them 'rubber-boarders' (fake skaters). It is also interesting to look at the *Techies*, very specific media consumption. They tend to select what they watch very precisely, and waste no time on what they decide is pointless. Their attention is extremely hard to capture because they tend to watch TV, play games and read online magazines – all at the same time – while consuming their favorite beverages and snack items.

The life of the *Sports Guys,* as expected, is very much influenced by their sporting passion. Training takes most of their time, and sets the rhythm of their lives. Sport also teaches them a philosophy about how to view the world. They very much look up to their sports stars, and it is interesting to see the importance they place on the subtle symbols of their chosen sports – worn on their T-shirts and caps, or on display in their bedrooms. Unlike sports figures in the West, this group is significantly less influential in Hungary as regards driving fashion or other lifestyle trends into other segments. In many ways (as in music and in party habits), they simply follow the *Peacocks* lead.

THE TRADING GAME

TEEN SEGMENT	WHAT THEY TRADE AND SELL
ALTERNATIVES	MUSIC, INCENSE, HERBS, CLOTHING
MASTERS OF THEIR OWN UNIVERSE	COMPETENCE, NETWORKING
TECHIES	HARDWARE, SOFTWARE, AND SKILLS
SPORTS GUYS	SPORTS GEAR AND CLOTHING
FREESTYLERS	EQUIPMENT, GEAR, GADGETS, AND MARIJUANA
CAR GUYS	TUNING EQUIPMENT AND GAS
NEAT NESTERS	SCHOOL NOTES
PEACOCKS	PHONE ACCESSORIES, MUSIC, AND DVDS
DISCO/KOCSMA GUYS	CROSS-BORDER DEALS, CIGARETTES, ALCOHOL AND DRUGS
BREAKOUTS	STUFF THAT 'FALLS OFF A TRUCK'

Outcome

Following the *Insider* sessions, over 60 hours of audio and 50 hours of video footage were available detailing the lives of the ten teen lifestyle segments. Video editors spent several long nights reviewing the material in order to capture the most defining moments – the ones necessary to connect brand functional and emotional benefits to consumer needs.

Coca-Cola's marketing director wanted something more for her team than a mere report and condensed video clips. She organized a brand workshop with all the members of her marketing team, conducted in a teen environment. Brand managers and their advertising agency counterparts participated in discovery modules to further explore the lifestyle segments. They then went to work immediately on aligning the different brands within the Coca-Cola Hungary portfolio to target specific lifestyle segments. In this way, the marketing team was able to break out from the traditional mass approach of targeting teens in general with a wide-array of brands, to targeting specific teen lifestyle segments with much more meaningful brand messages. As a result of the *Insiders* process, Coca-Cola Hungary was armed with the crucial insights necessary to target specific brands to specific user groups. This strengthened each brand individually, as well as increased the strength of the brand portfolio as a whole.

BRAND PORTFOLIO – PREFERENCE INFLUENCERS

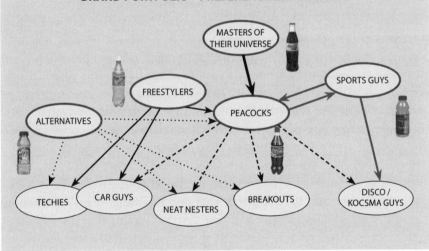

CHAPTER SEVEN

Exponential Positioning

People in the real estate business will tell you that the three most important factors to consider are location, location, location. Likewise, the three most important factors in marketing a brand are positioning, positioning, positioning.

Positioning is about the location of your brand in the customer's mind. Positioning strategy is the most important of all business strategies because it harnesses the power to understand, and then drive, customer behavior. The most common use of the science of positioning is brand positioning, but you can use positioning strategy to improve the perception of your company in the investment community, to secure enthusiastic cooperation from another department within the company, or even to position yourself and thereby enhance your own career. Think about the root word – position. How you position yourself, your brand, your company, or even your ideas will determine whether you have an advantage over the other guy.

Remember, you shouldn't worry about the other guy unless he is standing between you and the customer. That is positioning – he is positioning himself closer to the customer and therefore he is a threat to the success of your business. The best way to remove that threat is to find a way to position yourself even closer to the customer. Positioning strategy is like playing the Italian game, bocce ball. The objective is to get your ball closer to the customer than any other alternative.

Positioning is about seeing the world from the perspective of another person, the person whom you would like see to take some sort of action. It is their perspective that you must understand in order to put yourself in the most meaningful position for them.

You have the option of either trying to get the target to come to where you are, or you can make the move and go to where they already happen to be. It is much more efficient to move to where customers are in their current attitudes, perceptions and behaviors than to try and change them. Change, however, is probably what you require to grow your business. You must either get potential customers to stop buying whatever they are currently buying and switch to your product, or you must get existing customers to buy your product at a greater rate…or at a higher price. What you need to decide is how far can you move them and how far can you move yourself. To be successful, your position needs to be very close (closer than any other alternative) to delivering what the customers need when it comes time for them to make a purchase decision.

Your customers are constantly rearranging the positions brands hold in their hearts and minds in relation to their changing needs. They are constantly comparing your brand – consciously and unconsciously – to a field of suitable choices with influential information kindly provided by your competitors, as well as other forces in the market place.

Why brands?

Brands are your most important assets in business. They define your products and differentiate them from available alternatives. Your brand must have emotional attributes – a personality – as well as a functional role to ensure the maximum appeal to customers. How you position your brand becomes the single most important strategy you employ because it literally defines the customer value contained within your brand. Customers can, of course, buy a product that is not a brand, but they are assuming that one product is no different than any other in that product category. In many countries around the world, basic items such as sugar, flour, milk, meat and eggs are still sold in markets without any branding, just as they have been for thousands of years. The customer simply views the product as a commodity and will buy the cheapest eggs, milk, or sugar at the market. If there is any difference, it will only be on the basis of price. In other words there is zero brand value.

Brands happen

Assume a vendor in an ancient market takes the step of feeding his pigs extra corn before he slaughters them, and thereby makes the meat sweeter. Without any advertising, logos, or other marketing tools, his customers will begin to taste the difference, and they will develop their own method of determining which meat is sweeter. They will establish that the meat at a particular store, or available on a particular day, or perhaps wrapped in a particular type of paper, is sweeter. The market vendor will begin to get customer requests for the sweeter product, and he will see that it sells faster. He will recognize the basic principle of supply and demand and will, consequently, raise the price of the sweeter meat slightly over his other meat. His customers already recognize the meat is worth more and consequently, will be willing to pay more. You now have the makings of a brand and it is based solely on the perception of customer value – sweeter meat.

Does this sound a bit too basic? One of the oldest brands from the world's largest consumer products company started this way. In 1879, a worker at Procter & Gamble's soap factory in Cincinnati didn't mean to leave the mixer on all night, but he did and as a result mixed in too much air. At the time, Procter & Gamble's business extended down the Ohio River from Cincinnati, and then farther down the Mississippi River. Because most dock workers at the time couldn't read, shipping people at the factory would mark the crates of soap with X if was to be off-loaded in Moline, or XXX for Vicksburg, and so on. When the over-mixed soap showed up one day in stores along the river, customers noted that the new soap floated. Because the new soap stayed on top of the water it was easier to find when they washed their clothes in the river water. They told the store owner and he began making sure he bought more of the soap with the X's on the wooden crate. Procter & Gamble quickly realized that leaving the soap mixer on had produced a superior soap – a floating soap. They had learned a lesson in customer value, but they had yet to fully understand the concept of brand.

Years later when a new method for unloading crates at the river docks made the series of X's to mark the crates for offloading obsolete, the markings were eliminated. You guessed it – store owners up and down the river began to refuse the new crates of soap, insisting on the soap from the crates with the identifiable X markings – the soap that floated. Procter & Gamble, the company that is considered by many to be the best marketer in the world today, had inadvertently created a rudimentary brand with their markings of X's on the soap crates. When they recognized the reality that customers wouldn't accept unbranded soap (no X's), P&G rushed to create a logo for their boxes of soap to resemble the missing X's. Next, they developed one of the first customer communication programs to let their loyal customers know that the soap they preferred ('the soap that floats') was now in the crates with the moon and stars logo that the company had hurriedly developed to resemble the dock worker's crude communication symbols. Look at the back of any Procter & Gamble product you have in your home today and you will see this now famous moon and stars logo that communicates quality to customers around the world.

Brands happen – one way or another. Brand positioning is the science of getting out in front of that natural customer process to better understand this customer value process from the beginning so that you can communicate and deliver that unique value for your brand that is better than any alternative. The basic brand positioning process does three things:

1. It enables you to see the consumer from their perspective.
2. It clearly differentiates your brand from available alternatives with its own distinct identity.
3. It creates sustained interest in your brand by highlighting its most important features and benefits.

The positioning process

Brand positioning is comprised of three basic elements – target, frame of reference, and point of difference. Normally you start the positioning process with those you believe to be the customers for your products. Then you look at your competitors and try to establish how your product can be different, better and more special than what they are offering the same customers. You consider this point of difference as the most important element of your positioning and call it a USP (Unique Selling Proposition). Consequently, you will have a 'business as usual' positioning.

Exponential Brand Positioning offers a more powerful alternative because it equally explores all three of the basic positioning elements (target, frame of reference, and point of difference) to leverage the highest growth potential for your brand. Rather than lock yourself in at the start with an existing customer group, or a pre-established list of competitors as viable alternatives (the competitive set), start clean and find the most powerful positioning for your brand – consider each of the positioning elements as a potential key to capturing exponential growth.

Solving for X

The trick is in determining which element contains the power to drive exponential growth. Let's look at it like an algebra problem and solve for X –

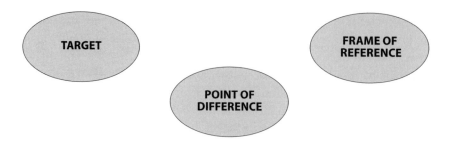

Figure 43: Brand positioning – solving for the exponential X

the *Exponential X*. Once you find the *Exponential X*, and unlock the full potential of your brand, the other two elements will become almost self-evident.

Jeep Cherokee, and the explosive growth of the SUV category almost 20 years ago, is a good example of the power of the *Exponential X*. Somebody very smart over at Jeep had the inspiration to think outside the box and came to the realization that there was a bigger potential target out there than the typical sportsMEN who had bought 99.9% of the four-wheel drive vehicles. Someone once asked Willy Sutton, the famous bank robber, why he robbed banks. His logic was perfect: 'Because that's where the money is.' The Jeep brand manager went to where the money was – suburban middle-class moms buy a lot of cars. And they buy a new one every couple of years. The *Exponential X* was the target – a totally new customer target for Jeep Cherokee. From that point of establishing a new and bigger target for Jeep Cherokee, it was a relatively simple process to nail down the other two elements – frame of reference and point of difference. Instead of looking at previous competitors such as Ford Bronco and Chevy Blazer, Jeep began looking at the world from the new target's perspective (suburban middle class moms) and their perspective of available choices. Minivans were very popular at the time with suburban moms. Based on this new target, and the minivan as the frame of reference, the Jeep marketing team established what features and benefits were needed achieve a superior point of difference. Immediately you think four-wheel drive. Close, but not quite. Four-wheel drive is only the functional support to a stronger emotionally driven point of difference – control and security. Moms driving with their children in a Jeep Cherokee feel more in control because they sit up higher and can see what's coming ahead. They also like the security of knowing that if the road or weather gets bad, they can get through it safely.

The Jeep Cherokee example is *Exponential Positioning* from start to finish. Jeep was, in essence, creating a new vehicle category with benefits for a new target. SUV (Sport Utility Vehicle) wasn't a particular sexy name for a car category, but it did define the playing field to Jeep Cherokee's advantage. Jeep has a sporting tradition and that has helped its defense against all the 'me toos' that quickly followed its lead in going after suburban moms. Additionally, the word 'utility' specifically addresses the ability of this new category of vehicles to successfully compete against minivans. And as a result, Jeep sells twice as many Cherokees than it did before it repositioned at an average price 30% higher.

Jeep started the repositioning process by looking at a potential new target for a good reason – flat sales in a seemingly mature category. When thinking about whether you want to try and move the target to your position, or move your position closer to the target, the Jeep Cherokee example is a very a good example of successfully doing the latter. By adding power windows and leather seats and calling it an SUV, Jeep moved within the frame of reference (or field of viable alternatives) for suburban moms and then used the higher sitting position and four-wheel drive capability to create a point of difference that was meaningful, deliverable and defendable.

It is possible to start with point of difference, a feature that your new product does better than any alternative, and then try to move customers to your position by highlighting an unmet and probably unrecognized need that your product can fulfill. However, another starting point that focuses on finding a lucrative frame of reference and then staking out a position once you've seen who's competing for the business is leveraging the frame of reference *Exponential X* element within the positioning mix. This begins by asking yourself what business are you really in? For example, is the Kitzbuhel ski area in the ski business, or in the broader family vacation business? It depends. If you are talking to 20-somethings from Munich, it is a ski area and competes against Sell am Zee, or San Anton with a point of difference based on adventure, après ski partying, or some other competitive advantage for young people driving in from Munich for the weekend. But if Kitzbuhel wants to attract Dutch families who spend a lot of money on vacations over a week or two, it will be necessary to compete against other wintertime vacation possibilities that may include sunny beach resorts. Club Med understands this and now has both cold and hot destinations. It positions itself within the broader vacation frame of reference with the point of difference offering a getaway regardless of the season with the advertising slogan: 'the cure for civilization'.

Because you don't start out knowing for sure where the *Exponential X* is in your positioning mix, you need to go through the open-minded process of exploring different alternatives for each of the three basic positioning elements. Let's take a look at each of the three and what you should be looking for when solving for X.

Target

These are the people considered to be the 'most likely' customers for the brand. The emphasis is on the *most likely* in the future tense. Don't get too deeply locked into the past because what you will sell is obviously happening in the future. Think ahead. But this doesn't always mean new customers. On the contrary, it is usually much more efficient to think about how you can position yourself to existing customers – to get them to buy your brand a lot more often.

But whether it is new customers or existing customers you are pursuing, you now understand the importance of looking beyond simple demographic characteristics, and are thus looking carefully at psychographics (values and lifestyles) as a more accurate indicator of buying behavior.

We've already established that customers change their needs and desires through the day, through the week, and throughout their lives. The more you understand the target, the more accurate you will be in establishing the most appropriate frame of reference and the best point of difference. The grouping of available alternatives changes during the day, and, consequently, so does the bundle of benefits necessary to become the preferred choice. Teenage consumers of Coca-Cola are drinking the brand for very different reasons when they are at home having dinner with the family than when they are out after a movie with their friends. Taste and tradition may matter at home, but image is everything when they are out with their friends.

The temptation in targeting is to go after new customers rather than the existing customer. It is almost always smarter and much more profitable to farm existing customer relationships. It is a lot easier to understand what is meaningful to existing customers to get them to buy a lot more, than it is to figure out what motivates someone new. For example, in the banking business in CEE, it will cost you well over €100 to capture a new customer. You can, however, cross-sell existing customers with new products and benefits for around €15.

With the collapse of the Berlin Wall and the emergence of Russia, China and so many other countries as new commercial markets, there has been a 'field of dreams' mentality in capturing new customers there. You remember the Kevin Costner movie *Field of Dreams* that contained the famous line: 'If you build it, they will come.' That may have been true of Costner's ghostly baseball park in an Iowa cornfield, but if you enter markets that appear on the surface to have a huge population that you believe will come running after your products if you would just build the factories and distribution facilities to serve them, it is probably you who is dreaming.

If your business is like most businesses, the 80/20 rule applies to you – meaning 80% of your profit is coming from 20% of your customers. So, before you go off and try to capture expensive new customers, ask yourself if you are capturing all of the sales and profits from your existing customers.

Frame of reference

These are the grouping of alternative products for which your brand can most effectively substitute. Understand that the choices available are from the customers' perspective... not yours. The biggest trap marketers find themselves in when establishing an effective frame of reference is that they start off by calling it the 'competitive set'. Customers don't see it that way. They don't care about the Cola wars or anything else the business press keeps talking about.

If you are objective and honest about looking at all the choices the customer has and about where your brand fits, or could potentially fit, you may find the *Exponential X* in the frame of reference.

When we started exploring a meaningful way for Hungary to successfully compete in attracting FDI (Foreign Direct Investment) against much larger markets such Poland and Romania, we came to see the frame of reference as the *Exponential X* in the positioning puzzle. We recommended changing the marketing focus from trying to sell the country of Hungary as a national market, to selling Budapest in a broader context as a business and cultural hub of Central Europe. It is within that frame of reference that the Hungarian Government can more successfully compete for FDI.

A key factor to remember in establishing the customer's frame of reference is the 'law of limited choices'. Customers are not comfortable considering more than five or six choices in total at any given time. This means that customers keep only a small number of choices cataloged as viable alternatives in their mind (i.e., the memory storage discussion in Chapter 4). Force too many choices on them at one time and they will simply shut down and withdraw their attention. Think how you feel when you walk into a badly organized video store and there are 2000 choices staring back at you. You might give it a try for five or ten minutes before you anxiously rush to make a single choice and get out of there. A video store that segments the choices into subcategories, such as new releases, comedy, drama, action and so on, will enjoy the benefits of a completely different customer experience.

The Internet has offered us uncountable choices, but the winning portals and sites understand the law of limited choices and break the navigation process into manageable frames of reference.

When I was the Coca-Cola marketing director for CEE, I had to fight a long and difficult battle to get the sales guys to eliminate up to 50% of the packages we offered in each of the markets. The customer would walk into the beverage aisle in Hungary, Romania, or Poland and be faced with a very confusing array of choices. We finally managed to cut back the number of packages we offered to customers under a program we correctly called 'the rational store' that resulted in significant increases in overall sales volume.

A good tool to help you see the field of choices from the customers' perspective and how they evaluate those choices is by creating a *Perceptual Map*. For most categories there are a couple of parameters whereby the customer evaluates alternatives. The customer understands that there is a trade-off relative to benefits. A *Perceptual Map* helps you see those trade-offs from the customers' perspective. Plotting the different choices and then verifying the conclusions with hypothesis research testing can be a valuable tool. The trick is to identify the two most important purchase decision criteria.

Figure 44 shows a *Perceptual Map* based on how potential capital investors in East Central Europe evaluate the field of alternatives.

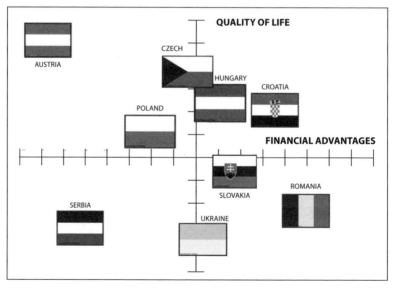

Figure 44: The CEE business investor's *Perceptual Map*

Although several countries are much larger than Austria, Czech or Hungary, the quality of life emotional benefit as perceived by the managers who will have to go to work in those markets is offset against the financial advantages for their company of being in a bigger market with more customers. Financial advantages also include the ease or difficulty in conducting business in practical terms such as taxes, tariffs, and clear government regulations that affect foreign investments. Using this frame of reference or *Perceptual Map*, Czech, Hungary and Croatia could craft a selling story to new investors based on benefits (emotional and functional) that can be perceived as better overall value than Poland, Romania, or Slovakia.

What was also important in developing this FDI *Perceptual Map* was that investment decisions are based on a combination of personal (emotional) benefits and business (functional/rational) benefits. Businesses do not make decisions – the people who work there do. To be successful, your B-to-B strategy – even on the scale of large FDI investments – must take personal needs and desires into consideration.

Point of difference

This is the primary benefit we want customers to associate with our brand to distinguish it from the available alternatives. Phillip Kotler, the distinguished marketing professor at the Kellogg Business School made an important point: 'The essence of positioning is sacrifice. What you give up is often more important than what you leave in.' Absolutely correct. Sacrifice less important features and benefits and get to the most important benefits of your product versus the other choices the customer is considering. How differentiating factors can be prioritized into lead and supporting roles is the subject of the following chapter on *Motivational Architecture*.

Features and benefits

What your product does (the soap that floats, for example) is a feature. What your product does for the customer (easy to find in dirty river water) is the benefit. Many companies sell features when the customer is looking for benefits. You tend to think about what your product does, while your customers are interested only in what it can do for them. That gap in perceptions can be a killer. Even if you manage to get beyond features, you will likely plow straight into the functional benefit limitation just as I just did with the soap example. A better, more emotionally connected benefit for the brand Ivory soap might be something like nineteenth-century moms being proud of being more clever and efficient because they were smart enough to buy 'the soap that floats'. It's hard to gauge for certain the emotional drivers of women washing their clothes in the Mississippi river during the 1880s, but you get the point – emotional benefits sell more effectively than functional benefits.

Support

This is the compelling and pre-emptive information that provides the validity for the point of difference, and for the positioning as a whole. It isn't one of the critical elements to solve for in the *Exponential X* positioning process, but it is important just the same. Support is where you can define the rational reasons that support the emotional benefit you rightly decided was your point of difference. Buying Hewlett Packard is the safest and most risk-free choice for a purchasing manager (the emotional point of difference) because it offers 24-hour customer service, free loaner equipment during down time, and other factors that *support* the point that Hewlett Packard won't leave you hanging in the wind.

The positioning statement

I want to take a moment to talk about the positioning statement not because I think it is so important that you put your positioning into an actual state-ment, but because you may come across such a statement in your work with other companies. Positioning statements are widely used even though the act of putting it into a specific structure has become somewhat obsolete with the advent of brand architectures as a defining positioning document that is easier to understand, and thereby execute brand communications.The traditional brand positioning format is as follows:

To _____ (target), *your brand*

is the _____ (frame of reference)

that _____ (point of difference),

because _____ (support).

Why is it always this format? Why do maps of the world put Europe on the upper half and Australia down below? You wouldn't recognize it as Earth any other way. If you are going to use a positioning statement, use the format that everyone recognizes and understands because gaining a clear understanding among everyone involved in selling your brand is half the battle.

Positioning statements are not meant to be great literature; they are meant to convey the key elements of your positioning in a succinct format. It is the positioning that defines the customer value of your brand. Get that right and solve for the *Exponential X* that will drive the exponential growth of your business. Don't spend a lot of time worrying about the actual statement.

Different customer targets – different positioning

I often hear the excuse for a weak positioning that the brand has different customer segments and therefore needs a common point of difference. That lack of focus on the needs of a single customer segment is what is known as a *weak positioning*. By definition, a positioning must be target-specific to be relevant. Pick the most important target and nail a highly meaningful point of difference for them. Then, if necessary, move on to a secondary target with a different positioning for each targeted segment. Multiple targets require multiple positioning.

I recently saw an international positioning statement for Pizza Hut that proclaimed its target to be both young families and teenagers. Think about it. Do you really think parents with young children will feel comfortable to be in the booth next to some smoking, groping, and potentially quite noisy 17-year-old teenagers? Or vice versa? I'm sure that whoever it was in Pizza Hut's international marketing department who wrote this positioning thought that the restaurants could appeal to both groups; he didn't want to leave anyone out. I can understand the motivation to capture as many customers as possible, but it has to be done in a more rational way. What Pizza Hut really needs to do is to have two separate positionings and, as a result, a meaningful plan to execute two restaurants in one. From five until seven in the evening it can, and should, target young families. You can imagine the atmosphere, the table decorations, lighting and featured products. From eight o'clock on it can shift positionings and become a cool teen place with different lighting, different music, and different featured food and drink items. Seems pretty obvious, doesn't it? And how tough would that really be? McDonald's does a redecorate in every store at exactly 10:30 when it moves from breakfast to lunch menus. It takes two minutes to reposition – everyday. McDonald's has also executed a different target positioning – toward teens – by running a successful late night program in the USA called 'Mac Tonight'.

Jeff Bezos, the CEO of amazon.com, boldly stated: 'We will re-merchandise our store for every customer.' Technology may make multiple target-centric positionings (mass customization) easier for online retailers such as amazon.com, but the question I would ask is: how close can the rest of us get to that ideal?

To sum it up

There are three basic truths about positioning:
1. Positioning is the brand. Who says so? The customer!
2. Your brand's positioning can never work for the other guy, or vice versa. Otherwise it isn't a position at all. A positioning must be ownable by a single brand.
3. Everything communicates. So everything must communicate the positioning!

And how do you know if you have a good positioning? The same way you determine if any other strategy is effective.
1. Is in meaningful (to the target as well as to you in accomplishing your business objectives)?
2. Is it deliverable? Can you really do what you say?
3. Is it defendable? Can you own the position today and in the foreseeable future?

CASE STUDY

Central European University Business School (CEU) – Solving for the *Exponential X* in positioning

By Ana Matos

Ana is a senior consultant and partner at the Garrison Group. She worked at Ernst & Young in Lisbon prior to joining Garrison Group in 2004. She has taught at both the CEU Business School and Corvinus University. Ana is a native of Portugal.*

* Ana can be contacted at ana@garrisongroup.eu

First MBA in Central and Eastern Europe (CEE)

As the first Business School in the region, CEU Business School has been in-volved in the evolution of the region every slippery step of the way. Unfortu-nately, the evolution of the school's curriculum has not kept pace with the evolving needs of the market. Founded in 1988 with the original name of the International Management Center by financier George Soros a year before the Wall came down, the school was truly revolutionary in offering an Eng-lish-language Western-style MBA. But that competitive advantage melted away over the years as more and more schools in the region developed their own MBA curriculum and a number of US- and UK-based schools opened extension programs in Hungary, Romania and throughout the other CEE countries.

Paul Garrison was appointed the Dean at the start of the 2007 academic year with the task of repositioning the school. A working team comprised of internal faculty and staff from the school as well as some volunteer Garrison Group associates and a McKinsey & Company team led by Katalin Walter worked *pro bono* on the re-positioning project.

Identifying the *Exponential X*

The project team went to work on a thorough analysis of the competitive set (*frame of reference*), the customer target and on assessing the strengths and weaknesses of the school itself. As discussed in Chapter 7, the *Exponential X* for the repositioning of the school could be any one of three positioning elements:

1. Target.
2. Frame of reference.
3. Point of difference.

Frame of reference, while important to the overall positioning, was discounted as the breakthrough *Exponential X* early on because it was clear that potential students really see the category as being defined by the MBA product category. Because they view the MBA primarily through the eyes of future employers who already have a clear understanding of what an MBA is and does in the workplace, trying to create a new product category for management education to supplant the widely known and accepted MBA was not seen as necessary or even viable. However, there was considerable discussion on in how wide a geographic area could CEU compete for students. Do potential students view CEU Business School as a Hungarian school, an Eastern European school, a European school with competitors such as HEC in Paris, IMD in Switzerland, and Instituto de Empresa in Madrid, or a global school such as INSEAD in

Fontainebleau and Singapore, as well as a number of high-quality US schools? But this question, though interesting, really leads to the more important question of from whose perspective is the *frame of reference* based? Consequently it became clear that understanding the needs and perspectives of the target customer would define the *frame of reference* as well as what that target would think and feel to be the most compelling *point of difference* for CEU Business School. The *Exponential X* for repositioning the school should be the target.

The Target

CEU Business School's past and current customer base (its students) are from over 60 different countries. The students truly are international with a class typically not having more than three students from any single country represented.

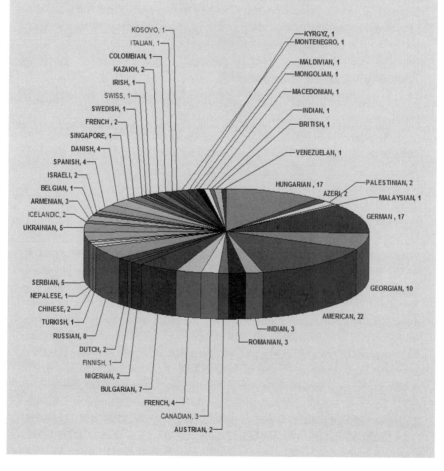

Seventy percent of CEU Business School students come from CEE and countries to the East where there has been a dynamic pace of change for almost 20 years.
- Constantly changing political environment.
- Intense real estate speculation.
- Rapidly evolving work force.
- Constant stream of new products and services.
- A sudden emergence of environmentalism and social responsibility.

The other 30% come to study at CEU to learn how that works…and feels. The needs and expectations of students vary greatly, depending on whether they come from the West or the East.

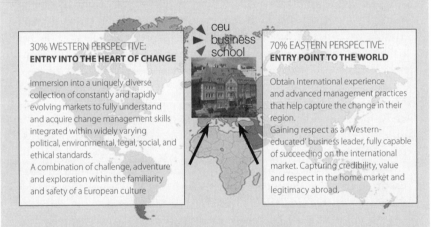

30% WESTERN PERSPECTIVE:
ENTRY INTO THE HEART OF CHANGE

Immersion into a uniquely diverse collection of constantly and rapidly evolving markets to fully understand and acquire change management skills integrated within widely varying political, environmental, legal, social, and ethical standards.
A combination of challenge, adventure and exploration within the familiarity and safety of a European culture

ceu
business
school

70% EASTERN PERSPECTIVE:
ENTRY POINT TO THE WORLD

Obtain international experience and advanced management practices that help capture the change in their region.
Gaining respect as a 'Western-educated' business leader, fully capable of succeeding on the international market. Capturing credibility, value and respect in the home market and legitimacy abroad.

After graduation, most of CEU Business School graduates will work in countries other than their own. Many will accept positions working across multiple borders and cultures immediately after graduation.

Frame of reference

The *frame of reference* for CEU Business School was actually determined based on the needs and expectations of the *target*. The challenge was to develop a product that would fulfill the expectations of two, very different, customer constituencies. But wasn't there an overlap that could be leveraged? If you were a student from the West coming to Budapest because you wanted to jump into the 'heart of change', wouldn't it be disappointing to find yourself geographically in the right spot, but surrounded with students like yourself who have not actually been raised in such a rapidly evolving environment?

So you would expect to benefit from classmates from the region. Conversely, if you were a student from the East coming to Budapest and CEU because you wanted to become 'Western educated' and have exposure to Western models and practices, wouldn't you be disappointed that all of the students in the classroom were similar to you and had not been raised in an environment of Western standards and practices? The reality is that although the two groups of students are very different and have quite different needs and expectations, they actually need a fair dose of the other to fully deliver on any expectation.

Another way to describe *frame of reference* is the field of available substitutes. Western students coming to Budapest are certainly adventurous and seeking an international career, but not so adventurous as to take inordinate risks or to venture too far outside of their comfort zones – like skiing out of bounds, but with a guide. Their choices were mostly schools from CEE with Western accreditation. Eastern students actually prefer schools even further to the West than Budapest and many put the USA at the top of the list. However, they also realize that the cost of going farther East significantly increases the cost of a top program (from approx $20,000 at CEU to over $40,000). And then finally, there is the question of acquiring a Visa; the US Visa has become increasingly difficult to get in recent years. So, for these Eastern students, the question of how far West they can get comes down to logistical and cost concerns more than anything else.

Based on this insight on the *frame of reference* for 70% of the target market (Eastern-originating students), it became clear that CEU Business School with its *point of difference* of offering a Western-style MBA was actually not really a *point of difference* at all, but merely a *cost of entry*. The *point of difference* was actually a fall-back position for most of the target of being simply less expensive than their first choice.

Point of difference

For any business, lacking meaningful product differentiation and having to rely on undercutting a stronger product on the basis of price is difficult and often not sustainable. What CEU Business School needed to do was to develop an MBA product that was *meaningful* to the needs and expectations of its target market, *deliverable* relative to where it was and what its core capabilities were, and last but not least, *defendable* relative to the competitive set on a much stronger financial foundation than low pricing.

The school began an in-depth look at the product it was providing and could potentially provide based on this assessment of the *target* and *frame of reference*. In lengthy discussions with HR professionals throughout the region, as well as getting input from a wide range of successful international business leaders, it became clear that most business schools focus on a very narrow interpretation of what comprises business education to the world of business. An MBA – Master of Business Administration – should literally acquire the skills and training necessary to become a 'master' of multiple functions within a typical business organization.

In recent years, many top schools such as Yale, Stanford and others have determined that this perspective of understanding business from within the typical functional areas of an organization is too limited; they should look more than they have done in the past at the integration of the business organization with suppliers and investors.

But businesses have to live in a broader world and – particularly in emerging markets – a rapidly changing world. Are business schools equipping tomorrow's business leaders with the skills and capabilities to succeed in a world that extends well beyond business? As the recent global financial crisis has so painfully illustrated, many business people lack the understanding of public policy and politics which have increasingly become involved in their businesses. And of course on the flip side, public-policy decision-makers and politicians certainly could use a deeper understanding of how business works, but that is a problem for the government administration and public policy schools. It is not only a question of spreading out into broader areas, but also of the necessity of going deeper, such as providing marketers with an understanding of sociology.

In the area of socio-political expertise, companies have been incredibly slow to grasp the impact social trends and public policy can have on their business. Society is much further along the green path while automotive industry, food processing or even tourism business leaders try to catch up. The tumultuous events affecting financial institutions are now affecting us all and it is already clear that public policy will be driving the solution rather than Wall Street. But how closely connected is the public policy department and the Business School in major universities? Isn't this a critical moment in time when business and public policy could benefit from some cross-pollination?

We have seen the re-emergence of local government's control of key industries around the world – from oil and gas in Russia (Gazprom) to financial services with the nationalization of banks in multiple markets. Add Hugo Chavez in Venezuela and Evo Morales in Bolivia and it becomes clear that future managers need to be extremely savvy about how public policy – and the threat of government intervention and regulation – impacts their strategies, especially in emerging markets.

In Europe, the expansion of decision-making and regulatory power of the EU is not just freeing up markets but also creating what Brussels perceives to be acceptable regulatory regimes across a continent of 350 million consumers. The newest phase in globalization (post-Internet globalization) will focus on environmental technologies and their global diffusion. Governmental and societal attitudes toward the adoption of new environmental technologies will be crucial to their successful adoption. All of the above require managers to think within and across borders, not just in terms of trade and investment, but also to anticipate the social and governmental impact of their strategies and tactics. And the same is true coming from the other direction, with government leaders needing to better understand the economic and business impact of their policies.

Because the student composition is so diverse at CEU Business School, the program was clearly providing the soft skills (cultural sensitivity), but was the MBA program providing the hard skills to succeed in such a diverse and rapidly changing environment?

CEU Business School ultimately decided on a *point of difference* for the school that it called *Transnational Leadership* – defined as the understanding of the broader (societal, economic, political and environmental) barriers and drivers of business growth in volatile markets.

Meaningful, deliverable and defendable

Introducing socio-political elements into an MBA program was CEU Business School's opportunity to leap ahead of more prominent schools in this area that were also determined to be highly meaningful to students from both the East and the West based on where and what they were likely to work on after graduation. So, clearly, a *meaningful* need existed, but how many MBA curriculums today can deliver political science, sociology, regional studies or history? CEU Business School determined that it was in a better situation than most business schools in Europe because unlike INSEAD, IE or HEC, CEU Business School is connected to a larger institution that offers graduate-level programs in sociology, public policy, environmental science and law. Few universities and even fewer companies have the benefit of sociologists or political scientists within their midst to help them chart a course through waters that have become incredibly convoluted. But CEU Business School does and as a result, this new positioning of *Transnational Leadership* effectively leveraged the broader capability of the university to deliver not only a more meaningful position for its graduates that will likely work in increasingly volatile markets, but also one that is *defendable* relative to the range of alternatives available to potential students.

The MBA curriculum was developed by program director Yusaf Akbar with the objective of providing the school's students with the necessary skills whereby they can move into and quickly adapt to a local market regardless of their country of origin. 'We need to help them get past the international manager trap that tends to homogenize differences with broad cross-border strategies and practices that so often lose their impact within individual markets', explained Professor Akbar. 'The debate about global versus local in marketing ended ten years ago – the reality is that you have to do both. In business strategy we also have to do both and unfortunately business schools and multinational corporations have been way behind on the local understanding piece. We need to think in terms of a new breed of transnational managers that can easily move from one country to the next, or even manage multiple countries at the same time. We need to build their capability to quickly assess in any country the socio-political realities that will surely impact his business – for better or worse.'

CEU BUSINESS SCHOOL TRANSNATIONAL MBA CURRICULUM

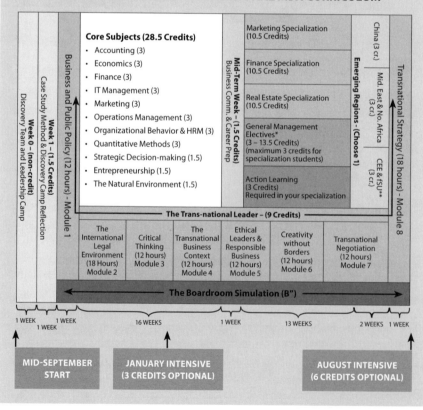

By analyzing the three integral elements of a brand position – *target, frame of reference* and *point of difference* – CEU Business School came to the conclusion that it was the unique diversity of its customer base today and going forward that constituted the *Exponential X* of the new positioning equation. From the critical perspective of a specific target comprised of 30% Western students seeking change-management skills and 70% Eastern originating students seeking international capabilities, and all likely to work in countries other than their own following graduation, an assessment was made of the range of possible alternatives in the market (*frame of reference*) and a corresponding *point of difference* that would be *meaningful, deliverable* and *defendable*.

CHAPTER EIGHT

Motivational Architecture

Once you have the elements of the position aligned and have identified the *Exponential X*, we can now power up the point of difference of your brand and thereby strengthen your overall brand positioning with a *Motivational Architecture*.

A *Motivational Architecture* is basically a brand blueprint that defines the hierarchy of brand benefits so that you can align those benefits to specific customer targets. Some call this a 'brand architecture', but in doing so, sometimes lose themselves in the interrelationship of different benefits and forget that the whole point is to identify the most compelling motivational hierarchy of the brand.

Your brand comprises many features and can deliver against a wide range of benefits – functional and emotional. The point of a *Motivational Architecture* is to organize all the available options so that you can separate great from good. The *Orbiter* tool discussed in Chapter 3 is a good mechanism to capture all the available brand features and benefits and link them to specific customer needs that you have identified in segmentation and customer targeting. But you still have a lot of options. Start the prioritization process of compiling a *Motivational Architecture* by establishing whether different features and benefits are according to one of the following criteria:

1. **Cost of Entry Features and Benefits.** These are the basic features and benefits that the customers expect when they purchase a similar product – category requirements. These features and benefits won't necessarily help you if you have them, but not having them could eliminate the chance of a sale.

2. **Differentiating Benefits.** These are the benefits that define your brand as different, typically with functional benefits such as taste, quality, design, etc. For most companies this is as far as it goes. But simply being different is not enough to capture exponential growth.

3. **Crucial Experience.** This is the most crucial and compelling point of difference for your brand that will drive long-term sales and profits. This is the winning combination of different, better and special all rolled up in a complete brand experience.

Apple is probably the only real brand in the personal computer business because it is the only brand that goes well beyond mere differentiation to get to an emotional experience focused on creativity and individuality. All the other lesser brands remain so because they have trapped themselves into competing on the basis of various functional benefits and price. Not coincidentally, Apple seldom needs to discount its prices and typically costs up to twice as much as competitive brands.

Remember that the benefit hierarchy from *Cost of Entry Features and Benefits* to *Crucial Experience* is done from the target customer's perspective. You must see features and benefits, and consequently the motivational hierarchy of those benefits through the heart, mind and gut of the target. Just as with the positioning statement when you want to pursue multiple target segments, you must have a different *Motivational Architecture* of brand benefits for different customer segments. Trying to be all things to all people is a sure-fire way to be nothing of significance to anyone.

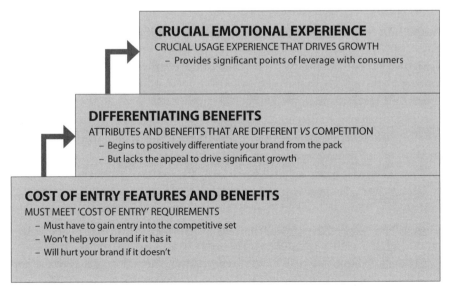

Figure 45: Effective consumer research will establish the benefit hierarchy of the brand – the *Motivational Architecture* (Source: Zyman Marketing)

When I first arrived in Central Europe with Coca-Cola in 1995, we were advertising that we were the original cola (*The real one*). We launched a major promotion centered on a traveling 'World of Coke' exposition that showcased the contour bottle decorated according to local customs around the world. While it is true that Coca-Cola is older than Pepsi and more 'real' (original), consumers couldn't have cared less. We also had big plans to build ice plants in several markets to make the product colder through the distribution of ice. It seemed that we had already placed a cooler in every third building in the region; why not pump the region full of ice as well? In the case of 'ice cold' we were only addressing *Cost of Entry*. Pepsi was doing exactly the same. You wouldn't buy a Coke or a Pepsi just because it was cold, but you probably wouldn't buy either one if it was warm, either. With the real and original concept we were just talking about an interesting point of difference, but as far as being meaningful to the consumer, it wasn't crucially important. Because it is true that Coca-Cola is the original, it could have been be possible that this differentiation could help re-enforce a higher level experience, but on its own, it just wasn't powerful enough. And we wondered why we couldn't grow market share versus Pepsi with volume swinging back and forth on the basis of a few cents of price discounting.

After careful study and research (*Value Diagnostics*), we found a crucial point of difference that we believed would drive preference, and consequently market share. We realized through our teen research that transitional difficulties and the exploding materialism had opened up huge gaps in society since the political changes of 1989/1990. There was a very visible differentiation between the 'haves' and the 'have nots' that was often thrown in the face of those who didn't have a nice car, or could not afford a holiday to the French coast. As a result, Romanian, Hungarian, and Polish teens all simply wanted to feel good about themselves, and to feel good about where they lived and what they had. They didn't want to be Americanized, or Europeanized, or capitalized – they just wanted to feel good about being who they were. It is true that they wanted to acquire more things, make more money and be part of the modern Western world, but they wanted to do all of that by being Romanians, Hungarians and Poles. Having learned that important customer insight, we launched our Coca-Cola brand-relevance strategy based on the brand's global values of optimism, continuity and inclusiveness. We drove local relevance to those core values by tying into the seasonal activities that local consumers enjoy the most. One outcome of that strategy was the launch of the Coca-Cola Beach House on Lake Balaton in Hungary and another one the Dnieper River in the Ukraine. We also developed a series of locally produced commercials which celebrate the fun of the inclusive local rituals and traditions which surround activities such as ice skating, and carnival – all including Coca-Cola, of course.

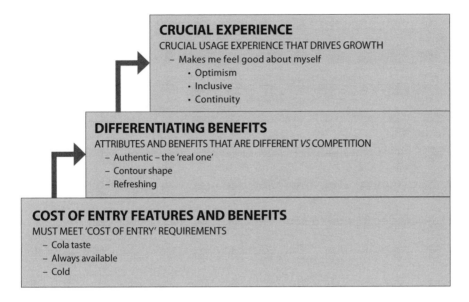

CRUCIAL EXPERIENCE
CRUCIAL USAGE EXPERIENCE THAT DRIVES GROWTH
– Makes me feel good about myself
  • Optimism
  • Inclusive
  • Continuity

DIFFERENTIATING BENEFITS
ATTRIBUTES AND BENEFITS THAT ARE DIFFERENT *VS* COMPETITION
– Authentic – the 'real one'
– Contour shape
– Refreshing

COST OF ENTRY FEATURES AND BENEFITS
MUST MEET 'COST OF ENTRY' REQUIREMENTS
– Cola taste
– Always available
– Cold

Figure 46: Coca-Cola CEE *Motivational Architecture.*

Getting to a crucial emotional experience that drives a more meaningful point of difference for your brand will require some serious gathering of customer insights. If you ask the right questions of the right people with your mind completely open to the answers, you will likely find it. This is why effective customer research, as part of the *Value Diagnostics* step, is so important. Without it, you will find it difficult to surface the insight you need for a brand experience revelation.

In *Exponential Marketing*, everything is connected. Each element builds on another to create greater momentum. The features of your product must connect to functional benefits. Those functional benefits, in turn, must connect to and drive emotional benefits. And finally, those emotional benefits must be transmitted into a crucial brand experience that only your brand can deliver on and own.

Advertising agencies will tell you that your brand must be single-minded and focus on a single USP. They are wrong. Powerful brands are complex with a myriad of interconnected features and benefits. It is your job as a marketer to organize these benefits and features into an overall brand experience.

Another good example of how lower level features and benefits connect to a higher level emotional customer experience is the personal computer business. Three competitors have staked out very different *Motivational Architectures* (Figure 47).

BRAND	FEATURES	FUNCTIONAL BENEFITS	EMOTIONAL BENEFITS	'OWNED' EXPERIENCE
(Apple logo)	– Funky design – Exuberant colors – Unique software and operating system	Doesn't fit in with the masses	I feel like I belong to a special club of creative people	CREATIVITY
(Dell logo)	– Affordable – Mass-customized hardware products and accessories	Tailor-made and assembled to my personal needs and budget	I feel comfortable that I have the right solution for my situation	FOR ME
(HP logo)	– History-reputation – Comprehensive integration of peripherals and processes – 24/7 customer service	Most reliable and durable technology, combined with always available customer service	I feel safe and secure that I made the best choice – can't go wrong	SECURITY

Figure 47: *Motivational Architectures* for Apple, Dell and Hewlett Packard

Do experiences matter? Absolutely! Take two prominent European furniture competitors – IKEA and KIKA. Which one do you suppose is the most successful?

KIKA thinks that it is in the business of selling sofas and tables. IKEA knows that it is actually in the business of creating and delivering inspirational living experiences for its customers. The showrooms in IKEA are displayed as living spaces with all the accessories and decorations you'd see in a real home – your home, it hopes. IKEA sells all of those accessories too, by the way. KIKA has only big rooms filled with lots of furniture.

IKEA also does a good job fitting experiences to different target groups. How about *Balancer* parents looking for children's toys and games? You don't have to guess which ones your children will enjoy; IKEA lets them experience the toys it sells in big playrooms. And then there is an IKEA restaurant with Swedish meatballs on the menu, where you can relax a bit – thinking about what you just bought in the show rooms so that you are in the proper state of mind before you go through the final area of the store set aside to sell you all those little odds and ends you need for the big items you have already picked out. IKEA gets it. KIKA isn't even in the same game.

SELLING A SOFA AT KIKA

INVOLVING THE CUSTOMER IN A LIVING ROOM EXPERIENCE AT IKEA

Figure 48: A brand experience is where the money's at

Brand imagery

Much of what will drive the experience will evolve from various image elements that are, or could be linked to your brand. There are four types of imagery available.

1. **Product imagery.** These are the feelings and attitudes directly related to the product's functional features and benefits. (i.e., Apple computers are creative).
2. **Usage imagery.** These are the feelings and emotions associated with actually using the brand (i.e., the sense of exhilaration and power when driving a 911 Porsche Cabrio on a windy country road).
3. **User imagery.** This is the connection with the type of people who use the brand – 'are they like me, or what I aspire to be?' (i.e., Nike women are firmly in control of their own lives).
4. **Associative imagery.** These are the links between your brand and the image of the other brands you choose to align yourself with (i.e., Michael Schumacher fills up at Shell).

The *Crucial Experience* for your brand may involve one or more of these imagery elements. For example, Porsche has done a very good job over the years of linking product imagery (the definitive 'sports car'), usage imagery (exhilaration), and user imagery (exciting and successful people) of the brand. All of these image elements matter a great deal to a Porsche buyer and consequently have become one unified brand experience.

169

Think global, act local

We have heard this phrase so often as something we should do in managing a global brand, but what does it really mean? What exactly should be global and what should be local? Leveraging the appropriate brand imagery elements is a pretty good mechanism to align your local marketing with the global brand to increase relevance to local customers. Two of the four imagery factors (product and usage imagery) are connected to the very essence of the brand, and should not be altered locally. The two remaining imagery factors (user and associative imagery) are ideal to connect your global brand to local users and the activities they enjoy – all connected to relevant usage occasions for your brand (Figure 49).

GLOBAL	LOCAL
PRODUCT IMAGERY • Feelings and attitudes directly related to the core Coca-Cola experience – functional features and benefits. (i.e., the unique Coca-Cola taste – the special burn and bite at the back of the throat)	**USER IMAGERY** • The connection with the type of people that drink Coca-Cola (i.e., young trendsetters knowledgeable about music and fashion)
USAGE IMAGERY • The feelings and emotions associated with Coca-Cola (i.e., optimism and inclusiveness – 'The Coke side of life')	**ASSOCIATIVE IMAGERY** • The links between Coca-Cola and the image of the other brands, activities and events you align yourself with (i.e., Coca-Cola and the Balaton – The Coca-Cola Beach House)

Figure 49: Global *vs* Local Coca-Cola

How do you know when you've nailed it?

Now that you have come up with what you believe to be a great *Motivational Architecture*, you need to ask yourself the same three questions for every other strategy in *Exponential Marketing.*

Is your architecture meaningful?

It your architecture meaningful to your company? Does it help the brand get to the business destination effectively and efficiently (i.e., achieve your goals and objectives)? Is it meaningful to your customer? The customer research you did should answer whether it is highly motivating and meaningful to the target customers based on all you know and have learned about your target and their needs.

Is your architecture deliverable?

Can the brand consistently deliver on the experience you've identified as the most meaningful? If it can, will the target believe it? The believability question is especially important in the high-tech world, where the customer has grown very skeptical of overly optimistic claims. A good rule of thumb is to under-promise and over-deliver. Don't get too carried away with what you think you can do – prove it one step at a time. We didn't start by stating Coca-Cola was essential to a perfect Hungarian summer experience; we started by setting up the Coca-Cola Beach House on the Balaton and we let consumers come to their own conclusions – carefully constructed and managed, of course. We also watched every detail and aspect of the experience the first year to determine what specific elements best delivered on the brand experience. Then we built on those in the following years.

Is your architecture defendable?

This is where a lot of seemingly great ideas come crashing to the ground. Be sure that what you promise is not just a category experience, but rather a brand experience that is linked to specific features and benefits that only your brand can provide. Think about the four image elements and how they can be ownable for you! People often ask me how the Coca-Cola Beach House was defendable. After all, couldn't Pepsi just as easily have built its own beach house on the lake? Sure it could have, but because we were first and the originators, Pepsi would have been seen as a copycat. Or as teen consumers prefer to call wannabes, 'a poser'. Definitely not cool. It would have been convenient for us if Pepsi had fallen into that defining wannabe trap, but it was too smart for that and rightly stayed away from the Balaton imagery we had linked quite effectively to Coke. Coca-Cola did the same thing with Santa and Christmas over 70 years ago and to this day you're not likely to see a blue Santa on a Pepsi display.

Starbucks in Europe quickly jumped to an experience-based positioning aligned with its 'Third Place Gathering Spot' focus that has done so well for it in the United States. But what was missing in the overseas positioning was the painstaking approach Starbucks had taken to establish a strong point of difference around the familiarity the barista has with his/her local clientele, the authentic devotion to unique coffee roastings and a strong sense of social responsibility practiced meaningfully on both the community and global level. Consequently, Starbucks found itself in Europe with a cool experience that was easy enough for competitors to copy because the important architectural building blocks of its people (the barista), social responsibility and coffee intimacy that combined allows Starbucks to differentiate itself from all others in the USA were not fully implemented in new markets.

CASE STUDY

Sony PlayStation *Motivational Architecture*: Repositioning the PlayStation brand in Central and Eastern Europe (CEE)

By Julia Vahidova

Julia is a consultant at the Garrison Group where she has worked in the beverage, consumer electronics and retail sectors, particularly in the area of customer insights. Julia is a native of Moscow. *

Before the release of the PlayStation, Sony had never held a large portion of the video game market. In 1994, the gaming world was split between Nintendo and Sega, when the consumer electronics giant bravely attempted to enter the highly competitive games console market.

As Sony's first foray into the video game market, the PlayStation was initially set to be an add-on for Nintendo's Super Nintendo Entertainment System video game console as an answer to Sega's Sega CD. When the prospect of releasing the system as an add-on dissolved, Sony transformed it into the PlayStation video game console. The PlayStation was released in Japan on December 3, 1994 and later in North America on September 9, 1995. The system was widely popular and became the best-selling home console up until that time.

By beginning of 2006, Sony Computer Entertainment has gone from being the aspiring new kid on the block to the leader of the pack. Its second-generation PlayStation 2 or PS2 was the world's best-selling game console, accompanied by the portable gaming device PSP. The company was planning to release the next-generation console PlayStation 3 (PS3) by the end of the year, upping the ante in the next-generation console war with Microsoft Xbox 360 and Nintendo Wii.

* Julia can be contacted at julia@garrisongroup.eu

PlayStation entered the CEE market in 1996 and by 2006 had achieved strong market leadership. But the market was stagnating. The Sony marketing team in the region was facing a serious question: how do you increase sales of PS2 in a highly competitive market that is already saturated with the product, especially if it is expecting introductions of the next generation of shining new-generation devices? The usual methods of decreasing the console price to increase sales were even less profitable because they were delivering less-than-expected quantity results. The team understood that instead of trying to sell more consoles and games to their core customer audience – the computer and videogaming addicts – it needed to broaden the target market and reposition PlayStation from a *gaming* device into a *social interaction* device. This had already happened in much of Western Europe, where PS2 karaoke and quiz games had a strong position in in-home social entertainment and provided the console with an image of a must-have at house parties and family gatherings. But it was yet to occur in CEE. The challenge for the team was to broaden the market in a similar fashion in the most efficient and effective way. The key was to understand potential new customer targets inside out and develop a stronger and more emotionally appealing proposition for them.

PlayStation's *Motivational Architecture*

The first step was to develop a lifestyle segmentation of its potential customer targets, which was then performed in all five countries participating in the project – Hungary, Poland, Romania, Czech Republic and Slovakia.

The rather obvious demographic target audience was young people between 13 and 35 who do not have kids – typically purchasing consoles for themselves. But the PlayStation CEE marketing team dug deeper and realized the importance of parents for the gaming category. In a lot of cases, parents were playing the role of gatekeepers for their children, having veto power on whether to buy or not to buy a console.

Beyond segmentation, the next step was to develop a successful marketing strategy for each of the three main PlayStation brands at the time – PS2, PSP and the soon-to-be-released PS3. The strategy had to be not only motivational for the primary target audience, but also for targeting parents – addressing their fears and concerns about video gaming while at the same time highlighting the emotional benefits of choosing a PlayStation for their child. For each of the brands, the team developed two *Motivational Architectures*, each targeting the most attractive customer segment from either a Youth or a Parent life stage. Finally, a comprehensive communications strategy was developed to ensure the most efficient and effective communications for all of the brands in the PlayStation family.

Customer target segment

The PlayStation CEE team developed a *Motivational Architecture* for the strong market-leader brand, PS2, targeting a specific customer segment called *Peacocks*: young people who like standing out from the crowd and showing off. *Peacocks* are very assertive and opinionated, pushing the boundaries and experimenting. They live in the moment and don't worry a great deal about the future. They are very social and outgoing.

The team chose this particular *Peacocks* segment because these young people are the top lifestyle influencers in terms of fashion and entertainment trends – including socializing, appearance, and gadgets and badges. Also, *Peacocks* are very premium-brand driven, which helps Sony minimize PS2 games piracy, something that was hitting very hard at the time; price is less of an issue among this segment. For *Peacocks*, life is all about peer connections and recognition. What they have is a reflection of who they are. Thus the team's objective was to make playing PS2 and exchanging games the key to driving *Peacocks'* image and social interactions.

HIGH FIRST-TIMER POTENTIAL AMONG THE MAINSTREAM SEGMENTS THAT HAVE PROVEN TO HAVE THE HIGHEST AFFINITY FOR PLAYSTATION IN CEE

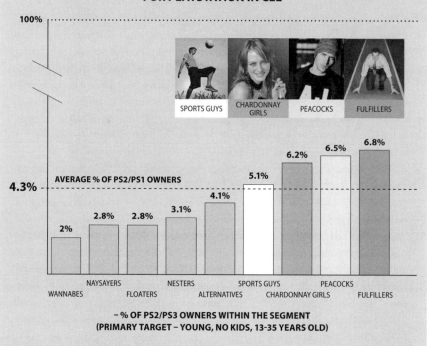

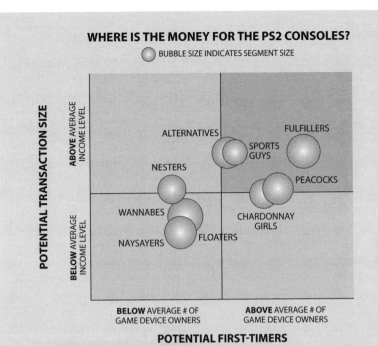

WHERE IS THE MONEY FOR THE PS2 CONSOLES?

BUBBLE SIZE INDICATES SEGMENT SIZE

POTENTIAL TRANSACTION SIZE

ABOVE AVERAGE INCOME LEVEL

BELOW AVERAGE INCOME LEVEL

ALTERNATIVES
SPORTS GUYS
FULFILLERS
NESTERS
PEACOCKS
WANNABES
CHARDONNAY GIRLS
NAYSAYERS
FLOATERS

BELOW AVERAGE # OF GAME DEVICE OWNERS

ABOVE AVERAGE # OF GAME DEVICE OWNERS

POTENTIAL FIRST-TIMERS

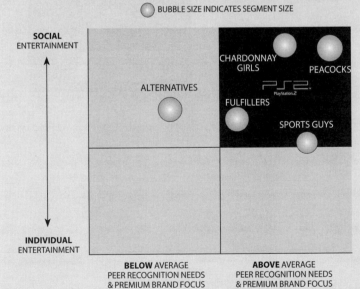

WHERE IS THE PS2 LIFESTYLE PENETRATION OPPORTUNITY

BUBBLE SIZE INDICATES SEGMENT SIZE

SOCIAL ENTERTAINMENT

CHARDONNAY GIRLS
PEACOCKS
ALTERNATIVES
FULFILLERS
SPORTS GUYS

INDIVIDUAL ENTERTAINMENT

BELOW AVERAGE PEER RECOGNITION NEEDS & PREMIUM BRAND FOCUS

ABOVE AVERAGE PEER RECOGNITION NEEDS & PREMIUM BRAND FOCUS

Usage occasion

In order to meet this objective, the team had to clearly see which usage occasion it would need to 'own'. Its current hardcore gamer customer audience was mainly playing at home alone and playing a lot, which gave them the 'uncool' image of being gaming geeks. To broaden appeal and capture *Peacocks* and the other segments that these trendsetters influence, PS2 had to be repositioned into a more social usage occasion. By prioritizing the different usage occasions on the scales of social and peer pressure, the team chose the occasion of *socializing with friends at home*, which included two possible situations:

1. Getting together before going out – meeting at someone's house, having fun playing PS2 and drinking while waiting for others to arrive. This occasion came from an insight of the *Peacocks* segment: they prefer to drink relatively cheaply at home and only then go out and spend less money in expensive bars they like.

2. House party – where PS2 would act as an entertainment for the whole team.

PS2 USAGE OCCASIONS

SOCIAL SETTING

PLAYING WITH RELATIVES

HOUSE PARTY

PS2
PlayStation.2

GETTING TOGETHER BEFORE GOING OUT

HANGING AROUND WITH FRIENDS

PLAYING ALONE AT HOME FOR A RECORD TO GET THE BETTER OF FRIENDS

PLAYING ALONE AT HOME AND/OR WHILE TRAVELING

INDIVIDUAL SETTING

LOW ⟵ ⟶ HIGH

PEER PRESSURE
(RECOGNITION / COMPETITIVENESS)

Once the brand team understood the usage occasion it needed to target for *Peacocks*, it became clear that the *frame of reference* for this segment was much wider than the direct competitors – other gaming consoles – than had earlier been imagined. Rather, it included everything that the target customers could do instead of using the console – going out earlier, watching sports, listening to the music and playing karaoke.

PS2 FRAME OF REFERENCE

WHAT COULD THEY DO INSTEAD?
(FRAME OF REFERENCE)

- **GOING OUT EARLIER (BARS/CAFÉS/CLUBS/CINEMAS/FAST FOOD)**
  - ENTERTAINMENT

- **WATCH SPORTS**
  - ENTERTAINMENT
  - COMPETITIVENESS

- **MUSIC (CDS AND MTV)**
  - HAVING FUN AND DRINKING (OR GETTING DRUNK)
    1. WHILE WAITING FOR OTHERS TO ARRIVE
    2. AT A HOUSE PARTY

- **KARAOKE**
  - HAVING FUN AT A HOUSE PARTY

Now that the *customer target, usage occasion* and *frame of reference* for PS2 were defined, it was time to create the *Motivational Architecture* for the brand that could successfully compete versus those broader alternatives.

Cost of Entry

One of the main reasons why PS2 became so successful is that it is a trendy console and a home entertainment device in one. Customers appreciated that PS2 provided a choice of options for different tastes and moods – they could choose from a wide variety of games, or watch a DVD, or just simply relax listening to their favorite CD. Even though the main competitors introduced their own consoles with similar capabilities, they were just not 'cool' enough; the cool new-generation consoles were yet to come. But although trendiness was perceived to be a good *differentiation* for the old target audience, it was merely a *Cost of Entry* requirement to the young vibrant youth that PS2 was now targeting. This segment would simply not buy a brand or a product if it was not trendy enough.

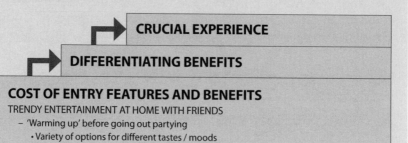

Differentiating Benefits

So, we established that PS2 had what is needed to be considered for purchase by the target customers– providing *trendy entertainment at home with friends*. But what did PS2 have that would differentiate it from the *frame of reference*? A deeper analysis of the benefits it could provide identified that playing PS2 was much *more fun and exciting* than the alternatives because it stimulated the competitive side of the *Peacocks* target segment. *Peacocks* want to be on top and to be noticed; everywhere they go they are looking for an opportunity to show off. So, 'beating the asses' off their friends and comparing each other's scores is a cool way of being the top 'rooster'. The drama and tension of the games when they are playing against each other is captivating, not only for the players themselves, but also the audience of other friends and maybe even a watching girlfriend. TV, music and karaoke are unable to match such fun and competitive drama.

But how about other game consoles? They also have fun and exciting games to offer customers. However, what those other game options could not match was the *range of games and peripherals*. Once hooked, consumers of gaming products are constantly looking for variety. *Peacocks*, in particular, get quickly bored with a game and need a continuous supply of new ones to keep them excited and motivated to keep playing. Only PS2 can provide them with the widest range of games and peripherals – from guns to video cameras and microphones. And only PS2 could provide the possibility of up to eight people playing simultaneously. Now the whole party could join the game and see who is best!

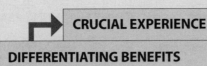

CRUCIAL EXPERIENCE

DIFFERENTIATING BENEFITS
MORE FUN AND EXCITEMENT
  – Drama and tension – competitive
    • 'Beating the assess of each other'
  – Widest range of games and peripherals
    • Multiplayer capabilities

COST OF ENTRY FEATURES AND BENEFITS
TRENDY ENTERTAINMENT AT HOME WITH FRIENDS
  – 'Warming up' before going out partying
    • Variety of options for different tastes / moods

Together with the *Cost of Entry* requirements, the above *differentiation* already raised the PS2's value equation above its competitors. But it still needed the *Crucial Experience* that would hit the head, heart and gut of the target customer – *Peacocks* – and drive the ambitious CEE region growth objectives for the brand.

Crucial Experience

After a thorough study of the target segment and its main emotional drivers, the PS2 brand team identified the key benefit that would ultimately drive the emotional connection to the brand – PS2 *makes the owner feel cool*. Those who have PS2 at home feel themselves *at the epicenter of attention* – everybody wants to hang out at their place and they are the masters who get to decide who's 'gonna be in'. Such experience of being among the 'most popular kids at school' is the most aspirational for the image-conscious and dynamic *Peacocks* that PS2 was targeting. The promise of this brand experience would hit them hard, driving the gut feeling of 'gotta have it'.

This emotionally driven purchase intent of 'gotta have it' would then be facing the attitude of the parents – in most of the cases moms – who act as gatekeepers to the purchase. They either serve as an enabler 'at the cashier' or 'veto' the console. Therefore the PS2 brand team needed to ensure that this secondary target – parents – would not become an obstacle and would be much easier to convert into a purchase.

The segmentation process, similar to that for Youth, identified that the most important Parent segment was *Guiders*: those mothers who are family coordinators. The *Guiders'* micro-managing attitude toward their family derives

PS2 MOTIVATIONAL ARCHITECTURE TARGETING *PEACOCKS*

CRUCIAL EXPERIENCE
'MAKES ME FEEL COOL' → 'GOTTA HAVE IT'
- I am the **epicenter** of attention
  - 'Everybody wants to hang out at my place'
  - 'And I get to decide who is gonne be 'in'.'

DIFFERENTIATING BENEFITS
MORE FUN AND EXCITEMENT
- Drama and tension – competitive
  - 'Beating the assess of each other'
- Widest range of games and peripherals
  - Multiplayer capabilities

COST OF ENTRY FEATURES AND BENEFITS
TRENDY ENTERTAINMENT AT HOME WITH FRIENDS
- 'Warming up' before going out partying
  - Variety of options for different tastes / moods

from their strong need to ensure the security and well-being of the whole family. They have an active and sometimes even hectic lifestyle because of the different things they have to manage within their life/day. At the same time, they have a strong sense of belonging and conviviality, wanting to provide joy and happiness to their loved ones. Such mothers are most likely to purchase PS2 for their kids on special occasions – either as a present on special dates (birthday, Christmas, First Communion, etc.) or as a reward for accomplishments (finishing the school year with acceptable grades, winning competitions in sports, music, etc.).

The strong barrier to purchase that *Guiders'* mothers have is their concern about unrestricted violent content coming into the home and stories in the press about gaming being too addictive, unhealthy, and a waste of time. In order to get their approval of the console, the PS2 brand team had to first appeal to their practicality and strong need for control and safety with some of the functional benefits of the console. But to ensure the purchase of PS2, the team needed to connect to the mother's emotional need to be loved and adored by her kids, with whom she feels more and more disconnected as the kids grow older. What the PS2 purchase could do is to transform the mother from an un-cool 'oldie' in the eyes of her kids into a cool modern mom.

PS2 MOTIVATIONAL ARCHITECTURE TARGETING *GUIDERS*

CRUCIAL EXPERIENCE
'I'M THE COOL MOM'
  – I'm letting my kids have fun in a modern and loving manner
    • 'They will be thrilled with this present'

DIFFERENTIATING BENEFITS
'PLAYSTATION IS A CLEVER CHOICE'
  – Convenient 'one-stop shop' for my kid's entertainment need
    • Multifunctional entertainment solution
    • Gaming, DVD, CD playing

COST OF ENTRY FEATURES AND BENEFITS
SAFE (CONTROLLABLE) ENTERTAINMENT OPTIONS AS A PRESENT FOR MY KIDS
  – But substantial enough that they will feel truly rewarded
    • Taking into consideration their options and wishes

It is very important that there are strong links between different *Motivational Architectures* that target different segments with the same brand; otherwise the brand starts to become schizophrenic and confusing to consumers with sharply contrasting personalities (the *Crucial Experience*) and related benefits (*Differentiating Benefits*).

Now that the PS2 brand team knew *who* to communicate to (the *target* segments) and *what* to communicate (the *Motivational Architectures*), all it needed to do was to understand *how* to communicate. The next step was to develop the PS2 *Communication Touch-Points* strategy that leveraged the marketing team's deeper knowledge of the target so that it could now deliver the more impactful brand proposition it had developed with its *Motivational Architecture* at the right time and at the right place to engage the *target* with the message to drive strong purchase intent.

CHAPTER NINE

Touch-Point Communications

Whenever I mention marketing communications, people inevitably think we are going to talk advertising. That's too bad because advertising may be the least important brand communication tool available, yet most big marketers spend up to 80% of their marketing budget on advertising – particularly television. Experienced marketers such as Coca-Cola, Nestlé, and Procter & Gamble know that 70% of the purchase decisions for their products are made in-store, yet they still pour the mass of their marketing budgets into television spots. They will, of course, tell you that this is necessary because, in order for a customer to consider the brand in-store, they must be predisposed to buying the brand through advertising. True enough, but don't you think it may be just a little bit out of balance?

Back to the future

The importance of marketing communication tools, such as packaging, POS, promotional programs and the like, isn't new. In fact, that is what most advertising agencies and their clients communicated to customers prior to the introduction of television in the 1950s. How television killed the advertising agency business could be a book in itself. Suffice it to say that agencies have fallen in love with the art of making little commercial 'films'. That is what they prefer to call your television ad, and it too often reflects the motivations of the creative people developing the ads. A lot of movie producers and directors got their start making commercials and few, if any, agency creative directors are unaware of that enticing fact. And who can blame them? Wouldn't you rather be making a big budget movie with Angelina Jolie than re-launching a laundry detergent? But marketing laundry detergents, soft drinks and mobile phones is what marketing guys do.

Marketing communications is about a lot more than advertising. Trying to get agencies and clients alike to break away from the mesmerizing lure of television advertising and to focus on other communication tools isn't a new problem. About 15 years ago, the concept of 'integrated marketing' came into vogue. The term was re-introduced by clients to focus more attention on other aspects of marketing communication that advertising agencies used to do quite well before that alluring siren – television – distracted them.

Money, as you would expect, became a strong motivator for agency managers, if not the creatives, to jump into integrated marketing with both feet. The very real threat that clients might start shifting their money to non-advertising areas, such as promotions and special events, hit the agencies like a hailstorm during a parade. Agencies came up with their own umbrella concepts to protect their core business – one agency called its solution the 'whole egg'. The whole egg idea was that the agency would acquire promotional agencies and design shops to do that other stuff, and thereby keep the client's budget under its own umbrella. Not only could it then keep its best creative guys focused on what they really wanted to do – advertising – it could also keep a close tab on the client's marketing budget to make sure this integrated thing didn't get too far out of hand.

Figure 50: A McDonald's tray liner

And as you can imagine, that is where it started to fall apart. Rather than see the need for the integration of the brand's positioning throughout the customer's buying process from need recognition through post-purchase behavior, the advertising agencies simply went about their business producing commercials, and then corporately delegated the junior agencies within their network to 'integrate' the television idea into all the rest of the available tools. You don't believe this is happening? Go into a McDonald's and you can see the advertising global campaign *I'm lovin' it* integrated into a wide range of areas, including the tray liners.

Tray liners? Instead of using the tray liners to sell the customer on a desert or a return trip (a good time for that, considering the medium and where the customer is during the buying process), McDonald's simply put a billboard image of the *I'm lovin' it* campaign on the tray liner (Figure 50). Is that integrated communications or POP used to 'sell' the advertising campaign? Talk about the tail wagging the dog! Rather than integrate the creative idea into a range of mediums, you should concentrate on integrating appropriate elements of the brand strategy into the customer buying process with the right message at the right time, in the right place to actually sell something. Agencies should focus their enormous creative abilities on making that buying process integration as high-impact as possible. To be fair to McDonald's, there are a lot more times when it gets it right – this just isn't one of them.

The myth of ATL and BTL thinking

Not only were some of us, as clients, pulled mistakenly into the whole egg concept, we created another 'tail wagging the dog' situation when we all started using the agency terminology to defining marketing communications as either ATL (above the line) or BTL (below the line).

What line are we talking about it? Surprisingly, very few people in marketing or in their agencies actually know. The 'line' originally referred to where the agencies made their profits when they were working with the old commission system. Some still use this obsolete commission system, but most of them have shifted to fee-based compensation. But ATL and BTL live on. ATL activities are those for which the agency once received a media commission – typically TV, radio, print and billboard. BTL was all the stuff they may have had to do, but didn't make a commission on.

This history is all fairly irrelevant today, but the carry-over implications of this 'above and below' mindset can damage your attempts to integrate your communications in order to address customer behavior. If you are an aspiring agency creative, where would you want to work – above the line working on big-budget television commercials and stunning print ads, or down in the basement (below the line) working on POP posters and shelf hangers? One creative director of a so-called agency 'hot shop' proudly proclaimed to me that his firm 'doesn't mess around with below the line'. He went on to explain that he'd prefer to let the smaller, less talented agencies pick up those 'crumbs'.

Whenever I want to find good advertising people to work on my business, or to hire creative directors when I ran an agency back in the USA for several years, I look for people who are motivated to inject creativity into everything they could touch or see. This is the mindset I am looking for. This type of person is thrilled to decorate a chair, or paint a bus. The canvas doesn't matter as much as the power of the creative idea itself. These people tend to do exceptional work, whether it is on a TV ad or a tradeshow brochure. They love the creative process for its own sake and they don't care a lick about being above or below anything.

But that type of creative purity is rare. Just as customers are emotional creatures who do what they want to do, and then look for rational reasons to justify it, we, as marketers and agency people, do the same. Face it – it is very cool to do advertising commercials. Your friends and family see them just before the movie starts at the cinema; you win ad awards at shows in places like Cannes, and if you are really lucky, you can go with the agency to a remote location shoot. How cool is that?

Recognize advertising for what it is and admit its emotional appeal. Just be smart enough not to give into it – like a drug. And as any recovering alcoholic or drug addict will tell you, the ability to recognize that you have a problem is the first step toward recovery. Advertising is very cool. It is also a terrific waste of money if you overuse it, or use it inappropriately.

Now that we have all of that out of the way, how do you exponentially gear up your marketing communications to deliver superior brand performance – *selling more stuff, to more people, for more money, more efficiently*?

Earlier in the *Exponential Marketing* process, there was an in-depth *Value Diagnostics* step. In that important step you learned about the customers' emotional as well as functional needs; and you developed a brand positioning and *Motivational Architecture* to address those needs. You also learned how to segment customer groups based upon their psychographics, motivations and attitudes, and then linked your brand benefits through the brand architecture. *Exponential Communications* is where you put your detailed knowledge of the customer buying process to work. Your marketing communications should align with the customer buying process step by step – from need recognition through post-purchase behavior.

Along this customer journey, you can insert some very important and very timely brand communication messages. If you know how your best customer prospects spend their days and nights, you have a much better capability of communicating your targeted brand message at the right time and at the right time of day in line with where they are in their purchase decision process. The only problem is that you haven't sold anything yet. What you have established, however, is purchase intent and the beginnings of brand preference. Take it one step at a time – you are currently a step ahead of most marketers because you are planting the seeds of purchase intent that you can soon harvest with actual sales if you take the time to close the loop, and close the sale with integrated messages inside the selling environment.

For most products, purchase intent is established 'outside the four walls' of the selling environment, while the actual purchase behavior occurs 'inside the four walls'. That is how you should target your communication objectives. Instead of an arbitrary determination of ATL and BTL, start talking about 'outside the four walls' communication tools, and 'inside the four walls' communication tools. The objective of 'outside the four walls' communication is to establish purchase intent. The objective of 'inside the four walls' communications is to do both – continue to drive purchase intent as you close the sale with actual purchase behavior. It is really pretty simple and straightforward if you think about it. The challenge is not just in recognizing the situations where you should create purchase intent or actually go for the final sale; it is also crucial that you integrate both the purchase intent and purchase behavior driving messages in a customer-involving manner.

Effective marketing communications links the important aspects of the brand architecture each step of the way from creating purchase intent outside the four walls of the selling environment to closing the sale inside.

Exponential brand communications understands the different customer experiences outside and inside the four walls; it leverages the most appropriate communication tools – the right message, at the right time, at the right place. It is about moving from interruption-based communication to engagement communications.

When you were a child, you knew precisely the best time to ask your father or mother for something. You knew the importance of timing and state-of-mind by the time you were four years old. Different requests required different circumstances and different times, but you knew even back then how important this was to achieving a successful result. You didn't interrupt your father the moment you saw him to blurt out your request. You picked the right time. If you wanted some money to go to the movies, it wasn't very helpful for you to ask your father three times regardless of where you found him and what he was doing, was it? You could have gone for frequency, as media people call it, by writing the request down on a several sheets of paper and posting it wherever he went during the day. Instead you timed and positioned your message with the right wording, at the right time and the right place. Shouldn't you do the same with your customers? You can manage communications with your father or your spouse and engage them at the best time putting the best 'spin' on you request precisely because you happen to know them so well. Now that you have *Strategic Customer Targeting* data that includes much deeper psychographics and lifestyle data about your best customer prospects, you now have the capability to engage them rather than merely interrupt.

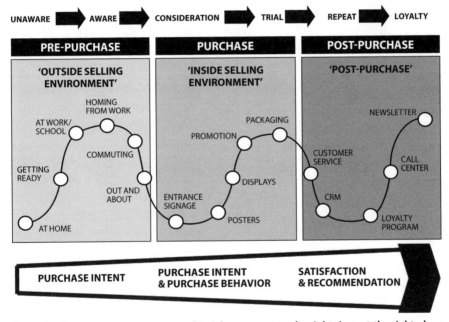

Figure 51: Forget ATL and BTL; target the right message, at the right time, at the right place

Traditional media

Advertising still has a role in the overall communication process, but it should be recognized as only one of many available tools. For many consumer product companies, advertising is still the most efficient medium to reach a mass of potential customers. The trick is to use it in coordination with other, more involving, mediums and by making the ad as experiential as possible for potential customers.

For many mass-marketed products, television is still believed to be the most efficient means of communicating. Through the advantages of linking sight and sound, the medium has the capability to be relatively involving for a one-way communication tool. In most CEE markets, television 'reach' can be misleading due to the low level of involvement the customer has with the media. It is true that almost all households in the region have television sets and they always seem to be on, but being on is not the same thing as being watched. Think about how many times you have gone into the home of friends or family members and had an in-depth discussion – all the while as the TV ran on in the corner. Many people feel comforted by having the TV on: they like the background noise; it is a part of the culture. But this means that you must be wary to count on it as a viable communication vehicle – it depends on the programming and the time of day. In CEE markets, you sometimes need to regard TV almost as you do billboards and radio. The customer is not always actively engaged with the medium, and because of that, you need to first call their attention to the TV before you can expect them to see your ad. It was for this reason that we used the popular *Always Coca-Cola* jingle in this region to break through to the customer in our TV ads – much the same as we use jingles on the radio in other markets.

Another problem with television in several CEE markets is targeting. Even when customers are actually watching the TV, they are usually watching programming that is very widely targeted. Most Western markets have programming that targets specific demographic as well as psychographics segments. Not so often in CEE. Here, television programming is almost always mass targeted – everybody, all the time. With mass targeting being the low-cost choice of programming managers, many advertisers are looking to more specifically targeted mediums, such as print and radio. These more discriminating advertisers will tell you that because they can ensure a minimum of bleed (that's what happens when the ad flows over to non-targeted people) in magazine and print, they can get a better cost-per-thousand reach than with television advertising. You will have to make this decision based on your own target customers. Nevertheless, don't be fooled into reach numbers that reflect televisions that are on rather than televisions that are being actually watched. The difference between active and passive viewing in this region is immense.

There are other important advertising mediums besides television, and although they are primarily still one-way communication, they can often drive more efficient brand preference. Radio is often overlooked and seldom used effectively anymore. With the increased drive time in most CEE markets, and some upscale customers stuck in traffic jams, radio is becoming a great medium for the right type of product. Again, the key is to try and involve your target customer the best you can within the limitations of the medium. With the right sound effects and voices in the old days, before TV, radio was called 'theater of the mind' – it allowed you to imagine a situation inside your head more vividly than if you actually saw it. Readers of good fiction will tell you the same – they like to read good stories and will often avoid seeing the story when it is made into a movie as it will never live up to the power of their own imagination.

Ask your agency copywriters to use their creativity to create some breakthrough 'theater of the mind' radio spots to involve your customer. And don't forget about your customers' state of mind while they are listening to the radio – it varies a great deal. For example, if you were IKEA and you wanted to advertise to *Balancer* parents a new children's bed that resembles a castle with a ladder and play area, when would you run the ad? You know that *Balancers* tend to live in suburban areas (green areas for kids) and work in the city (white-collar jobs), so commute times are lengthy. In fact, because *Balancers* are typically between 30 and 50, they really don't listen to the radio except in their cars, and then mostly to hear a bit of music mixed with news and traffic reports. So, the question is: which is more effective – running the castle bed ad during the morning drive, or during the evening commute home?

If you are seeing the world through the eyes of your target, you will ignore the advice of the radio sales rep and avoid the morning drive in spite of the fact it has higher listenership. Think about what is going on in the mind of a *Balancer* on the way to work – his children are still of great importance, but they said goodbye for the day 20 minutes ago. Now he is lining up his day, pre-thinking important meetings and activities, getting into the zone. On the way home, *Balancers* are still paying attention to the radio to avoid traffic jams so they can spend as much evening time as possible at home. They are getting into a different mind-set, thinking about the moment when they walk in the door and the kid yells out 'daddy'! Now, when do think your castle bed radio ad will best penetrate into their consciousness and create purchase intent?

Billboard is another misaligned medium due to what should be the most obvious of mistakes. In this case, though, it is usually the client that screws it up. Keep in mind the two-second rule. Two seconds – that's it. That is about how much time your customer has to read your billboard as they drive by – two seconds. Most billboards are approved by clients in the comfort of their office without consideration of the clutter and speed with which the advertising will be seen along a busy street. Look at the creative boards among a cluttered environment for the same two seconds and you will see for yourself. This is one medium where the agency almost always gets it, and the client seldom does. Agencies, as a rule, understand the need for brevity and strong images, while clients tend to fall in love with lots of product details that they have included in their agency brief. In the case of billboards, less is always more.

Print is the opposite. Agencies like to use less copy and stirring visuals in print ads just as they do on billboards; but think about the customers' state of mind when they are reading their favorite magazine. Are they on-the-go and rushing about, or are they sitting in their favorite chair with a cup of coffee and enjoying the read? In the print medium, the customer is probably ready for, and wanting more detail about the brand and category. Because most magazines are very targeted, this is a good opportunity to really sell the crucial elements of the *Motivational Architecture* with the appropriate level of support to create strong purchase intent. Use the medium and the focused time of your customer to work a little harder on communicating more important and relevant information. Think about the state of mind of the target when they see the print ad. Are they reading an informational newspaper or magazine (such as *Car and Driver* or a business journal), hence will they appreciate more detailed information. Maybe they are they escaping through the lives of celebrities in *Blikk* or *Hello,* and consequently you will need to think about more imagery that fits this occasion. Figures 52 and 53 depict ads that Publicis created for Heineken. They do a good job of aligning the brand with a specific medium and the consumer's state of mind when reading the medium.

TYPE OF MAGAZINE: MOVIE AND VIDEO MAGAZINE

PUBLISHING: MONTHLY

TARGET READER: 18–29 YEARS, MORE MALE

CONTENT: CINEMA, DVD AND VIDEO RELEASES, MOVIE TIPS AND CRITICS, MOVIE PREVIEWS, GOSSIP AND REPORTS ABOUT MOVIE STARS

'CAN YOU HOLD MY HAND DURING THE SCARY PARTY?'

Figure 52: Heineken ad for movie and video magazine

TYPE OF MAGAZINE: EVENT PROGRAM GUIDE FOR

PUBLISHING: MONTHLY, FREE

TARGET READER: 18–35 YEARS, LIKES TO GO OUT, ACTIVE, INTERESTED IN WHAT IS GOING ON

CONTENT: DATES AND INFORMATION ABOUT CONCERTS, THEATRE, RESTAURANTS AND OTHER ENTERTAINMENT EVENTS

'GET YOURSELF TOGETHER BY SATURDAY NIGHT…'

Figure 53: Heineken ad for event program guide.

Regardless of which media you use, you have the best chance of breaking through the medium's limitations by trying to involve your customers in the message. Act on the state-of-mind insights you have gained in your customer research and segmentation. Look at the Nescafé television ads. Can't you almost smell the coffee? And with Unilever's Magnum billboards (Figure 54) – you can almost taste the indulgence bordering on decadence.

Figure 54: A Magnum billboard from Unilever

These advertisements reflect the experiential use of traditional mediums because they involve the customers' senses in broader terms than you would normally expect from the limiting dimensions of a particular medium.

A word about the Internet

Some say that the Internet is to television what television was to radio 50 years ago. It is not. It is a completely different experience. Don't apply print, billboard, radio, or television thinking and creative to such a different and potentially valuable medium. This one has 'interactive' built into its name!

Plug your brand strategy and architecture into the technology. Don't just gather customer data for management purposes; use that in-depth knowledge to involve customers with highly targeted brand communications. The Internet has the capability and power of mass customization. Amazon.com re-merchandises its virtual store for each customer visit. You can do the same.

Just as you think of real walls (inside and outside the four walls) in a bricks-and-mortar retail store, think of virtual walls on the Internet. If the customer can buy at that moment during their journey on the Internet, then you are trying to communicate purchase intent and purchase behavior messages to close the sale. But if the customer is on another site and you want to bring her into your site with a banner ad, the message objective is purchase intent alone.

Words matter. Think in terms of a web *site* rather than a web *page*. A customer may read a page, but she can become more involved in a visit to a site. And a customer visit is much easier to turn into a brand experience.

Special events and sponsorships

This is where you can have a lot of fun in modern marketing communication. The brand strategy you want to leverage with events and sponsorships is *associative imagery*. What you are trying to do with associative imagery is to capture the user experience of a related activity and associate it with your brand in the hearts and minds of the customers. Think of how successfully McDonald's and Disney have leveraged each others brand equity to benefit their own brands. McDonald's virtually owns children in the fast food business with its Happy Meal concepts. The Disney movies tie-in (with characters and games inserts in the Happy Meal) is the kids' incentive that keeps Moms coming back again and again. McDonald's would have a tough time doing this without Disney. All it would be left with is a rather pale two-meter-tall, red-haired clown that actually frightens my four-year-old. Disney also benefits. The worldwide penetration of McDonald's outlets is an incredibly strong media tool to help Disney launch new movies and sell DVDs.

Special events are a great opportunity to create positive purchase intent that will be strong enough to hold the customer all the way through into the selling environment to the cash register. In fact, some of the most efficient special events break through the actual four walls and move from a purchase-intent activity outside, to a direct purchase driver inside the store itself. Knorr soups create purchase intent followed very quickly with purchase behavior through its successful in-store cooking events.

Most events are run outside the selling environment, but they are still very effective brand communication tools when executed properly because they involve the customer quite literally in a brand experience. At Coca-Cola we recognized a factor that made experiential communications even more important in CEE than in Western markets – the perceived lack of media objectivity in the region. We turned to special events and activities as the most persuasive of all the tools in our communication arsenal. We found that we could involve the consumer in a brand experience quite efficiently with programs such as the Coca-Cola Beach House (now Coke Club) and the Fanta Fun Taxis. We knew that over 20% of all teenagers in Hungary visit the Coca-Cola Beach House each year, while a total of 80% watch or hear related activities on TV and on the radio. They believe what they see and hear about Coca-Cola and summer fun because they have either been there themselves at some point, or have friends who have actually been there and told them all about it – word-of-mouth. The Coca-Cola Beach House was the killer weapon in winning the Cola war in Hungary. Don't believe me? Ask the Pepsi guys. Better yet, ask teenage soft-drink consumers.

One problem with most successful events is that you can get carried away just as with any other medium. The advertising guy tends to fantasize about being the next Spielberg when he is shooting your ice-cream ad, and the client starts thinking he has created the next theme park with his special event. Leave the film work to Spielberg and the theme parks to Disney. In both cases, your role is to create an involving brand experience – that's it, nothing more, nothing less.

At one point a few years back, the director of the event agency that ran the Coca-Cola Beach House was showing me the improvements for the coming year. He mentioned that he was cutting back the sandy area to make more room for experiential activities. It was my idea originally to put sand at the

Beach House and I was quite proud of how well it had been received. Naturally I protested that the people who go to the Beach House really like the sand. He calmly asked me if my intention was to have people lie around enjoying the sand, or to use the space more efficiently so that we extended the Coca-Cola brand message to a larger number of people through more efficient turnover events? He got it completely and pulled me back in from the land of theme parks and Mickey Mouse.

An important lesson in executing a successful event: when you have delivered a superior brand experience, don't screw it up by bringing the customer back down to the level of a simple advertisement. Involve customers in the brand and don't worry about the logo. If you involve them properly, they will remember your brand. And don't introduce skepticism into the experience by overselling – be subtle. This is where we screwed up the most at the Beach House; we put blazing advertising screens next to the band on the stage, or a sea of red banners ringing the lake. It's massive overkill and actually hurts the communication efforts by reducing a brand experience back down to just another brand advertisement.

Most companies can't afford to create their own event, so they tie in via a sponsorship to someone else's pre-packaged event. This is a dangerous, but sometimes necessary path. The first thing you should know is that the customer will not thank you for sponsoring their favorite event or team when you put your name on it – in fact, they will usually resent it. They expect that big companies and big brands will sponsor big events, and if they are anything more than neutral about it, they may even start to wonder if that is why your brand costs them so much. Mobile phone provider T-Mobile sponsors a free concert with big-name acts every year in Budapest for 400,000 people – just because. One unfortunate side effect of blowing a lot of money is that many customers link the cost of the huge concert to their frustratingly high mobile phone bills, which they consider more expensive than rivals Pannon and Vodafone. T-Mobile is not, in fact, more expensive on most tariff packages than its competitors, but perception is reality and its over-the-top marketing spending is contributing to that perception.

The other common event mistake is the sponsor's logo mistake. This mistake is based on the thinking that brand awareness is actually relevant. It isn't. I didn't say awareness is unimportant – just irrelevant. The brand name becomes relevant only when you tie it to some customer benefit, and most logos do not accomplish this on their own. Of course it won't be likely that customers will actually buy your product if they have never heard of it, but by the same token, just because they have heard of it, doesn't mean they will buy it. Most logos in a sea of other sponsors' logos don't go any farther than communicating a name and the fact that the company has a lot of money to throw around. You need to do a lot more than that to involve the customer in your brand and gain their purchase.

The truth is that much sponsorship is more about senior executives' egos than delivering effective and efficient brand strategies. There is associative imagery at work, but unfortunately, it is the image of the executive who is trying to benefit from the association with a high-profile sporting or entertainment event, rather than being involving and meaningful to the brand. Just like the customers' ultimate motivation in buying your products, a lot of executives buy sponsorship rights for emotional reasons and then look for rational reasons to support that decision. Responsible managers try to connect the event to their brand in a meaningful way. The ego thing is unfortunate because there are effective sponsorship activities and special events that will benefit your brand – just make sure you are in that camp. To the sponsorship salesmen out there: you need to work harder at building a lasting brand relationship that makes sense for your event if you want to keep getting sponsor funding.

The right brand strategy is to connect to the sponsored event or team in a real and meaningful way. Vodafone's decision to sponsor a traffic helicopter in one market (to communicate the convenience and benefits of being connected no matter where you are) makes sense to me. Activate the sponsorship and activate beyond the logo. Demonstrate within the activities around the event that you not only understand the customers' involvement with the event, you share it. The beer brand isn't the point of the football match, but it can be a part of the experience. What is crucially important is how the beer brand fits into, and becomes a part of the fan's overall football experience. Your job, if you are a brand manager for a beer, is to understand that experience, and to activate it in a meaningful way that involves your customer.

The Chinese got it right over 3000 years ago:

> Tell them and they will forget.
> Show them and they will remember.
> Involve them and they will understand.
> *Ancient Chinese Proverb*

All the logos and 'brought to you by' stuff is mostly a waste of time and money. It's just show-and-tell and lacks real customer involvement.

Ownability is a key component in any successful sponsorship or event. No, not ownership from a contractual standpoint – that's for the lawyers to work out. Ownability, or 'experience ownership', is what you should be seeking based on the event's emotional and functional connection to your brand's architecture. A quick acid test to determine the level of potential ownership is to ask yourself if your competitor could perform the same activity. Assuming your brand positioning is meaningful, deliverable and defendable, and the activity fits with your brand architecture, then it would obviously not work as effectively for the competition. And likewise for the events they are doing.

Look at all the possibilities in the market, and then compare the functional and emotional benefits of the activity that you want to connect with to create a meaningful experience for your customers. Ownability comes from a deep understanding of your brand's architecture as well as the architecture of the event or activity you want to associate with. Find the viable links – the aspects and experiences that drive the emotional appeal – and then build your marketing strategy around those connections (Figure 55).

COCA-COLA   LAKE BALATON

CRUCIAL EXPERIENCE	**CRUCIAL EXPERIENCE**
– MAKES ME FEEL GOOD ABOUT MYSELF – OPTIMISM – INCLUSIVE	– MAKES ME FEEL GOOD ABOUT MYSELF – ANTICIPATION – SHARED
DIFFERENTIATING BENEFITS	**DIFFERENTIATING BENEFITS**
– AUTHENTIC – THE 'REAL ONE' – CONTOUR SHAPE – REFRESHING	– AUTHENTIC – THE 'HUNGARIAN SEA' – SHALLOW AT ONE END FOR FAMILIES AND DEEP FOR ADULTS AND SAILING ON THE OTHER – SENSE OF TRADITION
COST OF ENTRY FEATURES AND BENEFITS MEETS MINIMAL BEVERAGE REQUIREMENTS – COLA TASTE – ALWAYS AVAILABLE – COLD	**COST OF ENTRY FEATURES AND BENEFITS** MEETS MINIMAL SUMMER PLACE REQUIREMENTS – SUMMERTIME FIT – CLOSE TO WATER – LOTS OF STUFF TO DO

Figure 55: Alignment of Coca-Cola and Balaton *Motivational Architectures*

To form a mutually beneficial partnership, start thinking in terms of a brand property rather than simply sponsorship. The word 'property' conveys the accountability and responsibility of a business asset. Sponsorship is just some place to put your logo. Connect with something that has special significance to the consumer that can be accessed to drive purchase intent through a viable and meaningful link to the unique *Motivational Architecture* of your brand. Remember, the objective is to involve the consumer in an experience. Choose what and how you associate your brand very carefully. Identify the deep connections that can last, or walk away.

Evaluating the effectiveness of 'outside the four walls' communications

How do you know what's working and what's not? To unleash the involving power of your brand, you will need to utilize both traditional and non-traditional mediums. Evaluating their effectiveness will be like comparing apples to oranges. The old advertising measurements will no longer be effective. A lot of mass marketers use measurements such as 'reach' and 'frequency' to indicate if they have achieved the proper communication levels to reach their targeted customers. The rule of thumb on this measurement is 70% reach with a frequency of three times. This formula assumes that if you reach 70% of the target with a compelling message, and then repeat that message three times, they will get it. Maybe yes, maybe no.

I'm okay with the objective of reaching 70% of the target, but some of the best advertising ever done – the '1984' introduction commercial for Apple Macintosh, for example – was most effective when shown just once. Telling somebody several times what they should get the first time can be nothing more than an excuse for bad creative. It is true that there is a lot of clutter out there and you may need to repeat yourself to break through, but is advertising frequency really a critical measurement? How does it directly relate to purchase intent or actual purchase behavior?

Other marketers have done away with frequency and replaced it with 'recentcy'. What this marketing-invented word means is that it isn't important how many times you reach the target customer, what's more important is how recently the message reached them prior to their purchase decision. I can understand how the proximity of the message to a usage occasion is useful with products like pizza delivery or booking a holiday vacation, but recentcy still isn't enough because it doesn't measure impact.

The biggest problem with any of these frequently used brand-communications measurements is that they are focused on the transmission of a brand message when it is the reception by the target we should be measuring – the advertising's persuasiveness in driving purchase intent. We need measurements that track the delivery of the message relative to the stage of the customer's buying decision in order to ensure that we provide the right message at the right time. Outside the four walls of the selling environment, we should be creating purchase intent, while inside the four walls we should be closing the sale in our communication tools by driving actual purchase behavior.

The problem with most measurement systems is that the more objective they are, the more precise they need to be. That means money. Procter & Gamble and Unilver have recently announced a joint program, with A.C Nielsen in the United States, to share the cost of an extensive customer tracking system that will attempt to determine the effectiveness of various brand messages that impact the customer as they go about their daily business. The right idea, but the logistics and systems necessary to do this sort of scientific-impact tracking is so expensive that neither of these two competitors can do it on their own. Not even in a country of 280 million people! Where does that leave you and your business?

Rather than trying for the 100% solution with the perfect quantifiable measurement tool, let's be more practical, and much more affordable. It isn't worth the cost of being so precise as long as you are focused on the right communication factors. Consider a more subjective brand communication measurement system that rationally focuses on the most important factors in driving purchase intent outside the four walls. Inside the four walls you can measure communications the old fashioned way – does it cause actual sales to go up, or not. Once again, it is important to separate the two objectives to measure inside and outside the four walls with communication tools that do what they are supposed to do.

Although we naturally prefer hard numbers and fact-based measurement tools that are very precise, we have become quite comfortable with subjective measurement tools in a lot of popular sports. Olympic judges can't possibly measure a gymnast's performance precisely with hard numbers. Imagine the costs of lining up some sort of laser tracking device to measure spins, jumps and turns. Instead, what they do is to agree on a set of parameters that can be weighted according to the judge's visual observance of the gymnast. Factors such as originality, degree of difficulty, how controlled was the landing, and so forth, serve as effective parameters to measure the performance of one gymnast compared to another. While one judge may disagree about how difficult a maneuver was, or how controlled the landing executed was, my point is that at least they are all looking for the same thing. This enables the different judges to measure the same performance.

Establishing subjective parameters can enable you to evaluate and compare the respective benefits of apples and oranges because they focus the evaluation on pre-agreed tangible and observable outcomes. The marketing communications measurement system you develop for your company should simply take into account what you probably already know to be the drivers of purchase intent and actual purchase behavior. Television and billboard advertisements, for example, are very different from one another, so you must evaluate their effectiveness based on a common set of parameters that you and your team believe will affect purchase intent.

Purchase Intent Measurements (PIMs)

PIMs is a planning and evaluation tool we developed a few years ago. It *objectively* and *subjectively* measures the impact of various communication tools in driving purchase intent outside the four walls of the selling environment in a very efficient manner. Key purchase intent influencers on the PIM evaluation score are:

- **Situation impact** – the situation and state of mind of the customers when the brand message reaches them.
- **Context impact** – the noise or clutter level within the medium that competes with your brand's message.
- **Content impact** – is the message meaningful (cost of entry, functionally and/or emotionally motivating according to the brand's architecture) to the consumers' needs?
- **Stamina impact** – will the persuasive impact of the message sustain itself within the mind of the consumer until they are inside the four walls?

As an example, we can evaluate the various communication tools during the Coca-Cola Balaton campaign.

MARKETING ACTIVITY	TARGET REACH (%)	PURCHASE INTENT IMPACT*	TOTAL IMPACT POINTS	PERCENT OF IMPACT	PERCENT OF BUDGET
BEING AT THE COCA-COLA BEACH HOUSE	20	9	180	14%	12%
HEAR BEACH HOUSE ACTIVITIES ON RADIO OR READ IN PRINT	80	3	240	18%	4%

MARKETING ACTIVITY	TARGET REACH (%)	PURCHASE INTENT IMPACT*	TOTAL IMPACT POINTS	PERCENT OF IMPACT	PERCENT OF BUDGET
WATCH THE BEACH HOUSE REALITY SHOW ON RTL CLUB	60	6	360	27%	18%
ADVERTISING TV ADS	70	4	280	21%	58%
INTERNET SITE	15	6	90	7%	1%
HORECA 'TOP 40' ARTISTIC SIGNAGE PROGRAM	15	3	45	3%	4%
BILLBOARDS AND SIGNAGE	70	2	140	10%	3%
TOTALS			1335	100%	100%

*BASED ON A PRE-DETERMINED EVALUATION METHODOLOGY

Figure 56: PIMs – measuring impact on teen purchase intent
with Coca-Cola summer communications

Reach, as an objective measurement, is still important, but purchase intent impact is the variable factor that can be best evaluated based on the subjective parameters discussed among your team and which are pre-established in advance of creating the ads or selecting the media. While there may be an argument about how high the stamina impact is from a creative standpoint, or how much clutter is really affecting the context impact, your team is debating the right topic – the effect of communications tools on creating purchase intent outside the four walls of the selling environment.

The Coca-Cola Balaton communications example shows that by factoring the impact of the communication tool versus the cost, we can get to a viable cost/benefit comparison. Although the Coca-Cola Beach House property is only marginally on the plus side of its cost (14% of purchase intent impact versus 12% of total campaign cost), it is the extension of this property into PR, radio and television programming that demonstrates the effectiveness and efficiency of this Coca-Cola summertime relevance program. In contrast, look at the disproportionate cost of regular television ads compared to the overall effect on purchase intent. This should be closely evaluated for use in future brand communication plans. The PIMs measurement system may not fit perfectly within the applications of your business, but it should provide some food for thought as to how you can break out of non-relevant marketing communications measurements and begin to develop a more appropriate communications evaluation system for your business. This alternative way of measuring the impact of disparate communication tools will enable brand planners to break out of the expensive broadcast media trap by evaluating the impact of non-traditional media and communication tools; tools that in today's environment may actually be much more effective in driving purchase intent outside the four walls, as well as more efficient in increasing sales inside.

Although many of the measurements in PIMs are subjective, the internal debate about what drives purchase intent relative to the use of various communication and sales tools is more constructive and much more meaningful to driving the business forward than the current practice – evaluating personal likes and dislikes of a new series of commercials by the management team, or by how many trade customers will attend a sponsored activity. I believe that you will find that the debate among sales, marketing and operational personnel in defining the parameters and criteria to measure the impact of various communication and sales tools will actually add value to the entire marketing and brand communication process.

Operational marketing

Close the loop and close the sale. The best return on investment (ROI) in marketing communication will always be on those communication elements closest to the actual sale. It is only logical (Figure 57).

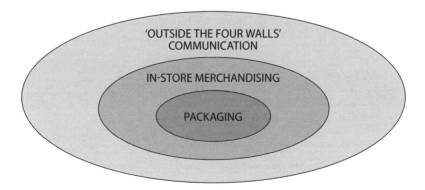

Figure 57: The marketing ROI bull's-eye

The problem is that many marketers look at in-store communication as a completely different communication process. It isn't. If you intend to get a good ROI from all the marketing money you spend outside the store, you must link it with the brand communication inside the store. 'Dance with the girl that you came with', as they say in the countryside. Good advice for marketers, too. If you believe that what you are communicating outside the store is effective, why wouldn't you re-enforce that success inside the store and make it easier to close the sale.

Your brand architecture is still the strategy driver. The key functional and emotional benefits that earned customer brand preference are the same benefits that will get you the purchase. Stay the course. The difference with 'inside the four walls' communications is that you can and must hit harder and more to the point. You must close the sale with a decisive call to action – generate trial, repeat sales, or a larger transaction size. You decide, but sell something! Do it by utilizing the right communication at the right moment during the buying process inside the selling environment.

Packaging is often under-appreciated and misunderstood. It is the decisive point where purchase intent and purchase behavior come together...or not. You win or lose the sale at that moment. Isn't that where you should absolutely be the most effective? Before you spend any money anywhere else, get your packaging right. And packaging isn't just a consumer goods game. Isn't the Federal Express truck a form of packaging? Look at how Frontier Airline – based in Denver, Colorado – uses graphics on its planes to convey its character and a sense of natural adventure. The package becomes a medium to communicate the fun adventure of traveling to Colorado where nature abounds! LOT is not communicating so much – just a logo (Figure 58).

Figure 58: The Frontier experience *vs* the LOT experience

Hungarian Tourism may not get it; but the Hungarian police force does. It gets the importance of marketing and brand image. At the same time that it overhauled its uniforms, it began a comprehensive crackdown on police corruption. If it wanted to be a modern professional police force, it needed to look like one. Everything communicates. Maybe Hungarian Tourism should hire a couple of cops to upgrade its marketing communications!

Don't get lost in contradictory and unrelated features and benefits when you develop your packaging. Stay focused on delivering on specific customer needs during the in-store decision process. The advertising agency, Publicis, has done a good job breaking out of the ATL and BTL trap. Its creative teams approach the entire buying process as a complete customer experience – *holistic marketing*. It thinks about the specific role in-store communications relative to the customer's state of mind with clear creative deliverables.

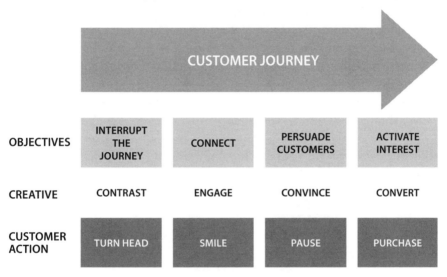

Figure 59: The role of communications in the store (© Publicis Advertising)

Occasion-based communications

Different customers shop for the same product in different outlets, at different times of the day, for different reasons. Customers themselves change throughout the day, week, month and season. Communicate with your customers with the right brand message addressing their needs at that moment, and on that occasion. Have the right package as well as the right brand message to match the occasion.

Join in the selling environment – fit in. Incorporate your brand message into the environment at a specific usage occasion for maximum effect rather than awkwardly trying to compete for attention. Customers are there for a reason. Fit in rather than resist and risk distraction accompanied by customer and retailer alienation. If you choose to execute an in-store event, make sure that the activity is both occasion- and brand-centric.

Work within the needs of the value chain. Work with your trade partners to develop innovative solutions to sell more of your products to shared customers, rather than pushing programs to get them to simply bring in more inventory. It really is a partnership; just as you can and should rely on them to provide overall shopping behavior data in their stores, they are looking to you to learn how they can sell more from a particular category. Utilize the information from your *Value Diagnostics* research on category and brand influencers to show retailers how they can sell more.

Diverta, a multimedia retailer in Romania used *Strategic Customer Targeting* to better understand the types of customers that shop different areas of its store so that it can better cross-sell from one product category area to the other (Figure 60).

Price is informational – it should not be the primary reason to buy! Keep price communication in the right context – after you have communicated brand value – *more for more and worth it*. Again, stay the course and keep your brand strategy close at hand as you execute your *Exponential Communications*.

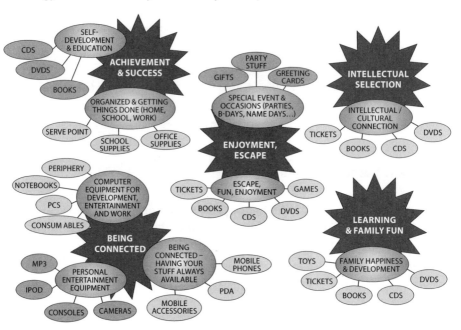

Figure 60: Orientation and attraction points that could guide different types of customers in-store (multimedia retailer example)

Coca-Cola brand experience on the 'Hungarian Sea'

By Katalin Halász and Mátyás Szalai

As the Hungarian marketing manager, Katalin led the transformation of the Coca-Cola Beach House into Coke Club. She is a ten-year veteran of the company and was recently promoted to regional marketing manager with multicountry responsibility in CEE. Katalin is a native of Hungary.[*] Mátyás is a consultant at the Garrison Group, where he works with FMCG and retail clients. He is an accomplished music composer/producer with compositions currently featured in several PlayStation games. Mátyás is a native of Hungary.[**]

As the proverb says: 'One swallow doesn't make a summer', but in the ten years that the Coca-Cola Beach House has opened its doors, the start of the summer season is no longer a question for thousands of young adults in Hungary. The Coca-Cola Beach House was established in 1997 at Hungary's biggest lake, Lake Balaton (fondly referred to as the 'Hungarian Sea'), with the initial idea to create a place where Hungarian teens could truly feel good about themselves, and feel good about where they lived and what they had. It offers a sandy beach (not a natural feature of the lake), beachside concerts and parties, as well as a variety of sports and leisure facilities. Rather using traditional advertising to simply tell consumers that Coca-Cola is the perfect soft drink for summer, one that fits their unique Hungarian lifestyle, Coca-Cola opted for a more involving event where consumers could live the Coca-Cola Hungarian summer experience.

Re-launching the 10-year-old Beach House as Coke Club

The Beach House formula worked very well for 10 years – its organizers managed to create a whole concept including an open-air club and beach. The Beach House was easily the hottest spot in the Hungarian summer: people could enjoy the free concerts on Hungary's first sandy beach, which also doubled as an open air club. More

---

* Katalin can be contacted at katalin@garrisongroup.eu
** Mátyás can be contacted at matyas@garrisongroup.eu

than anything else Coca-Cola did in those years, the Beach House took Coke from a parity market position with Pepsi to an almost 3:1 advantage. However, the continual transformation of people and trends required some serious renovation to the concept after 10 years of playing to a full house. The Coca-Cola Company reached the conclusion in 2006 that the Beach House property was outdated, out of touch with the current attitudes and lifestyles of young adults, and could no longer be counted on in its present form to serve as an innovative and inspiring place which could contribute to building brand affinity and helping Coca-Cola ensure its long-standing position as an icon of positivity and optimisim. Just as Coca-Cola had recently done in revamping its own image with the highly successful *Coke Side of Life* global campaign, the Coca-Cola Beach House concept in Hungary needed something more exciting and engaging for today's Hungarian reality in order to re-spark the connection with young adults. Like the rest of CEE, a lot had changed from 1997 to 2007. A simple refurnishing of the Beach House wouldn't be enough; a complete re-building, re-naming and re-positioning was required.

Before jumping into the ideation process involving all the small steps included in the re-building process, we needed to stop for a moment and think about what the vision, goals and objectives were with this new concept of Coke Club. Coke Club intends to develop and nurture a culture – to be the universal icon of positivity in a seemingly cynical and divided world. What objectives would help us reach this vision in Hungary?

1. To build and elevate Coca-Cola involvement among young adults from loyalty to advocacy.
2. To invite young adults to experience what it means to live on the *Coke (positive) Side of Life*.
3. To increase Coca-Cola's brand preference (a KPI – Key Performance Indicator) among young adults.

The philosophy behind Coke Club

In the myriad of global happiness surveys, Hungary features low down on the list and unfortunately has the distinction of having one of the highest suicides rates in Europe. It is definitely in need of a place that demonstrates that life can be approached in a more positive way. Coke Club's objective, while recognizing it is only a soft drink, believes that it can still have a role as a positive force in changing the ingrained behavioral codes of pessimism and cynicism into a more spontaneous, open-hearted and colorful approach. Coca-Cola could become an icon of positivity by 'institutionalizing' Coke Club values, attitudes and lifestyle portrayed in a real place that is well known and loved by Hungarian youth – the Balaton. Coke Club should strive to become a gentle teacher, share its commitment, and inspire others to join the *Coke Side of Life*. It could be a strong but *Innocent* (architype) leader who believes that positivity can be brought out in everybody and that young people can still achieve their dreams, whatever they might be. Therefore,

Coke Club needed to innovate, become an eye-opener and a place where there would be no conventions; a place that would fill everybody with memorable positive experiences; a place that would support spontaneity; a place where the rule is that there are no rules. Coke Club could redefine the terms 'concert' and 'festival'. It could develop the culture, and this could only be done by an iconic brand that not only serves its customers, but leads them, too.

Young adults should feel secure at Coke Club, because the brand's promise is to accept everyone as they are. Coke Club fosters an environment of openness, where there is no place for preconceptions, where you are free to be yourself, and where you want to share and connect with others.

What do we want to communicate?

How would these objectives help us to get to our destination? The following consumer take-aways were needed:

- Embed the notion that Coke Club is a club, where unique programs and projects happen and where people can gain a meaningful and unique Coca-Cola experience.
  - Desired consumer response: 'I cannot miss out on this and I will recommend it to my friends.'
  - *Peacocks* consumer target: 'Now I know that Coke Club is a club where cool and trendy things happen that I can use to boost my image.'
  - *Alternatives* consumer target: 'Now I know that Coke Club is a club where I can experience something unconventional but of good quality and culturally/intellectually interesting.'
  - *Freestylers* consumer target: 'Now I know that Coke Club is a club where I can participate in adventurous, trendsetting programs.'
- Show off the opportunity to become part of a real Coke Club.
  - Desired consumer response: 'What a cool idea that I can be part of a club where I can feel special, and meet and share experiences with people who are like me.

- Illustrate the uniqueness of Coke Club to consumers via positive gestures and showing the openness of Coke Club.
  - Desired consumer response: 'How great it is to feel special and valuable at this place; Coke Club does something for me.'

As a result of this strategy, the creators came up with the following content for Coke Club itself:

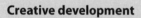

- The club will be open not only at night, but in daytime, too: from 10am to 4am every day throughout the summer.
- It will have cultural events: special dance performances, open-air cinema, and other unique performances like ballet in the sand – most of the visitors would never see a ballet performance otherwise, but Coke Club will bring it to them.
- It will have music: concerts with a strong focus on DJ culture, MTV Icon program (famous Hungarian popsongs played by alternative and up-and-coming bands).

Creative development

Meanwhile, the creative development to identify Coke Club's interpretation of the Global *Coke Side of Life* campaign had been launched with the core creative idea: *Coke Club is your living room extended right onto the beach and concert stage. It is a place where you can be either relaxed or wound up; where you can stay connected; and at the same time enjoy intimacy. A place where you are free to be spontaneous and open for whatever life brings.*

The Coca-Cola Company wanted to avoid traditional, mass media tools, and focus more on meeting young adults when and where they are most open to receiving its messages. The use of innovative media solutions, and those that would build fame and reputation were set as objectives.

1. Spread the knowledge about the new name and about the philosophy of Coke Club.
   - PR support launched the campaign-building expectations about the new club with articles by cultural icons who helped develop the Club concept.

- Strategically placed posters and others visuals were used around pedestrian and public transport areas.
- VIVA (Music TV in Hungary) program was produced at Coke Club.
- A live radio was broadcast from Coke Club by Radio Café.
- Guerrilla marketing was launched via the first ever commercial Video Blog – Feri Tivi – with daily humorous reports about the transformation of the Coca-Cola Beach House into Coke Club over a 22-day period leading up to the opening.

CokeClub®
SIÓFOK, NAGYSTRAND

2. Reverse the outdated perception that had become ingrained in the Coca-Cola Beach House after 10 years by building a radically different new Coke Club, positioning it as a lifestyle benchmark for clubbing in line with the Coca-Cola brand attributes of optimism and inclusivity, but also the important Coca-Cola value continuity – always there with you through the years, and always in tune with the times. Always!
- Print advertisements focused on image enhancement *vs* the old Beach House in lifestyle magazines.
- Mega billboard site on the highway, which goes toward Coke Club.
- Image and programming appearance in the supplement of a National Daily on the day when university entry exams were published.
- Partnership with IWIW (International Who Knows Who) social network site, creating Coke Club membership and downloadable program sheets.

3. Invite young adults to come and experience what it means to live on the *Coke Side of Life* in Coke Club.

- Grand opening party to which media and VIP celebrities and IWIW members were invited to generate WOM (word of mouth).
- Special Coke Club summer edition prints of two selected program magazines were produced.
- *'Don't Panic'* programs available at universities, cafés, music stores and art cinemas.

- Online communication emphasized announcing the program with a focus on the main concerts.
- Coke Club micro-site was developed.

The results

The following results were achieved after the first year (in relation to the country's population of 10 million people):

- Total number of visitors: 250,000
- Outstanding media value generated by PR: €1.2 million approx.
- Internet: 150,862 total visitors to Coke Club micro-site.
- Internet: 69,171 webcast visitors to concerts transmitted from Coke Club.
- Internet: Guerrilla marketing, video blog (Feri Tivi) had more than 840,000 downloads. Feri became a media personality and received 1200 blog comments.
- Internet: IWIW social networking had 198,000 registered Coke Club members and 1,200,000 program datasheet downloads.

But did it revitalize the brand as planned?

- Due to the success of Coke Club, the Coca-Cola brand became even more relevant to local consumers:
  - Coke is a brand I love: +6pp (teens), +4pp (young adults)
  - Coke is for someone like me: +6pp (teens), +4pp (young adults)
- Among teens, Coca-Cola managed to increase its 'favorite brand' status by 4pp, and Coke Club contributed significantly in communicating the 'optimistic' approach of the brand.
  - Coke inspires living with opportunities: +7pp (teens)
  - For people with a positive approach: +10pp (teens)
- Coke Club helped in differentiating the brand, and contributed to improving the brand's value-for-money ratio.
  - Coke is different from other brands: +10pp (teens), +11pp (young adults)
  - Coke is worth what it cost: +11pp (teens), +10pp (young adults)
- Coke Club enhanced the innovative image of the brand among teens:
  - Coke is always doing new things: +4pp (teens)
  - Coke makes moments more special: +8pp (teens)

- Because of the the image improvements, Coke Club helped to increase consumption frequency within the core target groups that helped the brand to achieve 3% volume increase *vs* the previous year during the summer period.
  - Coke drinkers: +3pp (teens), +8pp (young adults)

And the business results?

Because of the campaign, by the end of the second season the total sales volume of Coca-Cola products increased by +3%, which resulted a 4.8% increase (from 17.1% to 21.9%) in market share of Coca-Cola™ products and a market share of regular Coca-Cola increase of 2.7%.

Pantene delivers what it promises: How communications work outside and inside the four walls

By Sam Moorthy

Sam is the managing director of Icons & Images – a communications consultancy that works with the Garrison Group and others on client-agency collaborative relationships, and communications-related training. Sam has a long career in the agency business with stints in Central and Eastern Europe and India for Grey, and O&M before that. Sam is a native of India.*

P&G launched Pantene in CEE in the early 1990s. As a brand of scientifically developed hair-care products – shampoo, conditioner and styling – it revolutionized the CEE hair-care market. Pantene brought beauty-salon-type hair care and results to the mass market; and in doing so it developed a strong and loyal following.

Business grew rapidly in the first few years and the brand continued to launch consumer-relevant and distinctive initiatives on a regular basis. In addition, Pantene successfully stood up to challenges from other hair-care brands and launches, such as Organics, Elsève, and Fructis. Though business growth might have slowed a bit, with volumes and shares growing less strongly than earlier, Pantene continued to enjoy consumer loyalty.

---

* Sam can be contacted at sam@garrisongroup.eu

A communication challenge

Pantene has always offered consumers healthier, more beautiful hair. Although aspirational, communications conveyed this promise in a credible way, with statements like: 'It won't happen overnight, but it will happen one day', assuring consumers that they would start noticing results after 14 days. These were very specific, deliverable promises and helped build credibility in the brand and indeed in the category. However, as more brands entered the hair-care category, offering better looking/healthier/stronger/more beautiful hair, media soon became crowded with 'shampoo commercials'. Over time, consumers found it difficult to distinguish between communications from various brands. In addition, brand claims started becoming edgier to get that bit of extra attention from the consumer. Communications started looking similar, both visually and in the claims that were being made. Slowly, confusion with the communication was replaced by apathy and lack of interest, even disbelief in the claims various brands made. This was potentially dangerous as the category risked becoming generic and commoditized. Pantene had to regain consumer belief in the category overall, and re-establish itself as a brand with proven performance superiority within it. Communications had a huge task.

Pantene successfully employed a combination of 'outside the four walls' and 'inside the four walls' communications to better connect with the consumer and re-establish its unique identity and benefit; the brand emerged in a stronger position. The starting point was to recognize its own strengths and the connection the brand enjoyed with its loyal consumers. Communications could then build on this base and address the disbelief and apathy among the less loyal and disenchanted consumers.

The consumer

In broad general terms, hair-care product consumers are women – students and white-collar workers – living mainly in urban areas. They have university or secondary school education and a higher level of general awareness. The Pantene consumer specifically, is also aware and conscious of good health and a positive self-image. She is outgoing, leads an active, sporty life and is trendy in outlook and behavior. She is aware of and believes in new technology. She likes to remain looking young and attractive to the opposite sex but is unlikely to go in for cosmetic surgery or similar treatments. She is confident, self-assured and believes in looking after herself well. She is likely to spend a lot of money pampering herself – cosmetics, beauty treatments, spas, etc.

A detailed consumer-understanding exercise revealed that the major barrier for communications was disbelief in Pantene's performance superiority. The non-loyal consumer simply did not believe that Pantene delivered the benefit of healthy hair better than her current brand; so she had no reason to switch to it and stay loyal to it. Consequently, while she was aware of Pantene's 'healthy hair' benefit and its scientifically developed formula, since she decided which brand to buy at the store shelf, she was disproportionately influenced by what she saw there – display, shelving, POS material, pricing, etc. Pantene had to carry forward the consumer's positive disposition into the store and leverage that at the point of purchase.

In order to retain her loyalty or to win it back, Pantene's communication clearly had to work in concert outside and inside the four walls; and had to progressively ensure a purchase. The key questions were:

1. What should this message be?
2. How could it be tailored to re-build belief in Pantene's performance superiority?
3. How would communications inside the four walls build on the communications outside?

Communications development

The communication direction was decided based on qualitative research among loyal and non-loyal Pantene consumers. Three directions were tested – the one on air at the time (to be used as a benchmark) and two others. The *Measurable Results* (MR) campaign was the winner and was chosen based on how well it built belief in Pantene's performance superiority, and how unique it was compared to competitive messages. It focused on improving health, was insightful, addressed the main doubt in consumers' minds, and was distinctive.

At a very basic level, MR recognized that Pantene consumers took a variety of steps to look after themselves and improve their overall health – such as a healthy diet, lifestyle or exercise routine. Often compliments from family and friends told them that they were on the right track, and that the results of their efforts were noticed. Equally, they liked to measure the results and know for themselves as well: check their weight, measure their waistline, etc. While this objective measure worked for most health improvement routines, the customer was unable to know for sure if using Pantene was making her hair any healthier. The MR route offered her precisely that.

Communications implementation

The starting point for the MR campaign was a TV commercial that posed the question: 'You know how to measure the results of your diet, but how do you measure the results of your shampoo?' This immediately addressed the issue in her mind and set the stage to differentiate Pantene. The TV campaign launched a new variant, and made a specific promise: '10 times better protection against damage and split ends.' It then went on to introduce Pantene's unique measurement tool – the Sonic Comb – and explain how it could be used to measure hair health and the improvement a shampoo has made. It was designed to make her question her current shampoo choice and whet her appetite to find out more about Pantene. The TV campaign was supported by a comprehensive communication plan including:

1. Advertorials in beauty magazines introducing the concept of measurability, promoting the website and providing details of where hair-health measurement could be done.
2. An interactive component designed to explain how the Sonic Comb worked, to reassure consumers, since the concept and tool were new.
3. POS material focused on measurability, to emphasize the difference from other shampoo brands.
4. Consultants available to measure hair health and answer questions on the topic at specified times in specified stores.

This communication plan was implemented over a three-month period, and ensured that consumers received one consistent message across various media, exploiting the uniqueness and strengths of each medium to deliver that message in the most compelling way. Thus the TV campaign introduced the concept of hair-health measurability in the context of other health-related steps that are measurable. The interactive communication introduced the measurement tool in greater detail and answered questions on how it worked. The advertorials leveraged third-party credibility of the press and placed measurability in the context of health and beauty. Finally, the POS ensured measurability and Pantene's willingness to prove what it promised, were top-of-mind when the customer made her choice. Interactive communication, advertorials and POS also encouraged customers to get their hair tested by beauty consultants. This gave Pantene a powerful means to spend quality one-on-one time with them, not only answering questions and converting

them to the brand, but also understanding their concerns and hair-health related issues.

Communications results

Interactive communications and in-store contact worked well to drive customers to consultations. On average, beauty consultants spent about five minutes with each one, talking to them and testing their hair.

This was truly quality time spent with each customer, much more than would've been possible going door-to-door, or in a beauty parlor. It had more impact than any TV commercial alone, or that any communication outside the four walls could have achieved. It yielded very good results that traditional DM (Direct Marketing) exercises or CRM (Customer Relationship Management) programs would not even dare dream of: 65% of customers who went through consultation converted to the brand.

Country	Unique website visits	In-store contacts	In-store consultations
Hungary	36,230	28,400	11,358
Czech Republic	4,158	38,900	15,557
Croatia	2,437	11,000	4,400
Slovenia	7,113	11,700	4,684
Slovakia	1,654	12,300	4,924
Total	51,592	102,300	40,923
Avg./hour	-	19	7.6 (5.3 to 9.9)

Business results

Pantene shipped 50% extra volume during the period the MR campaign was running, compared to the previous period.

Country	Volume index
Hungary	148
Czech Republic	170
Croatia	175
Slovenia	110
Slovakia	112
Total	149

Conclusion

In order to reclaim its performance superiority status, regain customer belief in its claims, and retain customer loyalty, communications had to work at various levels. Pantene designed a communication program that understood and used various media, and delivered a consistent message outside and inside the four walls. This helped the brand not only convert consumers successfully; it also re-established its performance superiority and differentiated it from other shampoo brands. Crucially, Pantene reclaimed its position as a brand that truly delivers on its promised benefit, and sustained the improved volume and value shares resulting from it.

CHAPTER TEN

Performance Alignment

Now that you know where you want to go (the *Destination*), the means to get you there (*Customer Value*), how you can activate that value (*Motivational Architecture*) and how you can best communicate that value (*Exponential Communications*), you still need to get it done. Getting it done will require the support and commitment of a lot of people, both inside and outside the company. It is not enough to tell them what you want to do; you have to get them involved. Remember the Chinese proverb: 'tell them and they will forget; show them and they will remember; involve them and they will understand.' This also applies to involving the different people and departments within your company.

Performance Alignment is the final planning step in the *Exponential Marketing* process. It is appropriate that we end up with aligning structures and capabilities where we started – with the destination. The destination, inclusive of the goal, the key objectives and the value platform, is the magnetic north of your alignment compass.

Starting with *Destination Planning* allows you to focus your efforts on what you must do to exponentially grow your business. Obviously there are support functions, financial controls, and regulatory requirements that must be met within the operation of any business, but imagine the efficiency as well as the effectiveness that could be captured if you could harness even 70% of your organization's capabilities in driving toward the destination. You just might get there.

Your job in *Performance Alignment* isn't to cut costs, though cuts may be required, or to layer on structures and add lots of new people with new capabilities. Your job as a leader is to guide the evolution from what your business is, into what it must be to reach your destination. And you probably don't need many new people to do that. In most cases you will find that existing employees will be able to learn new skills faster than new employees, if they understand the necessity of the change and the importance of their individual contribution.

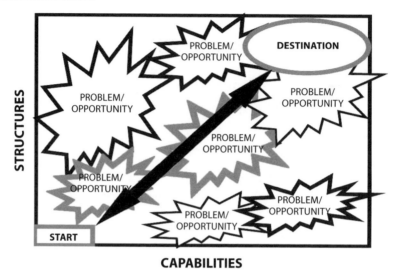

CAPABILITIES

Figure 61: Align capabilities and structures to the *Destination*

Change

A leader, by definition, must take the organization someplace and, to some degree, that process requires change. How you, as a leader, manage change with different constituencies (internally and externally) will make all the difference in whether the destination is achieved, or not.

Doing the same things every day will not deliver new results. To change the result, you must change the things you are doing. As Albert Einstein famously said: 'The significant problems we face cannot be solved at the same level of thinking we were at when we created them.'

Every human being is genetically programmed to resist change and maintain a state of equilibrium – the status quo. Homeostasis evolved so humans can survive under constantly changing conditions We all have a fear of leaving our comfort zone. As you begin to implement your new strategies and establish a new way of thinking, you must understand the underlying fear of change. Change usually brings stress, pain, and fear.

- Fear of the unknown.
- Fear of being redundant.
- Fear of not being able to keep pace.
- Fear of not understanding the new rules.

- Fear of more change that inevitably follows initial change.
- Fear of failure.

What we are really talking about is lack of knowledge. Change is most aggressively resisted when people do not understand the WHAT, WHY, WHERE, HOW, WHEN. Most organizations sit on the details about an impending re-organization for some very good reasons. What they oftentimes are overlooking – or don't understand – is the disruption and tension this causes throughout the entire organization. The quickest way to grind all productivity to a halt is to announce an upcoming re-organization. Even more disruptive is the inevitable leaking of an impending re-organization that management is trying to keep the lid on.

In times of change, communication within the organization needs to increase exponentially. You don't have to spell it all out before all the final decisions are made, but the more you communicate about how and why the organization will change, the better.

Thinking alignment

As you take inventory of the people you have, and begin to align them to the capabilities now required, make sure you take into account their individual ability to adapt, and to grow. The management analogy that there are racehorses and mules in an organization and that you shouldn't confuse the two is utter nonsense. Much more than horses, people have an amazing capacity to adapt and can accept change if properly motivated and encouraged. Historically, there have been far more instances of people riding horses rather than the other way around. This analogy tries to make a point that people are exclusively either linear or spatial thinkers. People have both left- and right-brain functions, and while most of us can be pretty effective at either one, it's usually not at the same time. Try spending a couple of hours writing up your last two months of expense reports, and then go straight into a brainstorming meeting on new communication tools for your brand. You'll feel like you are moving in intellectual concrete for the first half-hour... at least. On the other hand, try to settle down and do the expense reports after the brainstorming session. You'll get frustrated very quickly with the minutia and will push it off to the side for later.

What this means is that we become oriented to a way of thinking that, in turn, becomes self-fulfilling on how we look at our own capabilities as well as the capabilities of others. So-called 'creative thinkers' who use their creativity to excuse their own lack of organization are just lazy. We are all lazy in some regard, but creativity has nothing to do with it. The super organized who have an almost frenetic drive to stay busy will say that they are not creative, but maybe they are just afraid to try something new. We are all creative in some way. Effective managers know how to encourage the 'organizationally challenged' to adopt some disciplines to make them more effective. These exponential leaders can also help the 'creatively challenged' learn how to feel more comfortable with offering their ideas.

Start with yourself. As you embark on a new way of doing things, do some self-discovery and learn how you can best get into the proper frame of mind to successfully complete both spatial and linear tasks. Personally, I find that I need depth of vision when I'm trying to think creatively, and that I am usually best at this sort of thing in the morning. Administrative tasks for me are usually best left until after lunch; I can stay at it for several hours once I start knocking items off my list one by one. That's me. You're different, and so is everyone you work with. Encourage your people to discover for themselves what works best for them as they shift between spatial and linear tasks, and then have them align their schedules and activities to maximize their effectiveness.

Structural alignment

Most organizations are patterned after the traditional military structure of 'command and control', but if you want to break out of the existing way of doing things – something your new destination and strategies will likely require – you will need an organizational structure that is flatter and more interactive. Flatter organizations rely more on the manager's ability to 'lead and influence'. Managers who lead and influence have a high degree of trust in their people and don't spend much time checking up on everyone just to make sure they aren't making mistakes. Paperwork and administration are minimized to include only those elements that are absolutely necessary rather than providing a mass of information upwards so that someone high above can feel more comfortable with how firmly in control they are. They have confidence in themselves, as well as in their co-workers.

Many otherwise successful organizations succumb to someone's need to create an empire. Miniature kingdoms in an organization usually lead to turf battles and often succeed in creating impenetrable borders within the organization, rather than encouraging the cooperation necessary to create sustainable customer value. In marketing departments, miniature empires inhibit the process of *Communicating Exponentially*, and of delivering value both inside and outside the four walls of the selling environment. The traditional fight between sales and marketing is over. It has been for a long time – it's just that some people are slower to recognize the inescapable fact that marketing is sales, and that sales is a lot more than entertaining customers. Sales people are front-line marketers. Brand managers must be effective as rear echelon staffers who provide the front-line sales guys with the tools and weapons they need to win in the trenches.

'Marketing is too important to be left to the marketing guys'. The wall Sergio Zyman was trying to break down when he first made that statement 10 years ago was the notion that only the marketing guys understand the customer.

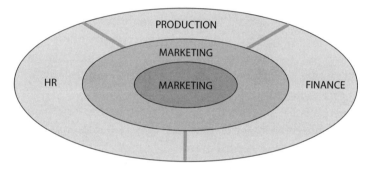

Figure 62: Marketing's role in the organization (Source: Philip Kotler's *Principles of Marketing*)

In a command and control world, the approach where marketing manages and interprets all customer information for the rest of the organization might be preferred (Figure 62). But in your exponential growth world, there is a fundamental need for everyone in the organization to understand and deliver on customer value (Figure 63).

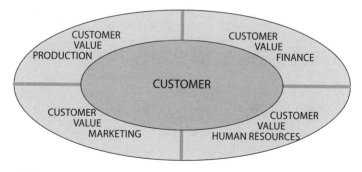

Figure 63: A customer-centric organization (Source: Philip Kotler's *Principles of Marketing*)

Motivational alignment

I have a simple HR philosophy that is closely aligned with my marketing philosophy. I believe that people will consistently take positive action if it is meaningful for them to do so. In other words, if it is in their best interests to do so. As we know from brand architectures, meaningfulness is usually driven by a motivating combination of functional and emotional factors. If you want someone to perform a job well – and be dedicated to that job over the long term – you must consider both their emotional and functional needs.

Just as an effective strategy involves a win-win overlap of being meaningful to the customer and being meaningful to the company, the same overlap must exist between the employee and the company. If employees believe that performing a job well – such as developing new ideas to deliver better customer value – is in line with what they want to achieve within their own personal and professional goals, they will move mountains for you and your business. And just like the process of getting to know your customers better, you need to better understand your employees holistically – their life goals as well as professional goals.

You have probably seen a lot of job descriptions. Most of them are task-driven and do not consider the emotional values a job may offer to a potential worker. Try adapting the same *Motivational Architecture* format you used to make your brand more meaningful, to making the position you want to fill more meaningful (Figure 64).

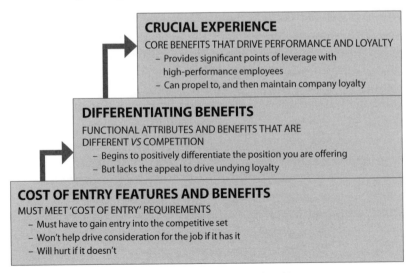

CRUCIAL EXPERIENCE
CORE BENEFITS THAT DRIVE PERFORMANCE AND LOYALTY
  – Provides significant points of leverage with high-performance employees
  – Can propel to, and then maintain company loyalty

DIFFERENTIATING BENEFITS
FUNCTIONAL ATTRIBUTES AND BENEFITS THAT ARE DIFFERENT *VS* COMPETITION
  – Begins to positively differentiate the position you are offering
  – But lacks the appeal to drive undying loyalty

COST OF ENTRY FEATURES AND BENEFITS
MUST MEET 'COST OF ENTRY' REQUIREMENTS
  – Must have to gain entry into the competitive set
  – Won't help drive consideration for the job if it has it
  – Will hurt if it doesn't

Figure 64: Employee *Motivational Architecture*

Just as in dealing with customers – everything communicates. Everything you do or say in the workplace will affect the value employees place on working at your company. For one thing, you will find that they probably are not favorably motivated by either word: boss or employee. Two very human companies, IKEA and Starbucks, have taken to calling their employees associates (IKEA) and partners (Starbucks). But titles are only interesting if you back them up in aligning the motivations of the job with the motivations of the people working in the organization. IKEA and Starbucks align motivations with training and progressive incentives from the most senior people in the company all the way to the cashier – which is one of the core reasons they are as successful as they are and have the kind of customer and employee loyalty that they do.

Don't underestimate the importance of simply enjoying your job. A great example is the Pike Place Fish Market in Seattle. If you think your job is difficult, try being a fishmonger. You start at the crack of dawn unloading smelly fish from the boats and then packing them on ice in the shop display windows. Then the customers come in with questions you have heard 2000 times before. They bring their indecisiveness and you need to deal with this in a positive and helpful manner to make sure you make the sale. You would expect employee turnover to be about 80% … per month!

But not at the Pike Place Fish Market! The owner decided some years back that how they all reacted to the job, to the customers, and to each other was basically up to each of them. They could choose to be miserable about what on the surface seems to be a pretty lousy job, or they could choose a different attitude. Choosing your attitude is just one of the four fundamental components that drives the FISH philosophy these guys created that has turned the situation around at the Pike Place Fish Market. This innovative, yet incredibly basic philosophy has not only resulted in unbelievable employee loyalty, but unsurpassed customer service levels that became the inspiration for Howard Shultz when he was creating the highly successful Starbucks chain so renowned for its employee loyalty and outstanding customer service. The four components are:

1. **Choose your attitude.** When you come to work each day, you have a choice. You can choose to make the most of it and enjoy what it is you do, or not. The choice is yours. It always has been, but some people just choose to blame others or circumstances instead of doing anything positive to improve the situation.
2. **Make their day.** This applies to customers and co-workers alike. Once you have chosen a positive attitude about how you approach your work, you

can create little opportunities throughout the day that will make a difference in the customer experience or in your daily interactions with your colleagues. The knock-on effect of making someone else's day is that you will find that it makes your day as well.

3. **Be there.** That's it. Just be there during those moments you are interacting with others. Don't play with your phone in the middle of a conversation, or answer emails on your computer during a meeting. Don't be thinking about what you will be doing later when you are assisting a customer, or bother with anything else that may be going through your mind at any given moment. Focus. Be there in mind, body and spirit in the moment and you will notice a huge difference in how people relate to you; they will appreciate you because you are actively demonstrating that you appreciate them.

4. **Play.** As adults, a lot of us have forgotten the importance of play. Play with the customers, make little jokes, create fun little rituals like they do at the Pike Place Fish Market such as when they all shout out customer requests in little rhymes as they toss a fish from the display area to the counter to be wrapped for purchase. You may not have fish to throw around, but I am sure you can find ample opportunities to play if you want to. Play means fun for everyone. Playing jokes that are funny at the expense of others is not constructive and adds no value. Fun is when everyone plays – including your customers!

This might all sound rather silly on one hand and too basic on the other, but it works because it is based on how people fundamentally relate to each other and the world around them. Maybe over time we have tried too hard on the thinking and achieving part as business people and not enough on the emotional benefits of simply enjoying what we do. Check out the FISH guys on the web; buy one of the books several people have written about them; or make a trip to the Pike Place Fish Market next time you are in the Seattle. But most of all, give it a shot, and try these fundamental workplace philosophies in your environment, regardless of your current position or task.

Exponential strategy

Like marketing and its core of providing customer value, strategy must also move from exclusive to inclusive – from the domain of a few to the involvement of everyone in the organization. A limiting factor in many companies is that they think about strategy in such lofty terms that it has become detached from what is really going on in the business. Strategy only sounds like a big word. Strategy is about finding the best way to accomplish something. It is the means whereby you accomplish an objective. A good strategy does a better and more efficient job of achieving an objective than a bad strategy. Pretty basic stuff. So, why make it complex and exclude everyone in the organization from thinking about how best to accomplish their particular objectives? Everyone in your organization can and should think strategically about what it is that they do. And to do that, you, as a manager, need to start by stripping all the lofty trappings from the word 'strategy' and get to what strategy really means at its core – finding the most effective and efficient means of accomplishing an objective. Tactics are the details of actually getting it done. To be effective, people – regardless of the level or function in your organization – need to be adept at both: strategies and tactics.

Now add *exponential*. Finding the killer strategy is not just about deciding the best course to get to a better place, but also about powering up the organization so that growth-generating ideas aren't being pursued only from above – instead, everybody is thinking about how to get there faster and smarter. Strategy shouldn't be 'owned' on the basis of corporate hierarchy. It shouldn't be something that is simply passed down from above. Strategy should become a way of thinking that is embraced and practiced at all levels in the organization.

Unfortunately, 'strategic' can be one of the most judgmental words used in business. Too often it is used to describe a person's depth of thinking. 'Linda is a strategic thinker and Jim is more of a tactician.' Who do you think is going to be picked for a promotion? The first truth is that the difference between a strategy and a tactic is often merely a question of how you draw your circles. One person's strategy might simply be another person's tactic. The second truth is that everyone has both a spatial and linear side to his or her brain. We all come from the factory hardwired with the capability to think both tactically and strategically. Don't make the mistake of using the word strategy as an attempt to separate the thinkers from the doers in your organization. I would prefer to have *doers* who *think* in my company, wouldn't you? Anyone can become 'strategic' in what they do if they are allowed to participate in how they accomplish their job. You can approach a task strategically, or tactically. It's best that you do both, one after the other.

The key to unlocking the strategic capability in your organization is to assign objectives rather than just merely tasks. Give a subordinate or a colleague an objective and ask that they come back with their strategy, as well as the details on how they intend to achieve that objective. Imagine the exponential power of that!

Most companies put a premium on the necessity for everyone below to understand the strategy from above in order to ensure that the tactical execution is strategically aligned. A strategic tactician? You're thinking that those two words go together about as well as 'pop culture', 'military intelligence' or 'jumbo shrimp'. Again, the key is that you don't assign a task, but that you encourage the different people in your organization to think about how they can best accomplish a particular objective. That objective may seem like nothing more than a small (tactical) detail to you, but it could be that you have not had the time or personal motivation to imagine other options about how that 'detail' could be done better. Or perhaps you simply do not know that area of the business well enough to come up with any 'strategic' ideas about how to do it better. But I'll bet the guy who does it every day could, and would… if you only encouraged him to do so. Everyone up and down the organization needs to think strategically, both in terms of how they align the execution of their objective with the strategy from above, but also in terms of how they can power up the execution to have a greater impact on providing – you guessed it – customer value. After all, improving customer value is what capturing exponential growth is all about.

When I was the managing director of Coca-Cola, a core strategy to win the market-share battle with Pepsi was to integrate Coca-Cola into the everyday lives of local consumers by making it more relevant to their daily needs and desires than any other soft drink. I presented this strategy to the chairman of the Coca-Cola Company in my annual business plan and he approved it. As strategically as I approached this relevance issue, the truth was that to the chairman, the local market-share battle was just another tactic within his core strategy of increasing Coca-Cola shareholder value. My relevance strategy had to link upstream to the global strategy by producing greater sales volume growth that would make our new plants more efficient to allow a faster return on invested capital.

Now let's take it a step further. My marketing manager was responsible for executing much of the tactical detail of my local relevance strategy. However, he didn't think of his responsibilities as tactical; he was thinking strategically. One of his strategies was to achieve greater relevance by building a strong association between Coca-Cola and Christmas. He recognized the opportunity of Christmas, not only in terms of the higher volumes that occur during the holiday period, but also because of the multidimensional appeal of Christmas across all age groups. Christmas is a time of the year when teenagers, moms, grandmothers and little eight-year-old brothers all come together in an emotionally shared experience. His specific strategy was to create an integrated marketing program that tugged on the emotional strings of our consumers through a seasonal tie-in with the local cultural icons. It was a strategic breakthrough for him, but it was still only a tactic to me – an executional detail of my local relevance strategy.

Let's take it even further to illustrate how the whole thing continued to grow exponentially as it gathered momentum. One level below the marketing director on the organizational chart, the brand manager for Coca-Cola took what was a tactical element of the Christmas program – the on-pack promotional gift – and built it into a brilliant in-home family involvement strategy. This brand manager recognized that getting the mother, father and children to spend time together in building a small model of a typical countryside town during Christmas – courtesy of Coca-Cola when they bought two, 2-liter bottles at the grocery store – would involve our consumers with the brand in a more meaningful and relevant way. And the strategic flow didn't stop there. The brand manager then assigned the tactical execution of his gift promotion strategy to an agency to turn it into a special event to draw greater attention to the promotion in the countryside. The event agency manager thought about all that had been done upstream, and how he could add value to the overall strategy. He then developed a Coca-Cola caravan promotion that resembled the Coca-Cola trucks in the television commercial. The strategy was to have families physically come out together to see the beautiful lights of the Coca-Cola caravan as it traveled through their own small town. They could then build a reminder of that family moment with the Christmas gift pack on 2-liter bottles, and buy more product.

On the sales side, the sales manager developed a strategy to leverage the strength of the television ads, the on-pack gift, and the Christmas caravan idea, to gain important end-aisle displays in all the major chain stores. I could go on to include several other people who expanded the impact of the program downstream by adding their own strategic thinking, and describe how the production guys figured out the best way to attach the gift packs in the plant, and so on, but I think you get the point. The power of strategic thinking flowed through the organization – gaining momentum as it passed into all areas of the business – and finally to the consumer by providing the best soft drink value available for Christmas time. And all of this resulted in market-share growth, more sales, and a more efficient plant with a faster ROI that allowed the chairman of the company to deliver greater shareholder value.

Trust the strategic thinking power of people you work with, and try this exponential strategy approach. You will be amazed by how much customer value power can be generated if you encourage people across your organization to think strategically about how they execute their tasks and functions. It is simple to do – only two steps are required to unleash the exponential power of strategic thinking throughout the organization:

1. Make sure that everyone understands the meaning of customer value and how it applies to each of them. This ensures that instead of just doing things, they are doing the right things – thus adding customer value.

2. Assign objectives rather than tasks. Ask people to think about their objectives and come back to you with ideas (i.e., strategies) about how they can build or deliver greater customer value in order to accomplish each particular objective.

It is essential to gain the enthusiastic participation in strategy of different people in the organization. This means that you must recognize and appreciate their individual contributions.

Before Coca-Cola, back when I started my career at Procter & Gamble, I was surprised that one of the most valuable incentives the company offered to employees was simple recognition. I remember that salesmen would joke about the recognition they would be rewarded with (rather than big prizes or monetary incentives) if they won a particular sales contest – but they would work their butts off to achieve what they jokingly called 'immense prestige'. Recognition is often the simplest and most powerful motivation of all. People inherently want to be recognized and appreciated for what they do. This doesn't mean that tying bonuses and profit sharing to performance is not important; it is. But recognition in itself is a powerful reward. Everyone is able to add strategic value if only you would let them, and they are more than willing to do so if you would simply recognize them for it.

So, do all these strategists running around in the organization need to see the big picture? Of course they need to, and it is your job as a leader to make sure they do.

Exponential leadership

Think more about 'leading' and less about 'managing'. Many managers pride themselves on their ability to keep their arms spread around a lot of difficult activities at the same time. They often feel irresistibly drawn to personally solve even small problems as they come up. They also tend to stay very busy. Leaders find a way to rise above all of that. They understand that simply having time to think, and the insights and ideas gained from that thinking, are invaluable. The most important managerial skill required for today's leaders in super-complicated and highly competitive environments is the ability to separate the 'must dos' from the 'can dos' and the 'should dos'. I'll take intense focus over incredible energy any day. 'Busy' and 'effective' do not automatically go hand in hand.

Exponential leaders go even further than mere focus. They have discovered the power of spreading and inspiring leadership throughout the organization. A very brief definition of a leader, rather than a manager, is that the leader has developed both the business understanding to figure out where to go and the human understanding to get everyone involved in the process of getting there. And as a result, she gets there faster – *exponentially faster*. These exponential leaders know that the secret of getting the emotional commitment from subordinates is to understand what motivates people as human beings. These leaders have the flexibility to adjust assignments to incorporate their employees' personal as well as professional goals – both matter.

Think less about control, and more about influencing. 'Command and control' managers believe they are avoiding problems and 'saving' the company by controlling activities so tightly that nothing can go wrong. At best, they achieve an error-free company. But what about finding new ways to do things that take customer value even higher? 'Lead and influence' managers grow value by encouraging others to do better.

Exponential leaders inspire leadership in others. They don't just personally light a fire in an organization; they create an atmosphere and an environment where thousands of fires are lit – everyday.

The exponential value chain

You know that you need to involve the customers to achieve customer value, and you know you need to involve your employees to do that. Think outside your company as well, because in most businesses there are a lot of contacts and factors that affect customers that you can't possibly control, but which you definitely should do your best to influence. They affect customer value – that's why they call it the 'value chain'. These are the suppliers upstream, distributors and wholesalers downstream and the retailers and dealerships right down to the customer. You must market through the value chain. The power of customer value grows exponentially as it goes through the chain when you ensure that everyone from distributors to front-line sales people, not only understand the brand architecture and its related benefits, they enthusiastically embrace it. The Chinese proverb advising you to 'involve them so that they will understand' applies for sales people, distributor reps, and retailers, just as it does with end-user consumers.

Marketing understands the target's needs and then meets those needs in a meaningful, deliverable and defendable way. Market to the customer. Market to the sales force. Market to the distributors. Market to the retailers. Just as you will enjoy customer loyalty when you market real benefits (functional and emotional) with customers in a meaningful, deliverable and defendable way, so, too, will you enjoy success when you market through the value chain with the same sort of value-added thinking.

I often hear marketers complain that the sales guys think they are marketing experts. More than those marketers realize! A sustainable advantage you can have as a marketer is to treat the rest of the organization – especially the sales force – as marketers. Be inclusive and involve them in the marketing – share the customer data and seek their counsel. Not only will the sales guys understand what it is that you are trying to achieve with the brand, they will become enthusiastic proponents of the brand strategy and all the unique ways they can power your brand's benefits on to the end-customer. They also know a lot about the customer and the rest of the value chain, so the communication should absolutely go both ways.

Once again, the power of *Exponential Customer Value* comes from getting everyone in the organization to understand why the customer values your brand. Marketing through the value chain is where the rubber meets the road in achieving *Exponential Customer Value* because these are the people – internally and externally – who are closest to your customers. Leverage the exponential power of involving every link in the value chain in the marketing and selling of your brand.

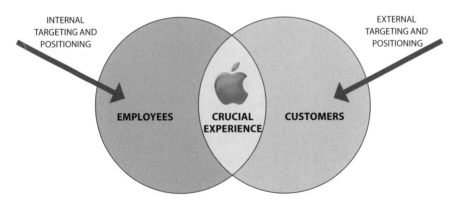

Figure 65: Apple builds on the strong overlap between employee and customer value/motivations

Do the math. If you work very hard as a good marketing manager, you can communicate effectively with a maximum of maybe 100 sales people to ensure that they understand and embrace the brand's value. Now imagine that these 100 sales guys go out and call on 1000 distributors' reps with all the necessary tools so that they can make sure those people understand and embrace the brand's value. The distributors and their sales people are then armed and ready so that they can then involve 25,000 retailers. Those retailers can now understand and enthusiastically embrace the brand, and they have tools and information they need to sell 10,000,000 customers. Get the picture? *Performance Alignment* is spending a lot more time than you probably have up until now marketing to the value chain.

I had a policy at Coca-Cola that each individual in the organization had to be able to participate with input into every marketing program before it was shown to customers. That wasn't easy to do because we had over 1300 people performing a lot of different activities around the clock throughout the country. Members of the marketing staff at Coca-Cola, including myself, would often travel out to the various sales centers to discuss what we were planning on doing in the days and weeks ahead. And, of course, we included production – even in the middle of the night with the graveyard (23:00–7:00) production shift. Not only did we get some good ideas from holding these input sessions, we also ensured that everyone understood what we were doing and why we were doing it. This knowledge empowered them to incorporate their understanding into how they preformed their own job, whatever it was. And with their input, they helped us do our job better and more efficiently. We also created a thousand points of communication to end-user consumers.

Think about it. The guy on the filling line who is watching the glass bottles go by and making sure everything is okay may also be the head of a rather extended family. Imagine one Sunday that at his family dinner someone remarked that they heard about a new activity Coca-Cola was running. In most companies he would have to shrug and admit he didn't know anything about it. We took a different approach and armed him with enough information so that he would not only feel good about where he worked and why he worked there, he could also spread by word of mouth why it is important and significant to Coca-Cola customers. Getting up in front of a hundred production workers in the middle of the night before they start their shift isn't just a good HR idea, it's good business; it's good marketing.

Remember the *Success Dashboard* from *Destination Planning*? If you believe that employees are your most important business asset – and you should –

then doesn't it make sense that employee satisfaction and motivation should drive your customer value platform? Take another look now at a *Success Dashboard* that does just that (Figure 66). And just as how you want your customer to think, feel and act is what determines your customer value platform, the same ingredients determine your employee value platform. And, just as you should use measurable objectives for customer actions, so should you with employee actions in the work place.

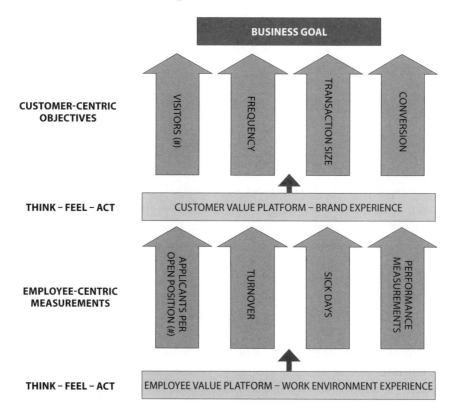

Figure 66: The impact of employee motivations on customer motivations (© The Garrison Group)

By utilizing *Exponential Marketing*, we were able to reverse our market share position for Coca-Cola in Hungary from a 36–54 disadvantage when I arrived to the 60–21 advantage Coca-Cola enjoys today versus its major competitor. It was also important that we quickly achieved double-digit volume and profit gains that demonstrated our effectiveness as well as the efficiency of our marketing. However, the most significant measurement for me was the employee turnover number of only 3% during the three years we implemented *Expo-*

nential Marketing in Hungary. Most FMCGs at the time were suffering from turnover of over 25%. It wasn't that people loved me – or any of the other managers; it wasn't even about how much we paid them. It was about each of us being able to win personally and professionally. Our management team learned to understand the motivations of our employees and we made a concerted effort to line up the roles they had in the organization with the goals they had as individuals. It's not easy, but none of this *Exponential Marketing* is meant to be easy – just effective.

What about corporate social responsibility (CSR)?

These days, companies are becoming increasingly concerned about CSR and the role of the company in the community. Some companies do it because they believe they can and should have a more positive role in society. Others see it mostly as a defensive move in the event something goes wrong within the operation of their business in the future; they can then fall back on the defense that they have been good corporate citizens. I prefer the first motivation; but regardless, it is truly a good thing that corporations are taking more responsibility for involving themselves in the communities in which they operate and sell their products.

In most cases, company management will get excited about this new sense of social activism and go on to develop some sort of corporate manifesto or mission statement that describes its noble intent… and then that's the end of it. That's too bad, because a real opportunity was missed by not integrating the CSR strategy into the business. Others, who are more personally committed and determined not to have just a flowery statement on their lobby wall, make a more determined effort to make social responsibility an integral part of business and how they work with external suppliers (i.e., Starbuck's Fair Trade coffee initiative) and with their employees (i.e., Coca-Cola lending employees to work with the United Way charity in local communities) and other operational aspects of the business. This is all very good and some consumers will actually recognize the effort and buy the company's products in support. But usually not. Consumers will buy the product for the same reasons they have always bought a product – because it provides meaningful value. Unless the CSR efforts of a company can actually affect the customer's perception of value, CSR should not be imposed on the brand strategy just because it is perceived by management to be the 'right thing to do'. In fact, CSR should not be imposed on any area of the business unless it can be determined that such activity will positively affect the business itself through better employee acquisition and retention, good local government relations, etc. That doesn't mean that a company shouldn't operate with integrity and comply with all local and global regulations and laws – it absolutely should. But a company should not take it as its 'responsibility' the solving society's problems above and beyond the interests of its business. Or if it does, then the shareholders must know this and agree to these actions that may negatively impact the financial performance of the business in the interest of the greater good. It may sound strange, but I would seriously question the integrity of a manager who pushed a company to support a cause or community activity he personally felt strongly about but had little to no real impact on the success of the business. Being a 'good guy' with someone else's money and resources to enhance your own personal standing in the community or sense of social worth is less than admirable, in my opinion. If you have a strong personal interest in a cause, then you should support it personally.

Businesses can and should do good things for their communities, the environment and their employees because it is in their business interest to do so. It saves the company money if it operates with greater energy efficiency. It saves the company money if it retains employees longer and those employees are happy. It can even make more money if those employees are so motivated that they develop new products and ideas that take the business to a whole new level. In many cases, a company can jump into a society issue such as assimilation of minorities, child labor prevention, global warming, etc., and improve its business performance sometimes in the short term, but more likely over the long term. I call this CSO (Corporate Social Optimization) and I believe that a company that benefits from doing good is much more likely to stay in business and continue doing good things. The key is to tie the doing good to doing good business – the two do not have to be mutually exclusive.

Most of the time, a company's CSR or even its CSO activities will affect the bottom line, but they will seldom have a major effect on the top line – driving new customers to the brand or getting existing customers to buy more or spend more money on the purchase. Customers will become increasingly aware of the role of the company in society and over time their positive feelings about these companies with translate into purchase decisions – even in emerging markets. But it will be a slow build and marketers have to be extremely careful about how they communicate these social values to consumers for a potential long-term payout when they need to keep their eye on the short-term goal of driving meaningful brand benefits to produce sales revenue today.

The brand halo

Feeling good about the brand you are buying and consuming is certainly an emotional benefit, but as we discussed in Chapter 8 *Motivational Architectures*, all three levels of the architecture (*Cost of Entry Features and Benefits, Differentiating Benefits,* and *Crucial Experience*) must be linked to one another – otherwise the brand will become schizophrenic, with certain aspects of the brand being completely unrelated to others. So simply plopping down an emotional experience related to a company's CSR activity on top of the differentiating functional benefits of your brand will probably not be effective; over time, you and your team will tend to focus only on the lower-level functional benefits due to the very real need to drive volume today. But the brand will be weaker in this instance because functional benefits have not been heightened to the level of an emotional experience.

Values related to how the company does business in the community (global or local) and how it treats its employees can have an impact on brand-benefit areas such as trust and continuity, for example, but it typically is not so directly related to the emotions flowing out of the functional benefits of the brand. Figure 67 illustrates how company reputation and the values of employees can create a brand halo that can extend down onto the brand to have some impact brand value.

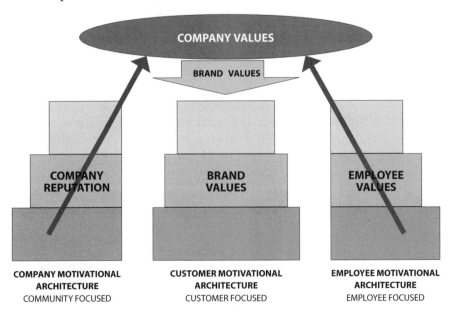

Figure 67: Integrating company reputation and employee values with brand value

So, the question is not whether or not you should become more involved in making a positive impact on the community and on the lives of your employees – of course you should. The question is how you choose to do that so that it also positively impacts business results. You must understand how social activism can affect your brand and also recognize its limitations. As with everything else in *Exponential Marketing*, the answer to what can and cannot affect brand value lies with the customer.

The power of momentum

The essence of *Exponential Marketing* is momentum in creating and delivering customer value. Momentum begins when you make the decision to grow your strategic brainpower by pushing strategic thinking out through the organization by assigning objectives rather than tasks. It takes hold when you establish the relentless conviction that increasing customer value is the only meaningful way to grow your business at the top line as well at the bottom line.

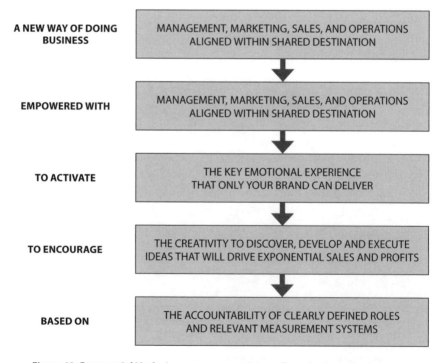

Figure 68: *Exponential Marketing* gets everyone internally and externally aligned in doing what they do best

And finally, as we all know, the most difficult thing about momentum is in taking that very first step – getting the ball rolling. So, get started. There is a lot of work to be done, and a lot of growth to be captured.

> *It's not enough to know, you have to apply your knowledge.*
> *It's not enough to want something, you have to do it.*
> Johann Goethe (1749–1832)

CASE STUDY

Raiffeisen Banks utilizes IT to plug marketing into the organization

By Julia Vahidova

Julia is a consultant at the Garrison Group where she has worked in the beverage, consumer electronics and retail sectors, particularly in the area of customer insights. She has also been active proponent in applying technological innovations as message delivery platforms. Julia is a native of Moscow.

Raiffeisen Bank has had a very rapid rise to third position in the Romanian market. The acquisition of the Romanian state-owned Banca Agricola network of over 220 banking outlets throughout the country and an employee headcount of over 4000 people gained Raiffeisen an almost immediate presence in the market. But with it came a massive integration challenge.

The first step in the integration was to establish operating standards in line with what the Vienna-based bank expected from its operations in 15 CEE countries. Almost simultaneously, there was a physical makeover that created the most customer-friendly banking environment Romanians have ever experienced.

After completing an exhaustive customer segmentation and insight mining process, the Romanian marketing director felt his small group of marketers located on the fifth floor of the bank's headquarters in Bucharest had found the pulse of the customer. His team then went about the process of developing *Motivational Architectures* targeting over different 30 banking products to 22 specific customer segments. The team briefed agencies and developed communication materials that connected emotionally and functionally to the customers as they moved through their daily lives outside the walls of the bank with targeted messages for Raiffeisen credit cards, consumer loans, and a range of savings products – just a few of the areas the bank addressed as a result of its enhanced knowledge of the customer base in Romania.

But beyond some posters and brochures inside the 220-branch network, most of the impact the team had was on driving purchase intent outside the bank itself. However, all the purchase intent in the world doesn't create any real value to the bank unless it is transformed into actual purchase behavior. For that the marketing guys needed the participation of all the people in daily contact with customers across the entire network. Rather than fight to increase control of what happens with customers inside the bank – the classic battle of pitching the marketing department against the sales department that is currently underway in many banks – the Romanian Raiffeisen marketing team went the other way.

It just took five minutes with the marketing team members to immediately recognize that they were definitely not the 'command and control' types – quite the opposite. Armed with customer information and insights that could be extremely beneficial to everyone from front-line sales people in the banks all the way to key account managers calling on SMEs (small and medium enterprises), the team looked for a 'lead and influence' mechanism to get that customer knowledge out to as many people throughout the network – all 4000 employees if possible. The question quickly became 'What's possible?'

The problem

Customizing product benefits and messages to specific customer segments in the bank may sound like a good idea, but making it happen is something else. How do you identify different customers on-site in over 400 branch locations now existing across Romania? How do you make the needs of different customers clear and actionable? How do you get the right tools to the front-line sales people at any given moment? What are the best cross-selling opportunities for a particular customer type?

In other words, how can you turn every sales officer at every outlet into a marketing person? How do you transfer your knowledge and make sure that they know all customer segments so thoroughly that they can determine what customer is sitting in front of them at any given moment, and what benefits of which banking products should be communicated to that specific customer? How can the marketing department in Bucharest help bank employees across 400 locations sell more banking products 'to more people, for more money, more often' and, don't forget, do this more efficiently?

The tried and not so true solution was to spend considerable money, time, and resources training sales people to improve customer service. But then, even after training, you still cannot be sure that they will use what they have learned and will not fall into the usual way of doing things because of time pressure or simple complacency. The sales force was already suffering from information overload, so piling on more books and more training was probably not the best means to the 'lead and influence' situation the marketing team was intent on creating.

The solution

If you want to turn your sales force into marketing guys, one of the first things you must do is to give them the tools to accomplish the job. Thus, the *Raiffeisen Marketing Toolbox* was born. The Toolbox was designed by the marketing department to assist the sales force, primarily the Front Desk Officers, in their everyday tasks – i.e., selling value-added products to customers. The Toolbox is driven by a software application that guides and arms the Raiffeisen sales force with the enhanced customer knowledge that is linked to the right product with the right sales message. The software was developed to support them during the entire selling process – from determining what kind of customer is sitting in front of them at any given moment, to providing the product descriptions and sales materials targeted to that specific customer. It also offers the sales officer the best potential to cross-sell products, thereby facilitating an important business-building post-sales element.

Built-in flexibility

The sales officers can approach the sales situation in two ways – from the perspective of selling to a specific customer and then accessing the appropriate product data (the customer block), or from the position of wanting to sell a specific product and needing to figure out who is the best customer to go after (the product block). The Toolbox is a multidimensional tool that can support the sale of a specific product, or can be utilized when the sales officer needs to sell  more to a specific customer target. Also included is a knowledge database that provides them with a wide range of support materials from self-training to branch identification standards.

For users, the Toolbox looks like a website. Sales officers open it with Internet Explorer and navigate it in the normal way – just like navigating the Internet.

Product block

In a bank – as in most other businesses – the sales force typically has objectives to sell more of a specific product over a given time period. The key questions are: how should they sell it, who they should sell it to, and which sales tools they should use.

The Toolbox supports this task right from the Start page. The sales officer can click on *Determine Key Product Opportunities* and then select the product he needs to sell. The first thing he'll see is a general *product description*. Although the description is not yet targeted to any of the customer segments, it still goes a step forward from the 'business as usual' way of describing only the features of the banking product, to communicating the key functional and emotional benefits from the product's *Motivational Architecture*. Thus, from the very beginning, the sales officer is already moving beyond the usual pure product-features-driven sales, and into the benefits that the product can provide to the customer.

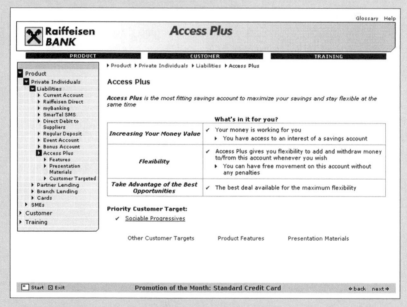

The next level of customization is in clicking *Priority Customer Target*. A *Priority Customer Target* is one of the segments that the Raiffeisen marketing team determined from in-depth research to be the communications focus for this specific product. This is the customer target that the sales officers should better understand in order to sell more. When they click on the link, they get to a page with deeper insight into customer needs – the key benefits and even the language of the description is closely tied to the psychographics of the customer; the customer then thinks and feels that this is a product for her with a focused proposition on how this product can better fit her life and her financial needs. This customer/product-specific page tells the sales officers what they need to communicate in order to complete their task of selling this product. It also contains a link to the full description of the customer target to give quick access to an even deeper understanding, if they need it. A link to the page with the product's *Presentation Materials* designed specifically for this customer target goes to the next step of arming the sales force with the communication tools needed to close the sale (leaflets, brochures, presentations, etc.). Here they can open the files and choose the most appropriate materials to print for the particular situation.

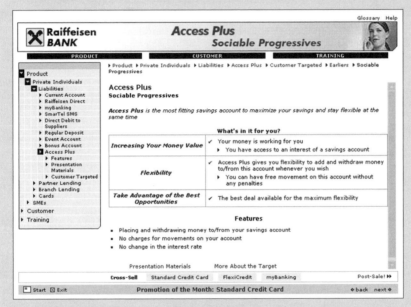

But if they still feel they need to sell this product to a customer target other than the *Priority Customer Target*, they can click the *Other Customer Targets* link and choose from the list.

Customer block

One sales officer's task is to sell more banking products to a specific target at the point where he encounters that customer. For example, depending on the location of their branch, some of the customers that come in may be identified as being from the segment called *Social Progressives*. The Toolbox can help the sales officer determine which products he should sell that type of customer and which sales materials he should use.

In order to determine this, he can open the Toolbox and click *Identify New Customer Opportunities* from the Start page. He can then navigate through the customer groups to the page for this customer segment.

Customer Segment Page

Here he can find a short description of the customer that quickly captures a few key insights. If he would like to get a deeper understanding, he can click on the *Detailed Description* link and find details on demographics, attitudes, values, hopes and aspirations, as well as lifestyle.

But if he feels he knows the target pretty well already from previous experience with the Toolbox relative to that customer segment, he can directly choose one of the *Recommended Products* to source product information that best fit this customer's needs, wants and lifestyle. The sales officer can then go to the *Customer/Product-specific* page to determine the best manner of selling this product to that customer. Or he can choose any other product that he thinks is appropriate to sell to the customer, based on the information easily at hand in the Toolbox.

Assisting the customer now

Another sales situation arises when the customer is already sitting, in the branch, in front of the sales officer. This situation is characterized by intense time pressure – the customers don't have much patience, and will not tolerate waiting in line for long. The sales officer can use the Toolbox to quickly identify what customer type is sitting in front of him, and proceed accordingly.

The Toolbox allows the sales officer to do that with a very quick and concise questionnaire. With the customer's permission, he takes a couple of minutes to quickly learn more about her with a few carefully chosen questions that identify the customer as belonging to a specific segment. A few clicks through the questions and the sales officer is linked directly to the page for the customer type in front of him.

Supporting tools

An important task for the banking sales force is to cross-sell other banking products to the customer. Prior to the Toolbox, cross-selling success would depend on the sales officer's knowledge of the customers and all the banking products, and his ability to understand which products were more likely to be sold to this customer – a lot to ask a sales officer when over 30 products are available and more coming available each month. Consequently, cross-selling is very hard to support. In the Toolbox, from every customer-specific page, the sales officer has a direct access to the cross-selling products that are most likely to appeal to the customer target he is currently dealing with. This makes it easy at any point in the selling process to offer the customer other products that she might also need, and to describe these products in the best possible way to close another sale.

The same approach was also taken to the *promotions of the month*. This bar always stays at the bottom of the Toolbox as a constant reminder to the sales force about this month's promotion; it leads to the description of the product, its features and benefits, and the essence of promotion – a 'Why not now?' call to customer action.

After the sales officer has profiled the customer, sold her the products she wanted, and cross-sold her products she may also need, he should not forget about the *post-sale* phase of any selling process. The Toolbox closes the loop by suggesting what to say to the customer after the contract is signed. He should invite the customer to contact him with any questions that may arise. It also gives the

sales officer the opportunity to send an e-mail to the back office in case there is a need to contact the customer with more information on her finances and banking products.

Next steps

The Toolbox that the Raiffeisen Romanian marketing team developed is in itself already a very powerful tool to accomplish the goal of integrating marketing into the selling process. But the marketing team is still searching for a way to do even more to make marketing – delivering customer value – everyone's job at Raiffeisen Romania. It is looking for more ways to make it even better and more effective.

One of the next steps to bring the Toolbox to an even higher level will be to integrate it with the customer database for a supercharged all-in-one CRM. Intranet capabilities (bandwidth) across Romania are still short of the high-speed connection necessary at this point, but not for long. Soon communication upgrades will open opportunities of even higher sales customization. The customer type would be stored in the database and it would be enough for the sales officers just to enter the customer's ID number and the Toolbox would immediately show them this customer's type, the products she already has with the bank, her contact information, and previous usage data necessary for better serving the customer, and therefore, better sales. The Toolbox would also recommend the cross-selling products based not only on the customer type, but also on the products she already has, the frequency and type of usage, and other parameters. The database would constantly be improving knowledge of which customers respond positively to which products and messages would be added to continually fine-tune the support materials contained in the original Toolbox.

The Raiffeisen Romania marketing team is very optimistic about how it can continue to add value – customer value – to the rest of the Raiffeisen organization. From the team members' perspective, they have just begun.

Published by Manager Publishing
Edited by Mary Murphy
Cover design by 7Field
Layout design, prepress by Layout Factory
Printed in Hungary by Dürer Nyomda Kft.

ISBN 978-963-9912-14-4